"Matt Woodley gives us a conte ___ any reader to both know and live out the truth of God with us in everyday life!"

Leighton Ford, president, Leighton Ford Ministries

"This commentary by Matt Woodley is one you don't simply want to reference but read. Woodley rightly manages to find the note of grace and promise in every passage. This is a book about the gospel—good news—of Matthew. I can't imagine studying the first Gospel without this book within easy reach."

Mark Galli, senior managing editor of *Christianity Today*

"Woodley's work brings both Christ and Matthew near; we experience them present with us, speaking to us about things that matter then and now."

Mark DeYmaz, pastor, Mosaic Church of Central Arkansas

"This journey through Matthew's Gospel combines effective commentary with engaging relevance. Whether you are officially a preacher or not, read this book with your Bible open and converse with Immanuel—you will want to share the blessing with others!"

Peter Mead, minister-at-large, Operation Mobilization, and preaching trainer, Langham Preaching

"Matt Woodley masterfully paints a portrait of our Lord through a relevant commentary on this important Gospel. This thematic study sheds new light on foundational truths, making orthodox theology accessible in our current cultural context."

Kevin Palau, president, Luis Palau Association

"Nine times out of ten, I am disappointed when I read through a commentary because it is either too academic for my purposes as a preacher or too generic for my purposes as a teacher. But not so with Woodley's commentary on Matthew! It is both educational and entertaining."

Derek Cooper, assistant professor of biblical studies and historical theology, Biblical Seminary

"Make your way through this book and you will not only find a readers' guide to Matthew and his most important themes, but you will find as well a telling critique of modern culture and church and their often misguided attempts to make sense of the mysteries of life."

Steven A. Hunt, associate professor of biblical studies, Gordon College

"With an engaging, well-written narrative, Matt Woodley invites readers into the story of Matthew's Gospel with a pastor's sensitivity. This is a substantive and accessible commentary that readers will find hard to put down."

Ed Cyzewski, author of *Coffeehouse Theology: Reflecting on God in Everyday Life*

"Matt Woodley's commentary is a wonderful resource for every pastor trying their best to communicate the good news of Jesus Christ and the values recorded in the Gospel of Matthew. I found this work to be theologically intelligent, spiritually insightful and delightful to read."

Kevin J. Navarro, senior pastor of Bethany Evangelical Free Church

"Matt Woodley provides a refreshing expository of an often familiar Gospel by provoking questions about the impact of God's coming kingdom in today's culture and society."

Mae Elise Cannon, author of *Social Justice Handbook: Small Steps for a Better World*

"As I read through Matthew Woodley's commentary on the book of Matthew, I was consistently surprised by his interaction with the text and the ideas and insights that developed as a result. This book is a gift and a challenge to pastors who want to think more theologically and to theologians who want to think more pastorally."

Tim Keel, teaching pastor at Jacob's Well Church

THE GOSPEL OF MATTHEW

God with Us

MATT WOODLEY

Foreword by Leonard Sweet

Afterword by Skye Jethani

To: Richard

From: Mama B.

Xmas 2015

InterVarsity Press
P.O. Box 1400, Downers Grove, IL 60515-1426
World Wide Web: www.ivpress.com
E-mail: email@ivpress.com

InterVarsity Press® is the book-publishing division of InterVarsity Christian Fellowship/USA®, a
movement of students and faculty active on campus at hundreds of universities, colleges and schools of
nursing in the United States of America, and a member movement of the International Fellowship of
Evangelical Students. For information about local and regional activities, write Public Relations
Dept., InterVarsity Christian Fellowship/USA, 6400 Schroeder Rd., P.O. Box 7895, Madison, WI
53707-7895, or visit the IVCF website at <www.intervarsity.org>.

All Scripture quotations, unless otherwise indicated, are taken from the THE HOLY BIBLE, NEW
INTERNATIONAL VERSION®, NIV® Copyright © 1973, 1978, 1984, 2011 by Biblica, Inc.™ Used
by permission. All rights reserved worldwide.

While all stories in this book are true, some names and identifying information in this book have been
changed to protect the privacy of the individuals involved.

Design: Cindy Kiple

Images: © ARS, NY. Stella Vespertina by Georges Rouault at Musee National d'Art Moderne, Centre
        Georges Pompidou, Paris, France. Photo, Philippe Migeat. CNAC/MNAM/Dist. Réunion des
        Musées Nationaux/Art Resource, NY.

ISBN 978-0-8308-3642-0

Printed in the United States of America ∞

Library of Congress Cataloging-in-Publication Data

Woodley, Matt.
   The gospel of Matthew: God with us/Matt Woodley.
      p. cm.—(Resonate series)
   Includes bibliographical references.
   ISBN 978-0-8308-3642-0 (pbk.: alk. paper)
   1. Bible. N.T. Matthew—Commentaries.   I. Title.
   BS2575.53.W66 2011
   226.2'07—dc23

2011023116

| **P** | 18 | 17 | 16 | 15 | 14 | 13 | 12 | 11 | 10 | 9 | 8 | 7 | 6 | 5 | 4 | 3 | 2 | 1 |
| **Y** | 26 | 25 | 24 | 23 | 22 | 21 | 20 | 19 | 18 | 17 | 16 | 15 | 14 | 13 | 12 | 11 |

CONTENTS

FOREWORD

Some people get downright silly about the Bible. I'm one of them. I believe this book, from Genesis to Genuine Leather, has the power to change lives.

I believe this Nook, or whatever form of virtual technology you use to read the most influential single work in the most influential language in the world, is the depository of divine revelation.

I believe that the Bible, whatever the version, can lead to conversion, though in my view the New English Bible engages the mind, the King James Version engages the heart, and the Jerusalem Bible engages the mouth.

I also believe, as Yiddish writer and Nobel laureate Isaac Bashevis Singer contended, "If you read the Bible as just a good book, as poetry or prose or history, then you are not anymore a religious person."[1] If I am to live and give my children a storybook existence, then every story needs a script. In a world of make-it-up-for-yourself unscripted spirituality, my storybook life is a scripturally scripted life. For the Bible tells us, from Genesis to the maps, the greatest story ever told.

A Scottish preacher once said, "Everything in the Bible is true, except for the facts." That's a pun and wordplay, of course, but I told you I could get downright silly about this book.

When people ask me "Who's your hero?" the first name that comes to mind is Tudor William Tyndale (1494-1536). In fact, every time I open my Bible I lift up a little thanksgiving prayer for Tyndale. I can read the Bible in English today because this Greek and Hebrew scholar believed that the average layperson ("a boy that driveth the plough" was his phrase) should be able to read the Bible in the vernacular. In the face of people like St. Thomas More, who denounced Tyndale as a "hellhound" who was "hellbound" to take the nation with him, Tyndale fled to Hamburg under a pseudonym to print his translation of the New Testament in 1524.

What did he get for this gift to the church? No Pulitzer Prize. No massive royalty payments. On October 6, 1536, he was strangled to death for his "heresy," then his body was brutalized by burning. Someone gave their life so that you and I can read the Bible in English today. You say, "What's the big deal?" Tell Tyndale it's not a big deal moving from one media form to another. By the way, Henry's second wife, Queen Anne Boleyn (1533-1536), secreted away a copy of Tyndale's 1534 English New Testament (1534), and it still survives.

In 2011 we celebrated the four hundredth anniversary of the King James Version of the Bible. In an irony so rich you can almost choke on it, over 80 percent of the New Testament, and 75 percent of the Old Testament in the "Authorized Version" of the Bible, were cribbed from Tyndale's translations. In other words, within a hundred years, the very people who killed Tyndale for heresy were "authorizing" his work.

In 2011 InterVarsity Press continues the release of new volumes in its Resonate Series, the first volume of which (Paul Louis Metzger's *The Gospel of John: When Love Comes to Town*) was released in late 2010. I am enormously excited about this series because it has invented a whole new genre of literature, a hybrid commentary where the best in biblical scholarship is coupled with theological reflection on the text that is accessible to that "boy that driveth the plough." What a novel and glorious experience to be reading a meditation which becomes an exegesis which becomes a devotional which becomes a homily—all in the space of a few pages. I fully expect this new form of "commentary" to become a standard form in the future. I also harbor dreams of the Resonate Series restoring to English-speaking Christianity some of its liturgical and devotional language which it has largely lost. It was that stately, magisterial register of the 1611 King James Version that made it so resonant and thrilling.

Leonard Sweet

SERIES
INTRODUCTION

We live in an increasingly biblically illiterate culture—not simply in terms of knowing what the Bible says but also in knowing how God wants to use his Word to draw us closer to him. The contemporary situation has drawn greater attention to the need for biblical and theological reflection that is culturally engaging. Yet the need isn't new.

In every age and in every region of the world, the church needs to be concerned for the biblical sense (what does this particular book of the Bible mean?) and its cultural significance (what does it have to say to us in our particular setting?), never confusing the two but always relating them. Only then can our reflections resonate well both with Scripture and with people's life situations. As you can imagine, it's a daunting challenge.

This is the challenge I face daily in my work as a professor at Multnomah Biblical Seminary in Portland, Oregon, and as director of its Institute for the Theology of Culture: New Wine, New Wineskins (www .new-wineskins.org). Many of my students do not come from Christian homes and have never been exposed to Scripture in a meaningful way, but they often come well-equipped to engage pop culture. Other students have been long entrenched in the Christian subculture and struggle to engage meaningfully in a pluralistic context that does not recognize the Bible as truthful and authoritative for life. Thankfully, Portland is a wonderful living laboratory in which to prepare for ministry within an increasingly diverse setting—ministry that brings the Bible to bear on that context in a theologically sound and grace-filled manner.

The aim of the Resonate series is to provide spiritual nourishment that is biblically sound, theologically orthodox and culturally significant. The form each volume in the series will take is that of an extended essay—each author writing about a biblical book in an interactive, reflective and culturally engaging manner.

Why this approach? There are scores of commentaries on the market from biblical scholars who go verse by verse through the biblical text. While these works are extremely important, there is an increasingly urgent need for pastors who feel at home in the biblical text to bring that text home to today's Christ-followers. They do this by interacting with the text expositionally, placing it within the context of contemporary daily life and viewing their personal stories in light of the original context and unfolding drama of ancient Scripture. There is also a need for people who feel at home in contemporary culture but who are foreigners to Scripture to inhabit the world of the Bible without abandoning their own context. God would have us live in both worlds.

Speaking of context, it is worth noting how this series emerged. I was participating at a consultation on the future of theological inquiry at the Center of Theological Inquiry in Princeton, New Jersey, when David Sanford contacted me to ask if I would serve as executive editor for Resonate. His timing could not have been better. During the consultation in Princeton, we discussed the need for academics to be more intentional about writing to popular culture and not focus exclusively on writing to our peers in the scholarly guild. We also discussed how greater efforts needed to be made to bridge the academy and the church.

In addition to dialoguing with David Sanford and sketching out what I would envision for such a series, I spoke with several biblical scholars during the consultation. One went so far as to tell me there was no need for another commentary series, for there was an overabundance of them on the market. But when they heard the vision for Resonate, they encouraged me to move forward with it. Like them, I believe a series of this kind could go a long way toward encouraging and equipping today's pastors and teachers to engage each book of the Bible in a thoughtful and rigorous manner.

Some volumes in this series are written by thoughtful practitioners and others by practically oriented academics. Whether practitioner or

academic, each author approaches the subject matter not from the standpoint of detached observer but rather as a fully engaged participant in
the text—always working with the community of editors I have assem-
bled along with managing editor David Sanford and general editor Dave
Zimmerman at InterVarsity Press.

Instead of proceeding verse by verse, the author of each Resonate volume draws insights from the featured book's major themes, all the while
attentive to the context in which these themes are developed. The authors' purposes are to guide, guard and grow readers as they move forward in their own spiritual journeys. In addition to focusing on the major themes of the book under consideration, each author also locates that
particular book within the context of the triune God's overarching narrative of holy love for Israel, church and world.

Our aim with this distinctive new genre is to have one finger in the
ancient Scriptures, another in the daily newspaper, and another touching the heart, all the while pointing to Jesus Christ. This is no easy task,
of course, but when accomplished it is extremely rewarding.

Each contributor to Resonate seeks to bear witness to Jesus Christ,
the living Word of God, through the written Word in and through his or
her own life story and the broader cultural context. So often we go
around Scripture to Jesus or we stop short at Scripture and fail to penetrate it to get to Jesus' heart—which is the Father's heart too. Instead,
each of us needs to depend on God's Spirit to discern how our culturally
situated words and stories are included in the biblical metanarrative, and
to learn how to bring God's Word home to our hearts and lives in a
truthful and meaningful manner.

We trust that you will find this and other Resonate volumes beneficial
as you exegete Scripture and culture in service to Jesus Christ, church
and world, and as God exegetes your heart through his Word and Spirit.
With this in mind, we dedicate this series as a whole to you as you embark on this arduous and incredible journey.

Paul Louis Metzger, Ph.D.
Executive Editor, Resonate

ACKNOWLEDGMENTS

As I poured countless hours into this book, many people poured countless acts of love and mercy into my life. So many friends fed me, housed me and taught me about God's grace. Chris Kelley (or should I say "Sergeant Chris"?), you taught me how to grow up by surrendering everything. Who would have imagined I could learn so much from an Irish farmer? Jim and Annette Glavich, thanks for the wonderful meals and healing conversations around your kitchen counter. John and Christine Hurtado, thank you again for your generosity, and for teaching me to risk again. Don and Joanne Uyeno, thanks for providing a place to focus on writing—which just happened to be Cabo San Lucas. Joe and Betsy Dyro, thanks for the writing room and for letting me steal your green olives. Carrie, thanks for helping me start my own journey of recovery-restoration. Leighton Ford, thanks for letting me spend three days with you—and for helping me to follow my "thread." Mom and Dad, thanks for loving me and worrying about me (but now you should listen to Jesus and stop worrying). To the Thursday night men's group in Bohemia, New York—thanks for your courage, your quiet support and for my weekly four minutes of pure honesty. Christopher West, you inspired me to sing "Blowin' in the Wind," my first musical solo. You have no idea how much that changed my life. Julie, thanks for teaching me more than you'll probably ever realize. And Therese, the little flower, more than anyone I know, you've taught me how to walk Jesus' "little way."

David Sanford, thanks for believing in my writing skills and for pitching my name to InterVarsity Press. Dale Bruner, we've never met but I read every page of your massive commentary on the Gospel of Matthew.

You're my Matthew-hero. Paul Metzger and Al Baylis, your "suggestions" and revisions often exasperated and irritated me, but now that the book is done, I have a confession to make: you were right 98 percent of the time (but I won't budge on the other 2 percent). Thank you for your love for Christ, your love for his Word and your love for the beauty of clear thinking. You made this a much better book.

Several Christian communities sustained and nurtured my soul over the past four years. Three Village Church on Long Island helped me stay and then helped me leave. Thank you for giving me the time and support I needed to make a major life transition. Crossover Christian Church led by Pastor Lesaya Kelly took me in and loved me. Christianity Today: you aren't a church, but you have given me rich Christian community. It's a privilege to share life with so many good friends who have such an incredible mission to build the church. I also want to thank all of my friends at Church of the Resurrection in Wheaton, Illinois. Walking with you through Advent, Lent and Holy Week has permanently changed the way I follow Jesus. Thank you Father Stewart Ruch (and the entire staff of Rez): I've always understood Advent, but now I finally get Easter too! And I can hardly wait for Pentecost. Finally, Pastors Kevin and Karen Miller (and Anne and Anne too), I could never say how grateful I am for your ministry of hospitality, prayer and presence. You have modeled to me the theme of this book—Immanuel, God with us.

Finally, I want to acknowledge my children—Bonnie Joy, Mathew, JonMichael and Wesley. I love you all so much. Of course my son Mathew (The Lesser) bears my name and the name on this book, but I dedicate this book to all of you. Keep walking the little way of Jesus. Keep doing great and daring things for him, but never forget to do "little things" for "little people" with the same spirit of greatness for Jesus. Receive his mercy and then fling it on other people, especially the poor and forgotten. Never forget to admit your weaknesses and cry out for help. And never forget the essence of this book: To come near to Jesus is to come near to a perfect love and a perfect power to restore all things. Jesus will take all the broken things in your life—and the whole world—and restore them. All your sad stories will come untrue. That is the little way of Jesus. He will never fail you or forsake you even to the end of the age.

THE RESONATE
EDITORIAL TEAM

Executive Editor
Paul Louis Metzger, Ph.D., professor of Christian theology and theology of culture, and director, The Institute for the Theology of Culture: New Wine, New Wineskins, Multnomah Biblical Seminary/Multnomah University

Managing Editor
David Sanford, Credo Communications, and advisor, The Institute for the Theology of Culture: New Wine, New Wineskins, Multnomah Biblical Seminary/Multnomah University

Old Testament Consulting Editor
Karl Kutz, Ph.D., professor of Bible and biblical languages, Multnomah University

New Testament Consulting Editor
Albert H. Baylis, Ph.D., professor of Bible and theology, Multnomah Biblical Seminary/Multnomah University

Editorial Assistant
Beyth Hogue Greenetz, administrative coordinator, The Institute for the Theology of Culture: New Wine, New Wineskins, Multnomah Biblical Seminary/Multnomah University

O God, who wonderfully created, and yet more wonderfully restored, the dignity of human nature: Grant that we may share the divine life of him who humbled himself to share our humanity, your Son Jesus Christ; who lives and reigns with you, in the unity of the Holy Spirit, one God, for ever and ever. Amen.

THE BOOK OF COMMON PRAYER

The great policies of world history are often turned not by the Lords and Governors, even gods, but by the seemingly unknown and weak—owing to the secret life of creation, and part unknowable to all wisdom but One, that resides in the intrusions of the Children of God into the Drama.

J. R. R. TOLKIEN

INTRODUCTION

During the past year I had the chance to work every weekend at a group home for six developmentally disabled adults. The staff members described the six adults, ranging in age from twenty-nine to fifty-six, as "high-functioning with mild mental retardation or Down syndrome." In other words, they could feed and bathe themselves as well as articulate their needs and opinions. Besides, everyone seems to think that developmentally disabled adults radiate a naive, sweet, happy, almost Christlike attitude. All of these factors, I assumed, would make my job fun and easy, hanging out with the residents, watching television, eating communal meals, taking them to worship services and bringing them to concerts at the beach.

I was wrong.

The job wasn't always easy or fun. For the most part, I was the one with "issues," not the residents. I could certainly *do* things for them—cook turkey burgers, wipe the bathroom floors, help them with their chores—but I found it difficult to *be* with them. In many ways they did exude a Christlike kindness, joy and freedom, but then they'd do something that would blow up my tidy assumptions. For instance, at times "William" would tell clever lies in order to pit staff members against his vindictive, overprotective older sister. After the death of his mother, "Robert" had watched his father and two siblings dump him in the group home and take off. He dealt with the sadness and loneliness by watching Johnny Depp movies. Whenever the residents acted manipulatively, expressed rage or withdrew into sadness, I felt overwhelmed by confusion, anger and inadequacy. Facing my own powerlessness and incompetence terrified me: I either wanted to fix them, numb my feelings or just quit.

Thankfully, I didn't quit (I needed the job). Instead I stayed long enough to learn a valuable lesson: authentic relationships require personal presence. In order to grow in love, the real me (as opposed to the pretend me), must show up and be present to the real you—not the you I think you are or want you to be. In other words, authentic love includes my willingness to be with you in all your beauty and promise as well as all your brokenness—your sin, mistrust, sadness, rage, doubt and anguish.

In the Gospel of Matthew, Jesus shows up and offers us God's personal presence. In the very first chapter, after providing a long list of imperfect people in Jesus' family tree, Matthew declares that the Messiah, Jesus, will be called "Immanuel (which means 'God with us')" (Mt 1:23). Throughout this entire book, from his birth to his death, Jesus is God with us. This is the story of a Savior and Messiah who performs many miracles, but perhaps these are the four greatest: (1) in Jesus, God wants to be with us; (2) God knows how to be with us; (3) through Jesus' death and resurrection, God is still with us; (4) in Jesus's ongoing presence through his Spirit, God is with us as we go into the world sharing this good news.

For Matthew these four miracles form the main themes in the story of Jesus' good news, the story of God not only living with us but also forgiving us, healing us, warning us and then renewing us and all of creation. Our encounters with the real Jesus (Jesus as he is, not Jesus as we want him to be) can be awe-inspiring, confusing, stretching, comforting, disruptive, painful and healing, but they're always supposed to transform us and our world. Jesus' kingdom of heaven is both large and small; it's personal and communal but also global and even cosmic. In Jesus' words, he will usher in "the renewal of all things" (Mt 19:28), a restored world and a new genesis.[1]

Surprisingly, although it's a huge story of good news and transformation, Jesus never asks us to follow him with a superheroic, overachieving, failure-free approach to the spiritual life. This "big way" route to discipleship eventually leads to spiritual burnout, disillusionment and self-righteous pride—i.e., "I can do it; why can't you?" For the most part,

Jesus asks us to follow him with our little faith, allowing the Father to work through our poverty of spirit, failures and suffering, our quiet obedience and trust, and our small acts of mercy toward sinners, outcasts, the poor and the forgotten. This "little way" makes discipleship accessible to all of us—except the self-righteous and the alleged experts.[2]

It's also important for Matthew to tell us over and over that the story of God with us isn't new. This Gospel creatively connects Jesus' good news with the story of the Jewish people as found in the Old Testament.[3] Ever the careful systematic thinker and organizer, Matthew patiently unfolds the story of Jesus as the Son of David, the one who gathers up and fulfills Israel's story (and thus our story too). Jesus will not only "give his life as a ransom for many" (Mt 20:28), standing with us by dying for us on the cross; he will also live the life we are called to live, thus fulfilling our broken stories.

This Gospel presents Jesus in a wide array of images besides God with us and the Son of David: a careful teacher, a warmhearted prophet like Jeremiah, a tender healer like Elijah, the messianic king who ushers in the kingdom of heaven and the divine judge who warns us to listen before it's too late.[4] Through these diverse images Jesus not only comforts the broken, forgives sinners and invites the weary; he also challenges the complacent, rebukes the smug and self-righteous and calls everyone to a life of quiet obedience. Jesus also prompts us to connect our personal relationship with him to the larger community of Christ-followers, embracing outsiders and fellow sinners and praying and working so the kingdom will come to earth as it is in heaven (Mt 6:10).

◆ ◆ ◆

New Testament scholars debate who wrote Matthew since the name Matthew isn't found in the text. Was it Matthew the tax collector turned follower of Jesus (see Mt 9:9-11)? That was clearly the consensus of the early church. Or was this book written by another early Jewish follower (or community of scholars) of Jesus? This latter viewpoint is the predominant view in many circles today. I side with the early church on this debate, although I agree with contemporary scholar Craig Keener, who accepts the possibility of Matthew's authorship but states that ultimately it doesn't affect "the authority nor accuracy of the Gospel, because it does not name its author (the titles were added to all four Gospels later)."[5] For the sake of simplicity, in this commentary I will follow the early church's opinion that this Gospel was written by Matthew.

The date of Matthew's Gospel is also controversial. Some reliable scholars date it before the fall of Jerusalem, or A.D. 70. Others date it later, perhaps in A.D. 75 or even late as A.D. 80 to 90. Probably the most honest position would be to conclude that the range extends from A.D. 65 to A.D. 85, and beyond that we don't know for sure.[6]

On the other hand, there's little debate that Matthew was writing to encourage and instruct a community of Jewish Christians who were aware of their allegiance to Judaism and to Jesus as the Messiah and Son of David. This reality helps modern readers understand the book's apparent harshness toward the Jewish religious leaders of Jesus' day. As a fellow Jew, Matthew writes to critique other Jews, especially spiritual leaders like the scribes and Pharisees. Israel's prophets did the same thing. (On a smaller scale, as a loyal and loving Minnesota Viking fan, no one criticizes the Vikings more than fellow fans like me because no one cares more about success than a true fan or insider.)[7]

Based on the overarching theme of God with us, I have divided Matthew into the following five major sections:

1. The Identity and Mission of Jesus (1:1–4:11)

2. The Public Ministry Jesus (4:12–11:1)

3. The Varying Response to Jesus (11:2–16:12)

4. The Growing Conflict with Jesus (16:13–25:46)

5. The Climax: The Death and Resurrection of Jesus (26:1–28:15)[8]

The first section, which includes everything before Jesus' public ministry, focuses on Jesus' birth, flight into Egypt, his baptism and his temptation in the wilderness. At each stage of this section, Jesus not only empathizes with sinners but also stands in the place of sinners—in all the anguish, sinfulness and temptation faced by human beings.

In section two, Jesus begins his public teaching ministry with a call to repentance (Mt 4:17), an invitation to discipleship (Mt 4:22) and with displays of his healing power (Mt 4:23-25). From there he moves into a long teaching section about what it means to live as a community gathered around Jesus (Mt 5:1–7:27). Jesus also reveals his mission in the way he treats outcasts, heals the sick, shows mercy to the desperate and calls people to a life of discipleship.

At the beginning of the third section (Mt 11:2), we find one of the first clear responses to the person of Jesus: the doubt of John the Baptist. Throughout this section we'll also see the growing conflict with the religious establishment, the struggling but imperfect response of the disciples, the clear-hearted faith of a desperate Canaanite woman and the emerging rejection from the Pharisees.

The fourth section begins with Peter's declaration about Jesus (Mt 16) and the revelation of Jesus' glory in the Transfiguration (Mt 17). From there Jesus provides extended teachings on topics related to life in the new community of his people—forgiveness, marriage, riches and discipleship. Jesus also emphasizes again our need to receive and live by grace (Mt 20). As chapter 21 begins, Jesus' message and identity place him on a crash course with the Jewish leadership. A series of confrontations (Mt 21–22) leads to Jesus' scathing indictment of the shallowness of their spiritual leadership (Mt 23). Matthew continues with two more chapters that, in the light of God's coming judgment, serve as profound wake-up calls that we start living as God's chosen people (Mt 25), waiting for the bridegroom and showing mercy to the suffering people on this planet.

The final section (Matthew 26:1–28:20) focuses on the death and resurrection of Jesus. The God with us of Matthew 1:23 becomes the God who is for us of the cross. For Jesus, love means presence and sacrifice. Love implies self-giving. So Jesus, Immanuel, gives himself for us in order to be with us. Jesus, the innocent one, is judged in our placed. As we'll see, Jesus' death and resurrection don't start a new story or even a new theme to the same story; instead, this section merely continues the promise and the theme begun in Matthew 1:23.

Throughout this Gospel Matthew invites us into a challenging adventure in which Jesus asks for nothing less than our wholehearted commitment. But then again, it's also an adventure especially designed for all the "little faiths" who never have to walk alone. Jesus doesn't just call spiritual experts; he continually calls the poor in spirit (Mt 5:3), the sick who need a doctor (Mt 9:9) and the spiritual beginners and children (Mt 11:25; 18:4). With particular clarity, Jesus himself provides the one and only requirement: "Come to me, all you who are weary and burdened, and I will give you rest. Take my yoke upon you and learn from me, for I am gentle and humble in heart, and you will find rest for your souls. For my yoke is easy and my burden is light" (Mt 11:28-30).

So based on Jesus' bighearted, merciful invitation, we come. We come not because we're worthy or qualified. We come not because we won't stumble or fail. We come not because our faith is big and strong. We come simply because he told us to. And that's always enough. As we come we pray, "Lord Jesus, I come with all my promise and gifts, and I come with all my sin and failures. I am finding rest in you. I am taking your yoke. I am learning life from you. Keep renewing me—and keep renewing the whole world—until you come again."

THE IDENTITY
AND MISSION OF JESUS

Matthew 1:1–4:11

It's a strange way to tell a story. In the first major section of the Gospel of Matthew (nearly four entire chapters), the main character in the story hardly speaks. Jesus' first words appear in 3:15—a quick sentence to his cousin John the Baptist to explain his own baptism. In the first half of chapter 4, Jesus speaks only three short sentences—this time to the devil. Although everything in this Gospel centers on Jesus, Matthew doesn't start with Jesus' teaching and self-proclamations.

Of course that doesn't stop Matthew from building his case for Jesus' identity and mission. With excitement and deep conviction, Matthew opens his story by giving his conclusion about Jesus' identity: Jesus is the son of David and the son of Abraham (Mt 1:1). But that's just the beginning. By the time this chapter ends, Matthew will also claim that Jesus is the Messiah (Mt 1:16), the Savior (Mt 1:21) and Immanuel or God with us (Mt 1:23). In chapter 2 these lofty titles of divine presence and power are countered with humble, earthy descriptions of Jesus: on five occasions he's called "the child"; he's a political refugee (Mt 2:19); he's a lowly "Nazarene" (Mt 2:23).

This opening section also makes an exciting claim about Jesus' mission—Jesus has come to fulfill the story of God's chosen people. The church has often struggled to articulate this aspect of Jesus' life. Sadly, many Christians assume that Jesus was starting a new story. Or they assume that Jesus plopped into history so we could get over that sordid, primitive, unspiritual, rule-based Old Testament Jewish thing. That's not Matthew's story of Jesus. According to this Gospel, Jesus enters the ongoing story of God's people and fulfills it. The first two chapters alone contain four out of Matthew's ten "formula quotations"—statements that claim that an Old Testament reference has been fulfilled in Jesus. But that's merely the tip of a very large iceberg.[1] On each step of his journey—his birth, his flight to and return from Egypt, his childhood in Nazareth, his temptations in the wilderness—Jesus is walking back through Israel's story. Of course Jesus is doing it right, while Israel (and all of us) failed.

As a result, Matthew proclaims that Jesus is the true Israel—God's true son—and the one who rescues Israel. Jesus is also the God with us who becomes a child and a refugee. It's definitely an exciting whirlwind of claims and conclusions about Jesus' identity and mission. Do these claims make sense? If they're true, will Jesus deliver on them? And if so, how will Jesus live among us? When he actually talks, what will he say? How will he treat people? What will he ask from us? Matthew more or less says, "Just wait and see. I won't give it all away in the first section of the story. But hold on: here it comes."

THE WORLD'S GREATEST ADVENTURE STORY BEGINS
Matthew 1:1-17

Every time I read a good story my heart thumps a little faster. Adventure stories, tales filled with daring quests and dangerous journeys, have always been my favorites. Even as a child, somewhere in the deepest, most secret places in my heart, I knew that life had to be a grand adventure story or it was no life at all. The ancients used to refer to a human being as a *homo viator*, or "a person on the way," a man or a woman on a journey, a quest, an adventure. Later in life, when I first heard that Latin phrase, it rang true with my soul. Yes, of course, I knew it all along: we're all *homo viators.*

I can still remember sitting in my suburban living room and reading the first line from J. R. R. Tolkien's *The Hobbit:* "In a hole in the ground there lived a hobbit."[2] Ten words into the novel and the story hooked me. Psychologists refer to this process as "narrative transport," or the capacity for a good story to grab us and move us.[3] This tale certainly transported me! What is a hobbit, I wondered, and why does he live in the ground? Will he leave his hole? If so, what surprises, dangers and delights will he encounter? And as I entered Bilbo Baggins's journey, I wondered: what adventures will befall me?

A few years later I read Henri Charriere's gripping *Papillon,* in which the author recounts his daring escape from the brutal prison Devil's Island. Captivated by Charriere's harrowing adventure, I longed to embark on a great and worthy quest—even if it just meant escaping from my suburban living room.

With daring quests stirring in my heart, I was deeply disappointed when I opened the New Testament, the grand story of Jesus, supposedly the greatest story ever told, and read a long and tedious list of Hebrew names. Where was the adventure, the danger and delight? Where were the *homo viators* in this story? Was this even a story? How dull! What a colossal flop!

Or was it? Years later when I read it again, I realized that Matthew, ever so slowly and gently, as if not to startle us, was sweeping us into the greatest adventure tale ever told. Matthew 1:1-17 does it all—provoking, charming and surprising us into the story of Jesus. The first two words *(biblos geneseos)* are also the Greek title for Genesis.[4] Matthew wants us to do a Genesis double take: the first creation and now, in Jesus, the new creation. In other words, the original creation—damaged, flawed, broken—is being restored and transformed in and through Messiah Jesus.[5]

Then Matthew quickly moves into one of those infamous biblical genealogies. We usually don't begin adventure tales with a family tree, but in the ancient world a genealogy grounded people in history. It told you who you were and where you came from.[6] Notice the two bookends of this genealogy in verses 1 and 16: they both refer to Jesus, who is called

the Christ. Like a roll of drums, the fanfare of trumpets or the announcement of a starting lineup, everything in this genealogy leads right up to
the nation's king and star.[7] When Matthew originally unfolded this genealogy, all ears and every eye would have anxiously anticipated the one
at the end, the one who held the position of greatest honor: Jesus, the
Messiah, the Son of David.[8]

By including three groups of fourteen names (see v. 17), Matthew con-
denses and highlights this genealogy in order to tell us a particular story
about Jesus the Christ.[9] It's a masterful adventure tale with two prominent themes.[10] First, Matthew wants us to hear the underlying story of
the sovereignty of God. Behind each name on Matthew's carefully selected list we find human stories riddled with sordid, scandalous, glorious and honorable details. Abraham displayed daring faith by believing
God's promise, but then he also doubted, lied and stumbled along the
way. Ruth evokes a tender story of friendship and loving-kindness, but it
also contains tragic deaths and Naomi's dark night of grief and loss.
David, Israel's greatest king, displayed valiant courage, but when Uriah's
name appears, we recall David's acts of self-deception, adultery, arrogance, betrayal and murder.

Matthew's selection of names is bittersweet, beastly-angelic—and
human. As this history illustrates, the human story is messy, unfaithful,
complicated and inconsistent. And yet with his predictable, measured,
orderly lists of names, Matthew also weaves another story. Summarizing this convoluted path to the Messiah's birth, he says, "Thus there
were fourteen generations in all from Abraham to David, fourteen from
David to the exile to Babylon, and fourteen from the exile to the Messiah" (Mt 1:17).

Matthew will continually remind us that Jesus fulfilled Old Testament prophecy (see 1:22 and 2:15, for example). But in this genealogy he
implies that Jesus' birth, life, mission, death and resurrection will fulfill
the entire Old Testament story.[11] No matter how dark and bloody we
make our own histories, Matthew wants us to know that three times
fourteen means there's a story and a storyteller, a plot and a plot-weaver.
Behind the mess and unpredictability of the human story, God is weav-
ing another story, a story of harmony and redemption.

Second, Matthew's new "genesis" also proclaims God's mercy for all injured and hobbling *homo viators,* people on the way. Notice, for instance, that out of the vast pool of people Matthew could have chosen for this introduction to Jesus, he selected some shockingly irregular people. Most ancient genealogies didn't include women at all, unless perhaps they were "great women," like Sarah, Rebekah, Leah, Rachel. But this genealogy doesn't mention any of these prominent "great women"; instead, Matthew intentionally includes four prominent but "irregular" women:

- Tamar (Mt 1:3), who acted as a prostitute by tricking her father-in-law so as to continue the line of her husband

- Rahab (Mt 1:5), a prostitute and a foreigner who also displayed courageous faith by protecting the Hebrew spies

- Ruth (Mt 1:5), another outsider from Moab (and a descendant of the incestuous Lot), who displayed a Godlike covenant loyalty to her mother-in-law and, in another sense, to all of God's people

- "Uriah's wife," or Bathsheba (Mt 1:6), the woman involved in David's scandalous affair and cover-up and who also, by God's grace, became the mother of Solomon.

Like all the men mentioned earlier in Jesus' genealogy, these women epitomize the human story—from soaring faith to sullied unbelief. These four women aren't notoriously wicked, especially compared to everyone else in this list of mercy-hungry wayfarers. But as non-Jews and ethnic outsiders, they represent an odd bunch of branches to graft into Jesus' family tree. And yet Matthew wants us to know that these irregular women belong in this story from the very beginning.[12] To paraphrase another New Testament writer, Jesus is not ashamed to call them his sisters (Heb 2:11-12).

Why? What's the point? From start to finish, this is the Gospel of divine mercy. This Jesus is pro-sinner. He is for us even in our sin and oddness. He is for the irregular and the preposterous. As a friend of mine said, "God chooses sinful, broken, unlikely people—who else does he have?"[13] So this is the story of Jesus' mercy. He saves his people from their sins (Mt 1:21). He identifies with sinners at his baptism (Mt 3:13-

15). He treats sick people, not the alleged healthy people (Mt 9:9). He dies pinned to a cross between two sinners (Mt 27:38). Look at this Messiah, this Jesus, this Savior, Matthew exclaims; he even has sinners in his family tree![14] And if our Lord and Master and Messiah lives and dies for sinners and oddballs, then his followers must love them too.

So don't let Matthew's dull-sounding introduction fool you. This is adventure-storytelling at its best. When Paul Auster started collecting stories for a National Public Radio project called "The National Story Project," he wanted stories "that defied our expectations about the world" or "that revealed the mysterious forces at work in our lives, in our family histories, in our minds and bodies, in our souls. In other words, true stories that sounded like fiction."[15] According to Auster's criteria, Matthew 1 does it all. Jesus' genealogy defies our expectations about the world and about God. This is not the God we would expect but a Savior who works mysteriously in our irregular, mercy-poor family histories.

"In a hole in the ground there lived a hobbit." Yes, a great fiction tale. Now hear a better story: one day in a hole in the Milky Way called planet Earth, among an odd group of people, Jesus the Messiah came to his people. It's a true story that reads like fiction. What adventures, dangers and delights will Jesus encounter? And if we follow him, what adventures shall befall us? Where will this Gospel of mercy lead us? Hold on, we're in for the tale—and the adventure—of our life.

WHEN LOVE FOUND A FORM
Matthew 1:18-25

After a long tour, Bono, the lead singer for U2, returned to Dublin and attended a Christmas Eve service. At some point in that service, Bono grasped the truth at the heart of the Christmas story. With tears streaming down his face, Bono realized,

> The idea that God, if there is a force of Love and Logic in the universe, that it would seek to explain itself is amazing enough. That it would seek to explain itself by becoming a child born in poverty, in s— and straw, a child, I just thought, "Wow!" Just the poetry

... I saw the genius of picking a particular point in time and decid-
ing to turn on this. . . . Love needs to find a form, intimacy needs
to be whispered. . . . Love has to become an action or something
concrete. It would have to happen. There must be an incarnation.
Love must be made flesh.[16]

With poetic beauty, Bono explained Christmas. That's the message of
Matthew 1:18-25. "There must be an incarnation. Love must be made
flesh." The God who is love enters our broken world, becoming as small
and vulnerable as a fetus in Mary's womb.

Verse 18 begins, "This is how the birth of Jesus the Messiah came
about: His mother Mary was pledged to be married to Joseph, but before
they came together, she was found to be with child through the Holy
Spirit." It's not make-believe; Christians have always claimed that this
story is rooted in history. At a particular time and place, God in the flesh
was born with a particular human body. Jesus also had two particular
people who brought him into the world: Mary and Joseph.

Although some people scoff, it's highly unlikely that a thoroughly
Jewish writer would invent this strange story. There were plenty of tales
about heroes conceived without a human father, but they were thoroughly pagan and therefore repugnant to Jews. Matthew would have
known the risk of opening the Jesus story to sneers and misunderstand-
ings, but he took the risk anyway (along with Luke) because he believed
he was telling the real, historical story of Jesus' birth.[17]

But Matthew wasn't just interested in history; he wanted us to grasp
the meaning of Jesus' birth through his names. The first name (see verse
21) is Jesus, the one who saves us from our sins. Once again, this wasn't
what Matthew's Jewish hearers would have been expecting. In fact, it
must have irked them. They wanted a Messiah who would save them
from the sins of others.

This isn't the message we want to hear either. We usually don't crave
a Savior who will help us identify our sins. My friend Doug is a Catholic
priest who perpetually hears rambling "confessions" that sound something like this: "Bless me, Father, for I have sinned. My last confession
was nearly a year ago. I've done a few bad things, but it isn't like I committed murder or robbed a bank (chuckle, chuckle). I suppose I did

scream at my brother-in-law during our Thanksgiving dinner. I said some pretty nasty things, but that was six months ago and I've gotten over it. Besides, you should have heard what he said to me. Why, that guy is such a jerk!" And so it goes.

Doug tries to remind people that Jesus came first and foremost to save us from our sins, not his sins or her sins or their sins. So Doug reminds his parishioners, "If you can't admit your sins, if you must constantly blame others, then Jesus has nothing to offer you." That's the point of verse 21: "He will save his people from their sins." In this story, Jesus will begin his new genesis by saving me from my pride, my lust, my oppression of others and my lack of love.

There's another name for Jesus in this story: Immanuel. In verses 22-23 we're told, "All this took place to fulfill what the Lord had said through the prophet: 'The virgin will conceive and give birth to a son, and they will call him Immanuel' (which means, 'God with us')." Immanuel literally means "with us, the God" or "the with-us God." We should swallow this meaning in its full potency, without diluting it to something like "in Jesus God draws near."[18] It means that Jesus is God with us as he swims in Mary's amniotic fluid, wiggles in the manger's straw, feeds the hungry and heals the sick. Jesus is God with us as he takes the bread in his hands and says, "This is my body broken for you." Jesus is God with us as he hangs from a cross, gasping for breath and shouting, "My God, My God, why have you forsaken me?" He descends into our messy world, standing in solidarity with human sufferers, plunging ever deeper into our pain and apparent abandonment.[19]

To see how radical this concept is, compare it with other worldviews. Within the framework of ancient Greek philosophy, the idea of a God taking on a body and then entering our world as a bloody baby was a mockery. One Greek philosopher sarcastically asked, "How can one admit (God) should become an embryo, that after his birth he is put in swaddling clothes, that he is soiled with blood and bile and worse things yet?"[20]

In Islam the incarnation doesn't fare much better. My good friend Omar, a kindhearted Muslim professor, appreciates the teachings of Jesus, but he cannot accept that God became small, vulnerable and weak.

By definition, Allah forever dwells above us. Allah sends angels and prophets and books, but Allah is too holy and we are too sinful for him to come to us. According to Kenneth Cragg, one of the foremost Christian scholars on Islam, although Muslims have a "great tenderness for Jesus" and they find the nativity story "miraculous," they still claim that the incarnation is simply an impossible concept.[21]

But the greatness of Christmas—and the entire New Testament—is this: God comes to us first as a fetus, then a potentially "unwanted pregnancy," then a slimy and wrinkled baby, then a twelve-year-old boy lost in the city (see Lk 2:41-48), then a preacher and healer, and finally a condemned criminal stripped naked, asking for water and screaming for God's presence. As the author to the Hebrews would say, "He had to be made like his brothers in every way" (Heb 2:17 NIV 1984).

A nice God, a decent God, a semi-loving God, a predictably righteous God would send us some help, maybe an angel or a prophet or a sacred text—at least some advice. We could respect and admire a God like that. But the Gospel of Jesus' mercy goes far beyond conventional righteousness, decency and niceness. At Christmas God became a naked baby. You can't get more vulnerable than that. It's beyond decent; it's a wild, lavish and dangerous love. We could respond with respect and admiration, but now we will also return love with love, because God is infinitely better than we could ever imagine.

Joseph grasps the ethical implications of this lavish, vulnerable love. For all he knew he was caught in a horrible dilemma. He wasn't anticipating a "virgin birth," and Mary hadn't had sex with him, so he could only conclude that Mary had been unfaithful. It's difficult for us to imagine Joseph's shame. Jewish, Greek and Roman law all demanded that a man divorce his wife or his fiancée in this situation, making her pay for the sin by impounding her dowry.

With his version of righteousness as decency, Joseph "had in mind to divorce her quietly" (Mt 1:19). In other words, in front of two or three people he would privately terminate the impending marriage. Although deeply wounded, Joseph would choose the righteous path, a path that would allow him to maintain his honor without publically humiliating Mary. All of that would have qualified him as a righteous person, but

Joseph heard God's call to a different standard of righteousness. In verse 20 we read, "But after he considered this, an angel of the Lord appeared to him in a dream" and told Joseph to take Mary as his wife. In verse 24 Joseph responds with obedience: "When Joseph woke up, he did what the angel of the Lord had commanded him and took Mary home as his wife."

Through the angelic messenger Joseph heard God's new standard, a standard based on risky, shocking, vulnerable love. Jesus will tell us over and over again that our new standard is the Father's heart (Mt 5:45). Based on the new standard of God's solidarity with sinners, Joseph chose to walk beside Mary, standing in solidarity with her in the stigma of her alleged "sin."

But Mary also serves as a human model for the new standard of righteousness. In many ways her beautiful obedience reflects Jesus' teaching throughout the rest of this Gospel. She almost slips by unnoticed, but that's the point: in her quiet, unspectacular response to these momentous events, she exudes meekness (Mt 5:5). She obeys with her deeds and not just her words (Mt 7:21-27). She doesn't draw attention to herself (Mt 6:1-18). She trusts her heavenly Father (Mt 6:25-34), and she lives under the persecution of Herod and probably others (Mt 5:10-12). In short, without saying anything, both Mary and Joseph embody the teaching of Jesus in the Sermon on the Mount and his call for righteousness that "surpasses that of the Pharisees and the teachers of the law" (see Mt 5:20).[22]

Bono was right. "Love needs to find a form, intimacy needs to be whispered. . . . Love has to become an action or something concrete." It was true for Jesus and it is true for his followers. Like Jesus himself, Christ-followers make love an action. Sometimes that compels us to move into places of pain, despair and trauma so we can incarnate the love of Christ by our presence. At other times we remain in ordinary places—homes, neighborhoods, schools, businesses and soccer teams—and by our connection to Jesus live as salt and light. Like Joseph, who followed the way of Jesus before Jesus' birth, we make love more than a concept. It's pure logic, it's also pure love and it's the pure way that Jesus came to offer this broken world.

THE STRANGEST CHRISTMAS STORY
Matthew 2:1-23

In his book *The Jesus I Never Knew,* Philip Yancey recounts flipping through a stack of Christmas cards and noting the most common scenes: New England towns buried in snow, nice and fuzzy animals (even friendly lions) cuddling like baby bunnies, and fat or cheerful angels floating on soft clouds. When the holy family made a rare appearance, Yancey notes that they exuded peace and patience.[23]

In contrast, Matthew draws us into one wild and crazy adventure tale. A small band of scholar-explorers, led by a magic star, leave their homeland on a chase for a newborn king. En route they meet a crafty villain bent on finding and killing this alleged new king. A cat-and-mouse game ensues, but the explorers outwit the villain. Embarrassed and enraged, the villain wipes out all the boys in a nearby village. The mothers wail inconsolably for their murdered sons. Meanwhile, warned by an angelic dream, the newborn king and his family hastily leave town, joining the ranks of world refugees as they flee to safety.

The whole story is just too wild and weird for fiction, but it's certainly consistent with Matthew's theme: Jesus is God with us. The real Christmas story is more interesting, dangerous, heartrending and hopeful than anything we could ever have imagined. The story in chapter 2 centers on three strong characters: the Magi, who represent the human quest toward God; Herod, who represents the human flight from God; and the child Jesus, who represents God's vulnerable love for us.

Like the Magi, people are still on a quest toward God. I think of my friend Linda, a brilliant English literature major who met me for two hours in the middle of finals week so she could discuss "spirituality." She arrived at Starbucks with five pages of neatly typed, well-researched questions: Why does the Bible seem to advocate slavery? Why does science contradict the Bible? How come good people go to hell? Why are there so many hypocrites in the church? Why does God allow natural disasters, like a massive earthquake in Haiti of all places? Is there a purpose to life? Can anyone ask honest questions and still be happy? Although she couldn't name her quest, she was grasping and longing for "something."

Linda has tapped into a long tradition based on some of our best stories—the exodus, the *Odyssey*, the *Divine Comedy*, *Pilgrim's Progress*, *The Lord of the Rings* and *The Matrix*, to name a few. Zen Buddhists call this sense of seeking "the red hot coal stuck in the throat." You can't swallow it and you can't spit it up; it burns you from the inside out. C. S. Lewis had a word for one aspect of this quest: joy, that aching and longing for something indefinable.[24] Novelist Walker Percy called it "the search," which he claimed "is what anyone would undertake if he were not sunk in the everydayness of his own life."[25]

In this passage in Matthew, the Magi represent a universal human drive to embark on a quest. Their stargazing wasn't recreational or philosophical; it signified the red hot coal stuck in their throat, their longing for joy, their participation in the search. After intently watching the stars and planets, after reading the signs and searching the clues, they embarked on a quest. "After Jesus was born in Bethlehem in Judea," Matthew tells us, "during the time of King Herod, Magi from the east came to Jerusalem and asked, 'Where is the one who has been born king of the Jews?'" (Mt 2:1-2). We don't know much about them, but we can assume this was a costly search driven by deep desire. In one sense the Magi represent all of us—seeking, questioning, longing human beings who awaken to life as a quest.

But they also represent something about God, for the Magi are not only seekers; they are questers who have been outquested by God. According to Matthew, God initiated their long and costly journey through part of his good creation—a star (Mt 2:2, 9). They may have spotted the star, but God used the star to guide them out of everydayness toward joy.[26] God also guided them through his spoken word, refining their initial quest through an ancient Old Testament prophecy recorded in Matthew 2:6:

> But you, Bethlehem, in the land of Judah,
>   are by no means least among the rulers of Judah;
> for out of you will come a ruler
>   who will shepherd my people Israel.

At each stage of their quest God sought the seekers, recapitulating the journey described by Augustine's prayer: "I should not have sought you unless you had first found me."

In Matthew's description of the Magi's journey we sense another story behind our stories of searching: God is seeking us. We start out the quest intending to discover something, but we end up being discovered. We think we are looking for something only to find that someone was looking for us. We assume we're ascending to God and realize that God is descending to us. This is divine mercy.

To Israel and the early church, the Magi represented the worst elements of pagan idolatry.[27] In fact, the prophet Isaiah seemed to relish the day when these foreign frauds would ignite like a pile of garbage (see Is 47:13-14). Like the imperfect, irregular and immoral ancestors in Jesus' genealogy, the Magi should have remained outsiders who could only sully God's "righteous" community. But in Matthew's Gospel, God's quest includes the unworthy and the unrighteous (see also Mt 5:45; 9:9-11).

By including them in this story, Matthew announces, "Here come some more sinners; here come more spiritual and moral oddballs; here come the pagan seekers, taken by God's hand, led through nature and then through Scripture, right to the little King Jesus." In contrast, he records this about the respectable Bible scholars: "When [Herod] had called together all the people's chief priests and teachers of the law, he asked them where the Messiah was to be born. 'In Bethlehem in Judea,' they replied" (Mt 2:4-5). In other words, they offered Herod impeccable theological data, but that knowledge didn't rattle their comfortable and privileged position; they didn't budge or begin their own quest. In this story Matthew foreshadows a frequent two-point theme: a warning to the "righteous" (Mt 9:9-11), the "insiders" (Mt 11:20-30) and the "firsts" (Mt 20:1-16) who may miss God's new creation, and an invitation for the "unrighteous," the "outsiders" and the "lasts" who are called to find true rest in Jesus (Mt 11:28-30).[28]

It's hard to miss the application for us: the questing God of Jesus, the God of grace, still seeks seekers, welcoming home sinners and outsiders. He still guides us step by step through nature, circumstances, relationships, failures, triumphs and especially the Holy Bible until we are led to worship King Jesus. The church, living at the foot of Jesus' crib and cross, should do no less.

Second, Matthew 2 also focuses on King Herod, who in many ways represents all of us in our rebellious flight from God. Unlike the Magi's long but joyful quest, Herod's story ends in tragedy. It's an ugly story, and most of us don't like sad, tragic tales. As a culture we crave happy stories—even sappy, shallow sitcoms—rather than classic tragedies.

By the time Jesus was born, Herod ("the Great," as he liked to call himself), had been king for forty years. For all his flaws, Herod had one thing going for him: he could keep order. His résumé included an impressive list of personnel shake-ups: he murdered one of his wives, arranged a "drowning accident" for a brother-in-law and hired hit men to strangle two of his sons. He even concocted a plan to ensure that everyone would cry at his funeral: as soon as he died, his goon squads would kill some popular local leaders, triggering a deluge of public grief. Herod's life was marked by a constant quest to avoid God, maintain control and devalue others.

But in Matthew's ironic take on Herod's reign, Herod also looks pathetically insecure. Throughout the story his fragile ego constantly wobbles on the edge of disintegration. In verse 3 we read, "When King Herod heard this [news of Jesus' birth] he was disturbed, and all Jerusalem with him." On the one hand, news about the birth of a royal figure would disturb Herod.[29] After all, he maintained power only through intimidation, terror and violence. But in this story, Matthew repeatedly calls Jesus not "the king" but "the child." That's the threat to mighty King Herod? A mother with a baby? It's Matthew's satirical way of showing who's really in charge. The little baby Jesus, hiding in the backwoods of Judea and suckling at his mother's breast, threatens Herod the Great.

Herod's insecurity propels him to devalue and then destroy the threat by throwing a nasty temper tantrum: "When Herod realized that he had been outwitted by the Magi, he was furious" (Mt 2:16). After narrowing his search for the baby, he orders his troops to enter the village and slaughter every boy under the age of two. Although this story isn't recorded outside the Bible, almost every New Testament scholar agrees that the attack was consistent with Herod's character and political tactics.

While the Magi represent humanity on a quest toward God, Herod represents humanity in flight from God. Unlike Herod, I'm not a brutal mass murderer, but like Herod, when left to my own devices I possess a tragic urge to resist God and devalue others. Like Herod, I'm not just an imperfect human who needs a little improvement; I'm a rebel who must lay down his arms.[30] I'm a runaway who must come home. Or, in the words of Martin Luther, I am *incurvatus in se*, curved in upon myself and bent away from God.

As a fugitive from grace and a human with a tragically bent heart, I simply will not respond to God's grace without outside intervention. My flight from God can be vanquished only by God's power. All of us, like Herod, are threatened by the presence of Jesus, which disrupts our kingdom of self. That's why our decision to "accept Jesus as our personal Savior" must start with God's intervention to get our attention and soften our hearts. For the most part, we're definitely on a spiritual quest—far away from God.

For instance, after considering the reaction of her "brilliant hilarious progressive friends," writer Anne Lamott decided that accepting Christ "seemed an utterly impossible thing that simply could not be allowed to happen." She describes Jesus as a cat who wanted to get picked up and let inside. "But I knew what would happen," Lamott writes: "You let a cat in one time, give it a little milk, and then it stays forever. So I tried to keep one step ahead of it, slamming my houseboat door when I entered or left. . . . [Finally] I hung my head and said . . . 'All right. You can come in.' Such was my beautiful moment of conversion."[31]

Like Lamott and every tragically curved-in-on-herself human being, we resist and even despise surrendering to God's presence. We would rather die. Opening our lives to God's grace requires a miracle. For many this miraculous opening comes through an experience of powerlessness—perhaps a failure, an addiction, a deep sorrow or a defeat.

By his own admission, my friend Chris was a stubborn, arrogant, self-willed, Herodlike fugitive from God's grace—even after he had accepted Christ. Finally, after a long, painful struggle with his addiction to alcohol, he faced his own powerlessness. His life had become unmanageable and his marriage unraveled. As he came face to face with his greatest defeat, he suddenly entered his beautiful moment of reconversion. In this season of utter powerlessness, Chris finally stopped running and surrendered to King Jesus.

But Herod doesn't bend, repent or surrender. To the bitter end he refuses the miracle of God's grace. It's a pathetic tale, but like Herod I too can grasp for control, refusing to surrender and spurning the miracle of God's grace. Herod's life is a grave warning: tragedies still happen, and apart from Christ I can become one of those tragedies.

Finally, Matthew's Christmas story also contrasts Herod "the Great" with Jesus "the child." In one sense, this chapter could be titled "The Tale of Two Kings." It's laced with irony because Herod, the pompous, brutal but phony king, seems to possess all the power; while, Jesus, the vulnerable, powerless, humble king, actually rules the cosmos.

From the moment of his birth, Jesus plunges into trouble, violence and uncertainty. Forget the perfect Christmas scene with a flourishing economy and a cozy family sitting around a fire opening a pile of presents. Jesus and his family are on the run, hated and hunted refugees, fleeing for their lives.

In verse 23 Matthew intentionally cites Jesus' hometown of Nazareth: an off-the-map, politically insignificant place in outpost Galilee.[32] The historian Josephus doesn't even mention it, and people of Jesus' day often disparaged it (see Jn 1:46). The name "Jesus the Nazarene" implied "Jesus, the Lowly Nobody."[33] But even while dying on the cross he remained "Jesus of Nazareth" (Jn 19:19).

Matthew wants us to know that despite despotic rulers, political refugees, ethnic hatred, the slaughter of the weak and the tears of heartbroken parents, nothing escapes Immanuel, the God who suffers with us and for us. God with us comes to places of violence and grief (Bethlehem) and places of insignificance (Nazareth).

At the same time, Matthew insists that this loving, vulnerable God is also the world's powerful, sovereign Lord. Even in the midst of human rebellion, hatred and violence, God's plan has not been thwarted. On four occasions in chapter 2 (see verses 5, 13, 17-18 and 23), Matthew reminds us that the entire story of God's people in the Old Testament is being relived in the events of Jesus' life.[34] Thus, history—even our personal histories, so littered with betrayals, failures and losses—cannot overwhelm the hope of God's story. Over and over again Matthew insists that as everything looks bleak, God is still among us working out a plan for world history.[35]

So even as Herod releases his death squads into the streets of Bethlehem, Matthew quotes from Jeremiah 31:

> A voice is heard in Ramah,
>   weeping and great mourning,
> Rachel weeping for her children
>   and refusing to be comforted,
>   because they are no more. (Mt 2:18)

The ancient quote from Jeremiah and the scene in Bethlehem are both thick with anguish. Inconsolable weeping pierces the air. But for Matthew God still proclaims hope. In Jeremiah's day the people of God had been shipped off into exile, but in Jeremiah 31:16-17 God promises the end of their grief: "Restrain your voice from weeping and your eyes from tears. . . . They will return from the land of the enemy. So there is hope for your descendants." In the same way, Matthew wants his readers (and us) to know that King Jesus will also walk the path of exile, loss and grief, but then he will return and find hope even in the darkest days.[36]

In a very practical way, Matthew's real Christmas story of God with us shapes the mission of the church. As Jesus identifies with his suffering people, the church discovers her mission to side with the vulnerable—the scorned (Mary), the sick and demonized (Mt 4:23-24), the poor in spirit (Mt 5:3), the persecuted and hunted (Mt 5:10-12), the anxious and "little-faithed" (Mt 6:25-34), the outcasts (Mt 8:1), the sinful and unrighteous (Mt 9:9-11), the "little children" (Mt 11:25-27), the burnt-out and burdened (Mt 11:28-30).

In the spirit of Jesus' identity and mission found in this chapter, Jean Vanier recently wrote:

> A society that honours only the powerful, the clever, and the winners necessarily belittles the weak. . . . The image of the ideal human as powerful and capable disenfranchises the old, the sick, the less-abled. . . . I also believe that those we most exclude from the

normal life of society, people with disabilities, have profound lessons to teach us.[37]

As we shall see, in Matthew's Gospel this doesn't just mean being
nice to unfortunate people. It is first and foremost a commitment to the
lordship of Jesus Christ, a willingness to live life with Jesus at the center. But whenever Jesus is truly at the center of our life together, we will
seek out, find and embrace those whom Jesus called the "little ones."
These little ones remind us who Jesus was (not only "the child," but the
hunted and hated refugee child), who Jesus came for (the weary and
burdened, Mt 11:28) and how we all must come to Jesus (as the "poor
in spirit," Mt 5:3).

For Matthew, the real Christmas story isn't a nice story with senti-
mental pictures; it's a dangerous tale. And once we agree to join with
Jesus, we embark on a dangerous path. It forces us to side with Jesus and
his little ones rather than Herod with all of his pomp and brutality. The
way of Jesus causes us to become vulnerable. According to Matthew, we
might even be killed for following Jesus the child. But that's another tale
for another chapter. When we next meet Jesus in Matthew 3, he's a full-
grown man. But approximately thirty years later he's fulfilling the same
mission he was in chapter 1: saving us from sin and walking beside us as
God with us.

THE GOOD NEWS OF REPENTANCE
Matthew 3:1-17

When the contemporary writer Kathleen Norris started a careful journey back to her childhood faith, she had to learn a jumble of "scary"
words. At first she felt "bombarded" by words like *heresy*, *repentance*
and *salvation*, words that seemed "dauntingly abstract" and even
"vaguely threatening." In Norris's experience they also "carried an enormous weight of baggage from my own childhood and from my family
history."[38]

I often meet people who, like Norris, feel vaguely threatened by the
call to repent. Unfortunately, our culture has largely lost the tough but
ultimately life-giving quality of repentance. In Matthew 3, "repent"

doesn't just mean "clean up your act," although it does imply readiness; it primarily means "come to the God who is coming to you." That's why Matthew quotes Isaiah 40: "A voice of one calling in the wilderness, 'Prepare the way for the Lord, make straight paths for him'" (Mt 3:3). Isaiah 40 announced a time when the Jewish exiles would joyfully return to their homeland. Now, at this point in Matthew's story, John the Baptist is announcing the joyful coming of the world's king, who ushers in the ultimate exile from sin and death. Both passages, Isaiah 40 and Matthew 3, declare the hope of returning to the God who passionately seeks us.

Although John is declaring a hopeful message in this passage, on another level he is acting completely inappropriately. He doesn't understand the rules of religious etiquette—and dress code violations are the least of his problems. In John's day, spiritually important events occurred at the temple, that magnificent white stone structure that dominated the scene in Jerusalem. The temple formed the core of religious life. If you wanted to get closer to God, if you wanted to join the "in" group of good religious people, if you wanted to look sophisticated or spiritual or righteous, you went to the temple. And as a good Jew, you didn't need to be baptized—that ritual was reserved for second-class, outsider Gentile converts.

Imagine the disgust people must have felt when John appeared in the desert and started his spiritual renewal movement. Instead of going to the temple, now you had to trek into the desert—that dry, ugly, godforsaken outpost in the sticks. When you finally arrived, you wouldn't find a slick, sensitive, smart preacher; instead, you'd meet the hairy, uncouth, insect-grubbing bozo of the backwoods railing at you about your need to repent. "Everyone," John would say, "must go down into the brown, murky waters of the Jordan River. Sorry, the king is coming, and even you 'good and righteous' people aren't ready. So stop acting like religious jerks and repent. Your family heritage and your spiritual résumé mean nothing to God. Everyone needs to get dunked, washed and cleansed. Everyone must die and be born again."

Imagine the shock of this message. It would be like God saying the following to a hip urban megachurch: "If you want to experience God's exciting new thing, drive to a small, dusty town off the beaten track. At the Second Church of the Sprinkled-in-the-Blood Church of the Holy Spirit in Christ, a tiny storefront operation three blocks west of the only restaurant-bar on Main Street, you'll meet a married couple named Clem and Bertha. These toothless recovering meth addicts live in the local trailer park and will be wearing old bowling shirts from the local thrift store. But they're my chosen instruments and their church is my chosen place. Drive there, find them and submit to their bilingual preaching and praying. In their presence, become like little children—vulnerable, ignorant, expectant and utterly astonished. Clem and Bertha will lead you to encounter my grace. That's right: renewal is coming, but it won't happen through you."

That was the core of John's message. God doesn't have to bless anyone. He isn't in debt to us based on our religious heritage or spiritual achievements. So John railed at the religious leaders' smug sense of security: "Do not think you can say to yourselves, 'We have Abraham as our father.' I tell you that out of these stones God can raise up children for Abraham" (Mt 3:9). Like John the Baptist, God is wild and free; he will pour out his Spirit wherever he finds open, thirsty and desperate hearts. Our wealth, our education, our impressive programs and palatial buildings won't help us because when God finds poor-in-spirit, hungry, merciful people, he will display his power among them (see Mt 5:3-10).

John's theme of repentance is disturbing because it casts us onto God's mercy and election—that is, God's ability to choose when, where and how he will save and bless us. It's also unsettling because repentance is connected to our sin. In Matthew 3:6 we're told that the people were "confessing their sins." It's painful to admit that we've missed the mark in our relationship with God. It's painful to confess our idols of comfort, pleasure, control, appearance and possessions. It's painful to look into the eyes of those we love and hear them say, "You failed me and you hurt me." Everything within us wants to protest, "But I was only trying to . . ." or "Maybe that's true, but *you* never . . ." It doesn't matter. We shot our arrow and it sailed past God's target, piercing a spouse, child or friend, an entire community or the poor and oppressed. After the arrows of sin go awry, we stand dumbfounded. We can only stammer, "I had no idea it would hurt so much."

According to the Bible, there are only two ways to deal with our sin: we can justify it or we can confess it. Justifying—in combination with denying, minimizing or excusing sin—leads to spiritual death. Confessing sin leads to life. That's the even greater thrust in John's preaching: Confess your sin, repent, get ready, because someone is coming. The king is coming. In John's words, "But after me comes one who is more powerful than I, whose sandals I am not worthy to carry. He will baptize you with the Holy Spirit and fire" (Mt 3:11).

Thus, despite his uncouthness, John's call for repentance leads to hope. Repentance really is a sweet relief. We try so hard to hide and justify our sins, blaming and projecting them onto others. We play games with God and others and ourselves. Repentance means we remove these defensive shields—our blaming and excusing. We stop playing games and come home to the God who is with us, and we also come home to our true selves.

True repentance leads to deep relational healing. There's a person behind our repentance; there's a presence waiting to find us as we repent and come home. That's why we need to test the authenticity of repentance by asking questions like, "Is my repentance only painful or does it also lead to joy? Does it merely produce shame or does it cause me to run to the Father who loves me? Does it lead to bondage, more guilt and regret, or does it lead to a deeper freedom in Christ who died for me?"

The fourth-century preacher and pastor John Chrysostom urged his listeners to repent with joy and hope:

> Like the prodigal, let us also return home . . . no matter how far we have gotten carried away in our journey. Let us go back to our Father's house, not lingering over the length of the journey. . . . Only let us leave this strange land of sin where we have been drawn away from the Father. . . . He finds great pleasure in receiving back his children.[39]

In Matthew 3 John the Baptist fulfills his role by helping us see our need for repentance. He gets us started on the journey back home to the

Father's house. In the words of Dale Bruner, "In John the Baptist, God
does us the honor of taking us seriously, grabbing us by the lapel and
telling us that we must turn around if we are to meet God from the right
direction. . . . God uses John the Baptist—to accuse us, to humble us, to
bring us to our senses and to reality."[40] But for all his brilliance and boldness John's message can't lead us all the way home. Of course John
knows that, which is why he says Jesus is more powerful and worthy
than he (Mt 3:11).

Based on his knowledge of the Messiah's power and glory, we can
understand why John balked when Jesus came to him for baptism. He
protested by asking, "I need to be baptized by you, and do you come to
me?" (Mt 3:14). Jesus insisted: "Let it be so now; it is proper for us to do
this to fulfill all righteousness" (Mt 3:15). John consented and Jesus was
plunged into the brown water just like every other needy sinner.

On one level, Jesus' baptism serves as an opportunity for Jesus (and
the entire human race) to hear the approval of God the Father: "And a
voice from heaven said, 'This is my Son, whom I love; with him I am well
pleased'" (Mt 3:17). Most commentators see a connection between the
Father's voice here and in Isaiah 42:1: "Here is my servant, whom I up-
hold, my chosen one in whom I delight; I will put my Spirit on him and
he will bring justice to the nations."[41] In Matthew 1 we read that Jesus is
the promised Son of David. In chapter 2 we read that he is the very pleasing Son of God and the true Israel (Mt 2:15). Now in chapter 3 we read
that Jesus is the "beloved" (the Greek word is *agapetos*—note the Father's affection) Son who also fulfills the role of Isaiah's suffering servant. Matthew wants us to know that many separate threads are coming
together to give us the final, beautiful, complete picture of Jesus.[42]

But this story also serves another purpose: declaring Jesus' mission to
save sinners by standing with us. Because of its potential to provoke mis-
understandings, Jesus' baptism with other sinners was a daring act. In
Mark's more explicit account, John proclaimed "a baptism of repentance
for the forgiveness of sins" (Mk 1:4). Of course this poses a problem because the New Testament offers us a sinless Christ (see Heb 4:15 and
1 Pet 2:22). The entire story of redemption hinges on Jesus' sinless nature. If Jesus is a sinner, even just a mildly messed-up sinner, he can't

help us because he's part of the problem; he's wedged in the bog of sin just like us. So from a public relations standpoint, Jesus' baptism was risky and potentially confusing. The people could already derisively call him "Jesus, the Nazarene" (Mt 2:23), the alleged Messiah and Savior with the sketchy family tree and the shameful birth. Now his enemies could smirk and say, "Our Messiah and Savior? Are you kidding? Did you know he stood in line with the rest of them, plunging into the murky waters just like every other spiritual loser and outsider?"

It was definitely a PR gamble, but Jesus and the early church embraced the risk. At his baptism Jesus made a clear statement of his intention and mission: he wanted to identify with us. Jesus' ministry is not just *to* sinners; it's *with* sinners. His baptism is a body-language statement that says, "I am with you. I am for you not against you." This becomes clearer when Jesus later refers to his death on the cross as "my baptism" (Mk 10:38-39; Lk 12:50). Jesus' river baptism prefigures his cross baptism: both were bodily expressions of his desire to be with us in order to save us.

So in his first public act Jesus allies himself with sinners and rebels. Over and over again, in his genealogy, his birth, his baptism, his eating habits and finally his death, Jesus plunges into the sinful mess of humanity. And following in the footsteps of Jesus, the church can do no less.

INTO THE SOUPY FOG
Matthew 4:1-11

Back in 2002 the town of Inglis, Florida, made national news by banning Satan from its city limits. Carolyn Risher, the mayor of this sleepy town north of Tampa, got fed up with the prince of darkness wreaking havoc on her home turf so she booted him out for good. "Be it known from this day forward," the official proclamation read, "that Satan, ruler of darkness, giver of evil, destroyer of what is just and good, is not now, nor ever will be, a part of this town of Inglis." The reporter who broke the story for the *New York Times* cynically noted, "The language leaves Satan very little wiggle room."[43]

If only Jesus had it so good. Instead, right after his baptismal blessing when the heavens opened, the dove descended and the Father declared, "This is my Son, whom I love; with him I am well pleased" (Mt 3:17), Je-

sus "was led by the Spirit into the wilderness to be tempted by the devil"
(4:1). After fasting forty days, Jesus was in a vulnerable state, famished and
lonely, haunted by the distant memory of the Father's blessing. And this
was the moment when Satan approached like a lion circling a wounded
gazelle. Where's the mayor of Inglis, Florida, when you really need her?

For Jesus and the early Christians, Satan (a.k.a. Lucifer, the devil,
Beelzebub, the deceiver and the prince of darkness) wasn't the butt of
secular jokes, a complex metaphor for cosmic evil, or a wimpy spirit that
we can intimidate with official proclamations. Throughout Matthew's
Gospel (and all of the Gospels) Satan and his minions are real and possess real power.[44]

But Satan's temptations usually aren't obvious. We probably won't
hear a sinister voice whisper, "Hey, buddy, there's a Chase Bank across
the street. Why don't you put on a fake mustache, buy a black squirt gun
and go rob that place? Think about it, my friend: you could move to Rio
and live comfortably for years to come." Instead, the essence of temptation is more like a pervasive, soupy fog. In Satan's soupy fog we get confused and disoriented, our head spins, our heart gets twisted and our
lives take the plunge into apparent godforsakenness. This is what we're
more likely to hear: "God is not for you or with you. And because either
God is not good or you are not worthy, this Immanuel does not walk
beside you in your sin and abandonment. In the midst of the cold im-
mensity of the cosmos, you are alone. You cannot trust in the care of a
'heavenly Father' who calls you his beloved and includes you in the fellowship of other beloved ones. So look out for yourself, grab what you
can and chart your own path through this world."

This was the primordial temptation, the original soupy fog encountered by Adam and Eve. In Genesis 3 the serpent sowed seeds of mistrust
with a simple question: "Did God really say, 'You must not eat from any
tree in the garden?'" In other words, "God's not good. God's a prude, a
cosmic killjoy. Just go grab that fruit. You deserve it." It was the same
soupy fog God's covenant people encountered in the Old Testament.
"What kind of God would lead you into the desert and then ditch you?
Don't you see? You're on your own."

Is God good? That's the central question behind every temptation and the taproot of every disorder in our souls. Can I trust God? For most of us, it's a conflicted and even agonizing question. We certainly have our doubts. We've been told, "You have to rely on yourself. Trust leads to betrayal, so keep your heart closed." These conclusions often stem from deep wounds in our heart—abuse, abandonment, rejection, betrayal, disappointment. All of these act like arrows to pierce our heart with hurt and fear. It's often easier to numb our hearts, shutting down our trust and turning back to a lifestyle of entitlement and self-protection. In other words, if God isn't my good Father who provides for my needs, then I will get my needs met my own way.[45]

In Matthew 4, Satan follows a similar tactic with Jesus.[46] In the first temptation ("If you are the son of God, tell these stones to become bread," Mt 4:3) Satan creates soupy fog about Jesus' relation to the Father. In essence, he challenges Jesus' identity with a taunt: "Assuming you are the Son of God, use your power to meet your needs and end this test. Surely as God's Son you deserve to satisfy your needs right now." This temptation cut to the heart of Jesus' mission. It was a clear attempt to derail his ultimate goal of being God with us, Messiah and Son of David.[47]

This ancient temptation feeds right into our hearts as well. Satan still uses it to derail us in our lives, turning us into consumers rather than disciples. For example, a few years ago, an ad that appeared in *Real Simple* magazine was headlined, "Things to do while you're alive." It then listed twenty-one items to check off before you die. Everything on the list represented the good life of the affluent consumer:

- See a Broadway show front-row center.
- Go to the Olympic Games.
- Float along the Nile.
- Fly across the Atlantic in a private jet.
- Get a spa treatment that requires a team.

At the bottom of the page the ad mentioned, "Whatever's on your list of things to do in life, do it better with Visa." Ah, the good life! And you can and should have it right now. Don't wait, don't agonize, don't worry about others, don't deny yourself because you deserve it right now.

By giving in to this temptation Jesus would have used his identity as the Son in a way inconsistent with the Father's mission for his earthly life. In the Old Testament, the people of Israel demanded bread right away without trusting the Father's love.[48] As a result, they died in the wilderness. But Jesus responded to this temptation by refusing to demand bread on his terms, choosing instead to rely on his Father and live according to his Father's will.[49]

After each temptation Jesus begins his response with the same formula statement: "It is written" (see Mt 4:4, 7, 10). Jesus shows us the way to deal with Satan's soupy fog: trusting his Father's love by knowing, clinging to and reciting Scripture. In this Gospel, Jesus will constantly rely on and quote his Bible—that is, the Old Testament. He obviously loved it, read it, studied it, memorized it and then lived it.[50]

In the second temptation, Satan tries turning this Scripture-quoting tactic against Jesus: "If [or "Assuming"] you are the Son of God," he says, "throw yourself down. For it is written: 'He will command his angels concerning you, and they will lift you up'" (Mt 4:6). If Jesus takes Satan's bait, he'll subvert the mission of God's Son, not only by ripping Scripture out of context but also by refusing to trust in the Father's love and goodness. So Jesus quotes Deuteronomy 6:16: "Do not put the Lord your God to the test" (Mt 4:7). It's a clear reference to a time in Israel's history when they did put God to the test, demanding miraculous proof of God's care rather than trusting and obeying God's love.

The third temptation is another example of Satan's soupy fog: "All this I will give you . . . if you will bow down and worship me" (Mt 4:9). This ploy also stems from the primal temptation to disparage God's good heart, luring us into mistrust and a sense of entitlement. "Just bow down and worship me," Satan offers. "You can have it all right now—no annoying disciples, no long journey through the pain of this broken world, no tears on a bloody cross."

Prior to the third temptation in this story, Matthew tells us that "the devil took him to a very high mountain and showed him all the kingdoms of the world and their splendor" (Mt 4:8). That is the way of Satan: tempting us to go up high, to set our own agenda and get our own needs met without ever going down. But throughout this Gospel, the Holy Spirit leads Jesus down before he goes up: down into the incarnation, down into Mary's womb, down into the stable, down into the bloody mess at the slaughter of the innocents, down into the waters of baptism, down into the presence of human disease and demonic attack. For Jesus, the way up is always down. He arrives at the resurrection life only by walking into and through the crucifixion. So Jesus descends into the ordinary, the broken and even the grotesque condition of his fallen world. Satan wants him to rise above it all. But Jesus, like a strong man lifting a boulder, must stoop low, getting his body underneath the dangerous load of sin and suffering, even allowing the load to crush him, as he finally rises again to lift the boulder out of the mud.

As Matthew's Gospel tells us so often, Jesus our Immanuel must be with us, standing in solidarity with a fallen and broken creation in order to raise and reconcile us to the Father's gracious heart. In Matthew 4:1-11 we see Jesus' deep solidarity with us on two fronts. First, Jesus stepped into Israel's story. As the children of Israel wandered in the desert for forty years and failed, so Jesus faced forty days and nights of testing and prevailed. Secondly, as Adam and Eve faced one temptation in paradise and failed, Jesus faced three temptations in a howling wasteland and prevailed. In both the story of Israel and that of Adam and Eve, humans wanted autonomy because of their failure to trust the Father's goodness and love. In contrast, Jesus trusted his Father and thus recapitulated— or took up and transformed in his own life—the broken stories of Israel, of humanity and of us personally. He lived the life we were called to live and thus achieved the mission of God's Son.

But he also lived our life by suffering with and for us. He walked right into the thick, soupy fog of our temptations, tasting all of it, drinking it to the dregs. As one New Testament writer declared, "Since the children have flesh and blood, he too shared in their humanity. . . . He had to be made like them . . . in every way, in order that he might become a merciful and faithful high priest. . . . Because he himself suffered when he was tempted, he is able to help those who are being tempted" (Heb 2:14-18).

At many points in our journey through life we will face the soupy fog of temptation. It will swirl around us and penetrate into us. We will question and then reject the Father's good heart, repulsing his hand of mercy and grace. As we attempt to meet our own needs our own way, we'll get lost in the fog, gashing our leg against a rock or plunging off a cliff. It happens so frequently we assume it's normal.

In his love and mercy, Jesus Immanuel walked into our fog. It swirled around him and threatened to destroy him, as it does every other human being. The fog of Satanic temptations left Jesus in need of assistance (see Mt 4:11), as it does us. But unlike Israel, unlike Adam and Eve, unlike you and me, Jesus never lost his footing. The fog didn't engulf him. By trusting his Father's love and goodness in the midst of howling temptation, Jesus showed us how to walk through Satan's soupy fog. As the fog-bearer and the fog-defeater, the triune God invites us with reassuring words: "Take my hand. Trust me. I've been through the fog. And I know how to lead you out of it."

THE PUBLIC MINISTRY OF JESUS

Matthew 4:12–10:42

For four chapters in Matthew Jesus has kept quiet about his identity and his mission. He hasn't made any public pronouncements; he hasn't taught anyone; and although things have been done to him, he hasn't done anything to anyone else. Then in Matthew 4:17 he opens his mouth for a short but incredible announcement: "Repent, for the kingdom of heaven is near."

The whole Old Testament tells the big, beautiful, hope-filled story of a God who would one day lovingly reign over his people and the peoples of the earth. God's reign would be marked by a peaceful "rightness" to the world—everything would be in its right place and every relationship would be on its right terms. And now Jesus was walking all over Galilee claiming that God's reign of love and rightness was here. Of course it had already been here, but not like this. It wasn't just a beautiful dream for the future anymore; in and through Jesus it was here and now and nothing could stop it.

Surprisingly, Jesus didn't quickly crush the opposition and roll out a huge program of instant redemption. Instead he started small and local

with three slow, quiet steps: he called some ordinary people to follow
him, he healed sick people (lots of sick people with various diseases, se-
vere pain, demons, seizures and paralysis), and then he gathered a community around himself. Obviously, this last step was important because
Matthew fills the next three chapters with Jesus' teachings to those who
had gathered around him (Mt 5–7). These teachings range from the
beautiful to the seemingly impossible, but they begin with one little
phrase: "Blessed are the poor in spirit" (Mt 5:3). In other words, we can't
do it but God can. This little verse contains the wide-open door, the
strong hand reaching down, the elevator lifting us up. This little verse
makes the way of discipleship accessible to all of us.

But Jesus didn't just teach; he demonstrated the power of the coming
kingdom. When Jesus showed up, stuff changed. Lives were transformed. Outcasts experienced Jesus' acceptance. The desperately sick
got healed. Sin-sick souls found forgiveness. All of these transformed
lives pointed back to Jesus' mission to preach the good news of the kingdom and heal sick people (Mt 4:23; 9:35). And the story keeps dropping
hints that the good news will include Israel as it also embraces all the
nations of the earth.

Jesus also drops plenty of uncomfortable words. Words like "follow me"
and "obey me" and "listen to me," even when it's inconvenient, risky and
dangerous—even when it might get you killed. Jesus didn't just want people to know about him; he didn't just want broken people to find healing
and acceptance (although that was part of it); he also wanted people to follow him. He wasn't kidding, either. At one point, a well-meaning disciple
wannabe eagerly offered his services to Jesus' cause, and Jesus basically
turned him down. "Foxes have holes and birds have nests," Jesus told him,
"but the Son of Man has no place to lay his head" (Mt 8:20). Jesus left no
doubt that he didn't just want a crowd of spectators; he wanted disciples
who would build their lives on his presence and his words.

STARTING WITH THE BIG STORY
Matthew 4:12-25

Everyone in my family resents my annoying television-viewing habits. I
often saunter into the living room during the middle of a show or movie

or game, suddenly get interested and then start asking pressing questions: "What's going on? Who is that? Why did she slap that man in the face? Why is there a polar bear on a tropical island? How did the Minnesota Vikings score four touchdowns?" Many years ago they made a pact: don't answer dad's pushy questions. Sometimes they'll roll their eyes and blurt out, "Dad, you can't just mosey into the middle of the movie/game/show. If you want to understand the whole story, start from the beginning—like the rest of us."

People can be so unreasonable! Although I must admit they have a point: it often helps to get a story's big picture before you can understand the details. For instance, a few years ago I tried to understand *Lost* by dipping into the third episode of the second season or the sixth episode of the fourth season, but it left me utterly bewildered. Then my daughter convinced me to sit with her and watch the entire first season in one weekend. Somewhere toward the end of the first DVD, I jumped off the couch and exclaimed, "Wow, this show is amazing! I finally understand *Lost*."

In the same way, when Jesus declares, "Repent, for the kingdom of heaven has come near" (Mt 4:17),[1] we can't understand the story of the kingdom until we get the big picture. The "kingdom of heaven" didn't start when Jesus showed up by the shores of Lake Galilee; God told us about the kingdom way back in Old Testament times. In startling, redemption-charged images, God provided a vision for a coming day when his rule would cover the earth like the waters cover the sea. For instance, the book of Isaiah promised that one day

- everyone would come streaming to the God of Jacob (Is 2:1)

- the nations of the earth would exchange their war instruments for farm instruments; they would cease to learn about war (Is 2:4)

- the Messiah would judge the poor with righteousness (Is 11:4)

- the calf and the lion would dwell together in peace (Is 11:6)

- the earth would be filled with the knowledge of the Lord (Is 11:9)

- the broken-hearted would be healed and the prisoners would be released (Is 61:1)

- God would create a new heavens and a new earth (Is 65:17-19)[2]

The big story of the kingdom of heaven meant that the triune God wasn't finished with his fallen, broken and rebellious creation.[3] One day, as God foretold so often in the Old Testament, he would come to his people and begin to reign as their rightful king. And then his reign would extend over the whole earth.

It's an astounding story and dream: all the broken things of the earth will be restored; all the sad stories and songs will be reversed; all the wars, hostilities, armed conflicts and places of torture will be converted into zones of God's peace; every traumatic memory and nightmare will be healed; every tear will be wiped away by God's tender hand; the poor and vulnerable will receive Messiah's protection while callous oppressors will receive judgment.

That was the dream, and the Jews kept the kingdom story alive, allowing it to burn in their hearts as they awaited its arrival. So when Jesus made his daring announcement in Matthew 4:17, we can imagine the electrifying excitement—or the appalling contempt. Some people would gasp with wonder and ask, "Is it really true? After all these years of yearning and longing, God's reign is finally here?" Others would choke with scorn; after all, what right did this lowly carpenter with a sketchy family tree and unsavory followers have to announce the inbreaking of God's kingdom?

The arrival of the kingdom in and through Jesus becomes the major theme of Matthew's Gospel. At the end of chapter 4 and then again at the end of chapter 9 Matthew pauses and provides a mini-summary of Jesus' life and work. On both occasions he uses almost identical words to say that Jesus went throughout Galilee, teaching in the synagogues and proclaiming the good news of the kingdom (Mt 4:23; 9:35). Jesus never said the kingdom of heaven would start after a person died or just managed to try a little harder. In his words and in his actions, Jesus declared, "The kingdom of heaven is here right now, in this place—even lowly Galilee, of all places[4]—in my presence, and it's for you. Yes, you ordinary, little, spiritually poor, mourning, meek, hungry, mercy-giving, peacemaking people." Jesus was the kingdom bearer; anyone who trusted him could enter God's promise of a new creation under the king's reign.

Jesus used the phrase "kingdom of heaven" in its broadest, most comprehensive sense. First of all, the kingdom was radically communal. Initially Jesus called a couple of brothers, Peter and Andrew, who ran a small fishing business. Then he included James and John, another set of brothers. Peter had issues with control and impulsivity. James and John, nicknamed "the Sons of Thunder," had issues with anger and volatility. By calling these four men—and then Matthew the tax collector, Mary and Martha, and the whole motley crew—Jesus was making a clear statement about his kingdom movement: it can't exist without community. Forging a community is part of kingdom living. Community is the place where our egos shrivel and die because God delights to throw us together with people who love poorly—and then they have to deal with our pathetic attempts at love. As Henri Nouwen once said, "Before you got up for breakfast this morning, you had the chance to forgive at least three times."[5] So right from the beginning, the kingdom was marked by the harsh, demanding but beautiful reality of shaping a new kind of community under a new kind of king.

Secondly, Jesus' concept of the kingdom of heaven was global. Jesus thought like a good Jew, his mind shaped and honed by years of reading Scripture. In Matthew's Gospel, Jesus seems particularly shaped by Genesis and Isaiah. From Isaiah Jesus learned that one day the king would reign over all things—machine guns and cruise missiles, wolves and cows and bears, the waters of the sea, global poverty, terrorist cells and oppressive regimes. Isaiah's kingdom images reflect the realms of politics, environmental wholeness, human rights and economics.

In a recent report, the U.S. Labor Department added twelve countries to its list of nations that use child labor or forced labor. It also warned that the global economic crisis could force more children at younger ages into situations of exploitation. Some of the worst offenders include the countries of Uzbekistan and Myanmar. Of course we're not talking about thirteen-year-old Johnny doing a few chores around the house; the Labor Department estimates that 215 million children, many as young as six years old, are forced to leave school and work long, grueling hours in indecent and unsafe working conditions. Some of the common products produced with the help of child exploitation include cotton, sugar cane, tobacco, coffee, bricks, gold, diamonds and coal.[6]

How should we, the followers of Jesus the king, respond to the exploitation of children? Do we ignore it and say it's not our problem or our nation's problem? No, because the coming king will redeem every facet of this broken planet. Do I neglect this story because God cares only about my personal relationship with Jesus? No, because the coming king cares about my salvation *and* justice for the poor and oppressed. If the kingdom of heaven has indeed come to us in the presence of Jesus, then as his followers we will care about the mistreatment of children around the world. We will also care about our choices as consumers and how those choices promote exploitation rather than compassion. I will consider these things because Jesus and his coming kingdom address large, global issues of economic justice, human rights and environmental wholeness. There is nothing that does not have kingdom implications. As Isaiah prophesied, one day "the earth will be filled with the knowledge of the LORD as the waters cover the sea" (Is 11:9).

Finally, at the same time, Jesus' call is also deeply personal, echoing in every human heart. In Matthew 4:18-19 this call to "follow me" extends to two ordinary fishermen.[7] In 4:23-24 Jesus demonstrates the power of the kingdom by "healing every disease and sickness among the people."

As a result, the kingdom comes into small and personal places, like our struggle with bladder cancer, depression, sexual temptation or drug addiction. It comes to a father fretting about his wayward daughter. It comes to my friend "Curt," who daily faces the fear of living with HIV and AIDS, the yearning to connect with a woman and be married someday, the struggle to pay his rent and medical expenses, and his intense battle to live in obedience to King Jesus. It's never easy, but if Jesus' kingdom power and presence won't flow to Curt and the rest of us through the community of Jesus' people, it certainly can't heal global issues of poverty, human rights and war.

So as his redeemed, kingdom-gripped people, we constantly pray, "Yes, come, Lord Jesus. Let your kingdom come!"

UPSIDE DOWN, UPSIDE RIGHT
Matthew 5:1-12

My friend Ray, a gruff recovering alcoholic, started attending our church's worship services to appease his wife and daughter. He believed in God (or his higher power), and he respected Jesus as a "great guy," but he kept complaining about Jesus' teachings. "Look, Jesus' teachings make for nice poetry on Sunday morning," he told me, "but I have three main beefs with Jesus' instructions: they're weird, unrealistic and negative. Hey, don't get me wrong, I like Jesus; I just can't live Jesus' way because I need a keep-it-simple God."

As we come to Matthew 5–7 and the Sermon on the Mount, Ray's gripe hits home. This sermon contains Jesus' manifesto for kingdom living, and the first twelve verses, which include the Beatitudes, set the stage.[8] Most people agree that the Beatitudes do make for lovely poetry, but was Ray right? Are they part of Jesus' weird, unrealistic and negative teachings?

These are the actual Beatitudes given by Jesus in Matthew 5:3-10:

- Blessed are the poor in spirit, for theirs is the kingdom of heaven.
- Blessed are those who mourn, for they will be comforted.
- Blessed are the meek, for they will inherit the earth.
- Blessed are those who hunger and thirst for righteousness, for they will be filled.
- Blessed are the merciful, for they will be shown mercy.
- Blessed are the pure in heart, for they will see God.
- Blessed are the peacemakers, for they will be called children of God.
- Blessed are those who are persecuted because righteousness, for theirs is the kingdom of heaven.

In Ray's defense, this does sound like a strange and unrealistic pattern for life. Jesus keeps calling his disciples "blessed," but most of us don't embrace his requirements for blessedness. I'm not sure if I'm ready to become fully pure in heart or merciful: that would mean I'd have to relinquish a truckload of impure desires and resentments. Nor do I ardently wish the Beatitudes on my loved ones—"Hi, Bob, I've been praying that you'll get persecuted today." At first sight Jesus' list seems counterintuitive.

But perhaps my friend Ray—and the rest of us—fail to see what Jesus was doing in his life, teaching, death and resurrection. Maybe the world as we know it is upside down, but we're so used to it that it seems right side up. When Jesus announced the coming of the kingdom (Mt 4:17), he initiated a revolutionary movement to set things right, to restore this upside down, off-kilter, broken world by turning it right side up.

When Jesus listed the Beatitudes, he wasn't just making nice poetry or giving good advice. He was declaring a manifesto of good news: "The world is changing and it's starting right now, right here, in my presence and in my Father's kingdom. The poor in spirit are getting blessed right now. The mourners are getting comforted right now. Those who hunger and thirst for righteousness are receiving satisfaction right now. Those who display mercy are receiving mercy right now. The kingdom hasn't come in its fullness yet, but it's starting to happen because that's the way it's supposed to be." Throughout the Beatitudes Jesus is more or less saying, "I'm turning the world right side up; I'm restoring everything to its proper position. Hang around with me, start following me and working with me, and let's transform this broken world into what it should be."

When you've spent most of your life upside down, walking on your hands with your face in the dirt, the good news of walking on your feet will seem strange. So, yes, Ray had a point: Jesus' teachings do seem weird to us. But that's simply because of our natural disorientation.

Second, if we're honest like Ray, the Beatitudes also strike us as unrealistic. In my own power, I don't tend to display mercy or find joy in persecution. If the Beatitudes are just recommendations about being nice and getting my life together, I don't need them. I've collected enough "you're messed up but try harder" advice.

It's important to note that the Beatitudes are preceded by Matthew 5:1-2, which in many ways serve as the interpretive key: "Now when Jesus saw the crowds, he went up on a mountainside and sat down. His disciples came to him, and he began to teach them." In other words, this sermon describes what happens when we come to Jesus. Throughout this Gospel Matthew provides clues that life in Jesus is much more than doing things for Jesus, although that's certainly part of it. Following Jesus also means—and perhaps first means—heeding his invitation to come (Mt 11:28) and the Father's call to listen (Mt 17:4). "Come" and "listen" precede "do" and "serve." We could call this the contemplative dimension of discipleship, the ability to be with Jesus, drawing life from him both alone and in community.

In a practical sense, we must sit at Jesus' feet and say, "Lord, we've tried to be good and happy and loving but we need help—lots of help! We need to learn life from you. So we're going to sit and listen. How would you have us live?" Jesus' description of life in the kingdom isn't about trying harder, gaining power and control and then mastering the spiritual life. It begins with an act of powerlessness and surrender.

Consider the first Beatitude: "Blessed are the poor in spirit, for theirs is the kingdom of heaven."[9] In Jesus' time there were two Greek words for poor: one referred to those with few resources; the other (*ptochos*) referred to the destitute, the desperate, the beggars.[10] Matthew 5:3 uses the second word. The key idea is that the poor in spirit know their inadequacy and so trust God as their ultimate refuge. In their powerlessness, they surrender to God and find confidence in him.

As a recovering alcoholic, Ray should have known this. Every addict must begin with the first step of any twelve-step program: admitting powerlessness in the face of an addictive substance or behavior and an inability to manage life as a result. In at least one area of his life, his addiction to alcohol, Ray was already living and breathing Jesus' teaching; he just forgot who came up with the ideas behind his twelve-step program.

In the words of Dale Bruner, "Every command in the Sermon on the Mount . . . drives believing readers back into the valley of the first Beatitude and its wonderful promise of kingdom belonging and kingdom resources."[11] In other words, once we accept and embrace our spiritual poverty, our radical need for God's grace, and once we surrender to Jesus and admit that we are powerless to save ourselves, that opens the door to everything else in God's kingdom. Consider a few examples:

- When we see God's offer of grace in the midst of our spiritual poverty, it's easy to mourn for our sins (Mt 5:4). Our tendency to run away from pain, especially the pain of our sin, starts to subside.

- When we believe that God is in charge of the world and our salvation, it's easy to be meek, to patiently trust God for his way and his timing to set the world right (Mt 5:5).

- As we receive mercy in the midst of our powerlessness, it seems utterly inconsistent to heap judgment rather than mercy on our fellow sinners (Mt 5:7).

- In this broken world of misunderstanding, hatred and prejudice, we must move into the conflict, becoming agents of reconciliation and peace (Mt 5:9).

- When we realize that Jesus saved us, out of love we'll follow him even if that means enduring persecution (Mt 5:10).

In living the Beatitudes I don't simply try harder to cut against the grain of my natural urges—acting merciful when I feel like smacking you in the face, for example. If following Jesus begins with spiritual poverty, the blessed powerlessness that sets us free in Christ, then Jesus' Beatitudes are realistic. We begin the rich life of the kingdom by admitting our spiritual poverty. We start the heroic journey of discipleship by acknowledging our spiritual inadequacy. And we do it in community because life in the kingdom of heaven implies doing life together with Jesus. That's realistic. That I can do.

Finally, according to Ray, Jesus' teachings are too negative. In his words, "I just can't walk around all day, weeping and mourning as I let people walk all over me and slap me on my right and left cheeks." For some reason Ray missed the key word in this passage: "blessed." Jesus repeats it nine times. Translators have debated how to interpret the Greek word *makarios*. "Happy" and "fortunate" seem too weak. Jewish New Testament translator Andre Chouraqui suggests that the Hebrew equivalent, *ashrei*, indicates the thrill of the traveler who's about to reach his goal. He's been on a long, hard journey, but he's on the right path and he's almost home. The Spanish term *bienaventurado* seems to capture this sense of joy. It's a word of approval, affirmation and confidence. Thus, my favorite translation for *makarios* is "Congratulations! You're on the right road. You're going to make it."[12]

This is the beauty and power of life with Jesus: his words of approval and promise become the truest thing about me, and these promises don't depend on my big-faith, heroic spiritual achievement. As the rest of the New Testament makes clear, we receive Jesus' affirmation and blessing as a sheer gift.[13]

If we don't live with this radically free and unmerited blessing at the core of our lives, then we enter into spiritual death. In the words of Henri Nouwen, "[Without Jesus' words of blessing] you will go on running helter-skelter, always anxious and restless, always lustful and angry, never fully satisfied. You know that this is the compulsiveness that keeps us going and busy, but at the same time makes us wonder whether we are getting anywhere in the long run. This is the way to spiritual exhaustion and burn-out. This is the way to spiritual death."[14]

Instead of spiritual death, Jesus blesses us with more hope than we could ever imagine. Notice the grand and confident reality that Jesus offers at the end of each Beatitude:

- for theirs is the kingdom of heaven
- for they will be comforted
- for they will inherit the earth
- for they will be filled (or satisfied)
- for they will be shown mercy
- for they will see God
- for they will be called childen of God
- for theirs is the kingdom of heaven

It's important to note that for Jesus these things will happen because God will do them—in the presence of God with us, they have already started to happen. The poor in spirit will receive and are receiving the ultimate expression of God's kingdom. Those who mourn will receive and are receiving comfort. The new heavens and the new earth promised by the prophets will belong and do belong to these people. They will make it on the journey because God will make sure they make it! And it all begins with the one thing we can do well: admit our own powerlessness.[15]

But this isn't a solo project, a private journey for me and Jesus. The

Beatitudes describe life together with Jesus at the center. Remember Matthew 5:1-2: "His disciples came to him, and he began to teach them." They came to him in community.

What does this look like in everyday life? A few years ago at one of our predictable all-church business meetings, we met Jesus in a profound way. After the meeting a few of us stood in the back of our sanctuary, chatting about the upcoming week. Suddenly a young woman shared that during the past week her mother had blasted her with deeply wounding words, calling her "worthless" and heaping scorn on her for her faith in Christ. After listening quietly, another friend said, "I'm sorry that hurt you. You know, I've lived most of my life with a strong message that I'm completely unimportant to my father." Another friend confessed she was struggling to balance her workaholic tendencies with the time needed to raise three children.

The conversation was honest and even raw. On one level, it was a descent into spiritual poverty and mercy and, for at least one of us, a descent into persecution. Then we huddled together, put our arms around each other and prayed, "Lord, we've tried to be good and happy and loving but we need help—lots of help! We need to learn life from you. So we're going to stay with you and listen." It was deep and rich and real. As the Spirit of God came among us, we also experienced the rich presence and blessing of Jesus. Indeed, we were on the way with Jesus—not alone but together. We knew that in the midst of our poverty, we were all blessed beyond measure.

THE GLORY OF SALT
Matthew 5:13-16

In his book titled *Salt: A World History*, Mark Kurlansky recounts a French folk tale about a princess who tells her father, "I love you like salt." Angered by this apparent slight, the father banishes her from the kingdom. But when he is denied salt, he realizes its value and therefore the depth of his daughter's love. Kurlansky concludes, "Salt is so common, so easy to obtain, and so inexpensive that we have forgotten that from the beginning of civilization until about 100 years ago, salt was one of the most sought-after commodities in human history."[16]

Ah, the glory of salt! For thousands of years salt represented wealth. Soldiers were paid in salt. Evil spirits were warded off by salt. For the Romans, a man in love was in a salted state. We really can't live without salt. Salt deficiency causes headaches and then nausea. If the salt deprivation continues, we will die.[17]

So when Jesus stood on the side of the mountain and told his disciples, "You are the salt of the earth," he was giving them a huge compliment and also a challenge. The Greek construction of the text is emphatic: "You, yes, you and only you are the salt of the earth. . . . You, yes, you and only you are the light of the world."[18] Notice the preposterousness of it all: after gathering a motley bunch of decent but deeply flawed disciples, riddled with self-centeredness, constantly vying for position, nursing grudges, fleeing danger and discomfort, whining like little kids, Jesus confidently told them, "*You*, yes you, are the salt of the earth. *You*, yes you, are the light of the world." Apparently Jesus could say this with a straight face because the disciples, despite their faults and limitations, were bound to Jesus (see Mt 5:1-2).[19]

That's the essence of life in the kingdom of God: everything gets turned upside down, which is really right side up. The poor in spirit get the kingdom. The meek inherit the earth. The hungry and thirsty get satisfied. In chapter 11, after noting the greatness of John the Baptist, Jesus comments, "Yet whoever is least in the kingdom of heaven is greater than he" (Mt 11:11). Little people, ordinary, flawed, even weak and preposterous people, become the beautiful, God-appointed heralds of a brand new world.

New Testament scholars debate exactly what Jesus meant when he called his disciples the salt of the earth. For the sake of simplicity, I'll discuss two broad categories of interpretation: salt is good, and salt is different. Salt exudes goodness and vitality because it's useful and valuable. Salt is a preservative, slowing decay and keeping meat edible. Historically salt has also been connected with the joy of new beginnings, and newborn babies were rubbed with salt (see Ezek 16:4). It's no wonder then that throughout history "procuring salt became a necessity of life, giving it great symbolic importance and economic value."[20]

I often wonder if our culture and our neighbors give us "great symbolic value" and consider us "a necessity of life." Do they see our good works and then give glory to our heavenly Father (see Mt 5:16)? Do our friends, coworkers and neighbors find us attractive, interesting, flavorful and compelling? In other words, do we truly reflect the character Jesus outlines in the Beatitudes? Are we poor in spirit? Do we display meekness and mercy? Are we committed to living as peacemakers? Or have we become salt that is good for nothing: dull, bland and flavorless?[21]

Every time I think the culture is giving Christ-followers a bad rap, I hear another horror story about our very unsalty behavior. After Harvard professor Kay Redfield Jamison courageously described her struggle with mental illness, she received thousands of letters. The most disturbing came from "fundamentalist Christians" berating her for turning her back on God. According to Jamison, "Others thought my illness just deserts for not having truly accepted Jesus Christ into my heart, or for not having prayed sincerely enough. I had left my heart open to Satan, and he had entered in. Madness and despair were precisely what I deserved and would have in this world and the next. . . . One woman, who included a prayer card with excerpts from the Bible, wrote that it was a good thing I hadn't had children as I had at least 'spared the world of one more crazy manic-depressive.'"[22]

If we get persecuted for this kind of behavior, we really can't complain about it. Jesus was without sin and yet sinners flocked to him. He even called sinners to repent—not exactly a church growth strategy—but broken people felt his compassion, not the terror of exclusion and judgment. As my friend and author Denis Haack notes, "Our message is the gospel of Christ, and since he is attractive, shouldn't our proclamation (and our lives!) be attractive as well?"[23]

If people in our culture are suspicious, cynical, bored, frightened or even repulsed by the church, we can start by asking Jesus to "re-saltify" us. We take our lives back to Matthew 5:3 ("Blessed are the poor in spirit") as we pray, "Lord Jesus, we are powerless to turn our lives into good salt; so by your power make us salty again."

Salt is not only useful and attractive; it's also different. Salt can flavor and preserve only because it has a different chemical nature from the substance it penetrates. Salt is most fully "alive" when it "behaves" like salt. When it loses its flavor, its distinctive character and chemical composition, when it stops acting like salt, then it's worthless. It isn't attractive, good, interesting or valuable. In Jesus' words, "[The salt] is no longer good for anything, except to be thrown out and trampled underfoot" (Mt 5:13). The Greek word for "good for nothing" or "becoming insipid" literally means "to become foolish."

If we just blend into the world around us, nobody will persecute us; people will step on us like road dust. Unsalty believers aren't attacked or ambushed or ridiculed or mocked; they're just shrugged off as irrelevant. They are so un-Beatitudelike, so insipid and dull, that there's no need to persecute them.

That's why Jesus started his kingdom manifesto with the Beatitudes. The goal is not to be different; the goal is to live life with Jesus, and that will make us different. When we face the pain of this broken world, we will be different. When we're hungering and thirsting for a better world, we will be different. When we're displaying mercy and living as peacemakers, we will be different. When we're meek and gentle in the midst of a pushy, violent culture, we will be different. When we're pure in heart, we will be different. And this differentness will often lead to one thing: trouble. Thus Jesus' blessing-warning in the last Beatitude: "Blessed are those who are persecuted because of righteousness" (Mt 5:10).

Salty Christ-followers don't seek trouble; they just know that, like Jesus, they're not always understood, appreciated or loved. Salt is a preserving force and light is a penetrating fire. Both salt and light can "sting" or expose. Seriously salty Christians can get killed, or at least mocked and excluded.

Back in the 1970s Oscar Romero was chosen to lead the Catholic Church in El Salvador because he was quiet and "safe." But after the murder of his friend and champion of the poor Father Rutillio Grande, Romero knew that the church as the world's true salt had to be different from the surrounding culture. In his words, "[The church] is not to be measured by the government's support but rather by its own authenticity." As government soldiers tortured and executed innocent people, Romero proclaimed in one of his sermons, "Like a voice crying in the wilderness, we must continually say no to violence and yes to peace." He traveled the countryside meeting the brokenhearted and visiting garbage dumps to comfort the suffering and reclaim the dead.[24]

On March 23, 1980, he criticized his country's military for its role in the violence and murder. As true salt and light, Romero said, the church could not remain silent: "In the name of God, and in the name of this suffering people whose laments rise to heaven each day . . . I beg you, I ask you, I order you in the name of God: Stop the repression!" The next evening, as he finished his homily during the Mass, a man in the back of the church waited for the right moment and shot Romero in the chest. Blood covered Romero's vestments as he gasped for breath. He died moments later.

Salt and light are good and noble. But salt can also sting and light can also expose corruption. When like Oscar Romero we hunger for a better world, when we resist violence and become peacemakers, when we display mercy rather than judgment, when we live with a pure heart, be ready, Jesus said: at the same time you will attract and you will repulse the watching world.

WHEN THE AUTHOR OF THE RULE BOOK SHOWS UP
Matthew 5:17-37

Many families have what I'll call an "Uncle Bill"—the odd or even semi-creepy distant relative who rarely shows up for family gatherings. Not that anyone actually misses Uncle Bill; most family members seem relieved when he skips Thanksgiving or Christmas dinner. The family doesn't treat Bill with outright contempt—actually, nobody even talks about Bill, unless it's in hushed tones so the children can't hear. People care about Bill, but it's awkward to have him around, and everyone acts more at ease when he stays away.

I often meet followers of Jesus who put the law of the Old Testament on a par with Uncle Bill. By "the law" (let's call it our "Uncle Law"), these Christians mean anything from Old Testament rules and regulations to the entire Old Testament. They know that Uncle Law exists; they know that somehow we are related to him, but dealing with the law feels awkward. Everyone seems a little more at ease when we can spend the holidays—or any day—with Jesus and without Uncle Law hanging around.

We tend to assume that Jesus is pleased by this blatant exclusion. After all, didn't Jesus tell us in the Beatitudes about a fresh and liberating approach to the spiritual life? Jesus seemed to focus on our inner life. In contrast, the law of the Old Testament seems to focus on the outer life. As a result, it feels like an exterior, phony, artificial and oppressive path to love Jesus and our neighbor. *Whew*, we think, *I'm so glad that my personal relationship with Jesus frees me from all those religious rules.*

There's one major problem with this attitude: Jesus loved the law. Matthew keeps telling us that Jesus' entire life, even the external events swirling around him, fulfilled the Old Testament. Jesus constantly breathed in the life-giving air of the Old Testament. He read it, studied it, memorized it, trusted his Father through it and fought Satan with it. And even as he died on the cross, slowly suffocating, gasping for air, his brain bursting with pain, Jesus managed to quote from the law.

Matthew 5:17-37 reinforces Jesus' pro-law convictions. He clearly does not say, "Once you have a personal relationship with me you can dispense with the law. Get rid of that batty old uncle. Just believe in me, focus on being pure in heart and merciful, and you can shed those cumbersome rules and regulations." Instead, right after the Beatitudes, that lofty and lovely introduction to the spiritual path, Jesus points us back to the law: "Do not think that I have come to abolish the Law or the Prophets [a shorthand way to describe the entire Old Testament]" (Mt 5:17). The verb tense for "do not think" implies, "Nip this thought in the bud" or, as I learned on Long Island, "Forget about it."

In other words, Jesus had no intention of tossing out the law and the prophets. So it made perfect sense for him to say, "Anyone who sets aside one of the least of these commands and teaches others accordingly will be called least in the kingdom of heaven, but whoever practices and teaches these commands will be called great in the kingdom of heaven" (5:19). If we were looking for a way to dump the law, or scratch it off our list of spiritual advisers, Jesus isn't offering any help. According to Jesus, this relative is here to stay.

Our culture sometimes forgets Jesus' deep connection with the Old

Testament. For instance, I've often heard people say, "Jesus never said anything about homosexuality. Obviously it wasn't important to him if you sleep with someone of the same sex. Come to think of it, Jesus never said anything about a heterosexual couple sleeping together before marriage either. Apparently Jesus practiced tolerant, nonjudgmental attitudes on these issues. Why shouldn't we?" On the one hand, this viewpoint affirms Jesus' radical love for imperfect people. Unfortunately, these arguments also assume that Jesus just plopped into history, rootless and traditionless. But Jesus clearly had roots: his entire life was rooted in Hebrew Old Testament views on God, marriage and sexuality. Rather than distance himself from these Old Testament viewpoints, Jesus reaffirmed them (see, for instance, Mt 19:4-6).

But Jesus did offer a radically new approach. It's found in the second half of Matthew 5:17: "I have not come to abolish [the Law or Prophets] but to fulfill them." According to one New Testament scholar, "fulfill" meant to complete, bring to its destined end or bring into being that which was promised,[25] just like a tree eventually will produce fruit.[26] But it doesn't come to fullness on its own. It needs help. And that's one reason why Jesus came: to show us how to live by correcting those who were misinterpreting the law. The Pharisees annulled the law by limiting it to mere manageable, outward observances that became burdensome for ordinary people.[27] With quiet and confident authority, Jesus claimed that he and he alone could tell us what the Old Testament really meant. He and he alone could provide the correct interpretation.

A number of years ago, when I was playing in a friendly men's softball game, the umpire made a call that incensed our coach. My coach didn't agree with the ump's interpretation of a specific league rule. The game stopped and a heated discussion ensued. Finally, the ump sighed as he pulled a rule book from his back pocket and proceeded to read page 27, paragraph 3b section 1. "As you can clearly see," he concluded, "this rule means that my call must stand." Unconvinced, my coach yelled, "But you're not interpreting that rule correctly." To which the ump replied, "Uh, excuse me, I think I should know: I wrote the rule book." After an awkward silence, my coach walked back to the bench shaking his head and pointing to the umpire as he told us, "Get ahold of that guy. He wrote the rule book!"

Jesus is saying that, when it comes to the Old Testament, he wrote the rule book. Of course this must have shocked Jesus' hearers. A man shows up in the outskirts of Galilee (not at the temple in Jerusalem) without proper credentials or pedigree, and he claims to offer the only correct interpretation of the Hebrew Scripture. Either this man is pompous and ludicrous on a scale unknown to the Jewish people, or he is none other than the long-awaited Messiah, God's mouthpiece. Either this man must be stopped, or we must stop everything and follow him. No wonder God the Father will say later in this Gospel, "This is my Son, whom I love; with him I am well pleased. Listen to him!" (Mt 17:5).

After establishing his identity and authority, Jesus proceeded to give his interpretation on six specific case studies. All six begin with the formula, "You have heard that it was said . . . but I tell you . . ." The "I" in each statement is emphatic, as in, "In contrast to traditional teachers of the law, I and I alone can tell you this." In other words, Jesus was implying, "Based on my authority and in the light of my coming kingdom, let me tell you what these Old Testament texts really mean."[28]

For instance, in Matthew 5:21-26, Jesus begins by interpreting the Old Testament command "Do not murder." Notice that he does not say, "If you put your faith in me, you can hurt and disrespect your neighbor—you can even murder your neighbor—but don't worry, I'll forgive you, because you are under grace and not the law." Jesus isn't teaching on forgiveness here; he's interpreting a small portion of the Old Testament. He's showing us what God meant by "Do not murder." In the light of God the Father's character and Jesus the Son's coming kingdom, the stark negative of "Do not murder" will grow into something more positive and life-giving than we ever could have imagined.

What did God really have in mind when he said, "Do not murder?" The young rabbi from Nazareth proceeds to give the right answer: "But I tell you that anyone who is angry with a brother or sister will be subject to judgment. Again, anyone who says to a brother or sister, 'Raca,' is answerable to the court. And anyone who says, 'You fool!' will be in danger of the fire of hell" (5:22). The Greek word for "angry" was a pres-

ent participle that meant "being angry." Since the Greek word is literally
orgizomenos, think of an anger orgy, an unrestrained feast not of sexual
lust but of anger and resentment.

Calling your brother or sister "Raca" fed the anger orgy and raised it to
a new level of contempt. "Raca" implied an irreparable defectiveness or
irredeemable worthlessness. The world is smeared with the slime of Raca
talk: "idiot," "moron," "retard," "worthless jerk," "pervert," "unwanted"—
I'm sure you can think of worse labels. We fling our Raca words on convicts, the elderly, the ethnically different, the uneducated, the overeducated, men, women, atheists, fetuses, immigrants, addicts, paranoid
schizophrenics and just about anyone on the wrong side of an issue.

Is there a better way? Yes, Jesus said, and it begins with the plain
brown seed of "do not murder." Put that seed in the ground, Jesus said,
and you'll harvest the fruit of respect, dignity, mutual honor and the
sanctity of every person made in the image of a glorious God. Certainly
you'll stop killing people. But you'll also stop any contemptuous name-
calling, placing people in tidy moral categories so they can be flushed
out of sight. Jerk? Loser? Good-for-nothing? Sicko? No, Jesus, said, he's
the beloved of God. God is blessing him with sunshine even as you pelt
him with contempt (see Mt 5:45).

That's why, Jesus continued, even if you're in the middle of a worship
service, if you've hurt your brother, if you've treated him with disrespect
or harbored contempt toward him, "First go and be reconciled to [your
brother or sister]; then come and offer your gift" (Mt 5:24). It can't wait;
do it now. Turn your enemies into friends. Convert your contempt into
respect. Jesus invites us to take positive steps to heal broken relationships. All of this fruit grows from one little Old Testament seed—do not
murder.

Take another case study. In Matthew 5:27 Jesus refers to another
small portion of the Old Testament—"You have heard that it was said,
'You shall not commit adultery'"—and tells us what God really intended
for relationships between the sexes. In light of the coming kingdom we
find the full flowering of God's beautiful plan. Jesus said, "Anyone who
looks at a woman lustfully has already committed adultery with her in
his heart" (Mt 5:28). Jesus isn't talking about an appreciative glance at

feminine beauty—or masculine attractiveness, since lust is an equal-opportunity sin. The verb used here for "looks" included not only the act but also the intent or desire to look, literally it meant, "is looking to desire" or "is staring." Clearly this act has moved beyond admiring to a leering, driving, must-have attitude.

Once again Jesus isn't just presenting a harder, deeper, more "spiritual" understanding of God's law. He's offering the right interpretation. What did God have in mind when he created us male and female, granting us the gifts of marriage and celibacy? Well, he certainly meant it when he said, "You shall not commit adultery." But God also intended that we reflect his original desire for the beauty of marriage, a lifelong covenant between one man and one woman. In Jesus' interpretation of marriage, there's a deep respect for the glory and value of one's spouse—or a neighbor's spouse, or a single person. Jesus' standard sets a high bar for the dignity of the person in front of me: he or she is the beloved of God, not an object for my sexual gratification.

In Matthew 5:34-37 Jesus gives another Old Testament interpretation, this time of the command about the keeping of oaths. On one level, Jesus merely wants us to keep our word. Don't bear false witness. Fulfill your vows. But based on God's original intent and in light of Jesus' coming kingdom, "Jesus is fighting for the integrity of speech . . . [because] a community is not stable when words cannot be trusted."[29] Jesus critiques oath-keeping because it's a slick way to avoid keeping the law. In contrast, the law was meant to make our speech resemble an Amish rocking chair—simple, sturdy, durable. In the end our speech may not win prizes for its beauty, but it's solid and trustworthy, marked by simplicity, clarity and honesty.

These three case studies don't just offer good advice for cleaning up our spiritual lives with a new set of rules: don't call people bad names, don't leer at beautiful people and don't tell lies, although Jesus' interpretation certainly does lead us to follow these rules and promote the dignity of other human beings.[30] But more importantly, everything Jesus says in this passage follows his teaching in the Beatitudes. His interpretation of "do not murder" and "do not commit adultery" flow from "Blessed are the poor in spirit, for theirs is the kingdom of heaven."

What difference does this make for followers of Jesus? Once again, Jesus' way isn't reserved for an elite cadre of spiritual superheroes. It's a path available for flawed and struggling nonheroes—the poor in spirit, the mourners, the meek, the hungry and thirsty, the merciful. These people inherit the coming kingdom of Jesus. How? Take one example: when you're poor in spirit, when you know how much you need God's grace, when you realize you have no claim on God for anything and yet he saved you, he loved you—no, he lavished you with grace and healing beyond what you ever could have earned—then how could you possibly look with contempt on another human being? You will obey Jesus' words in Matthew 5:21-26 because you have experienced and continue to experience God's abundant, undeserved grace. You were a pauper and he made you rich. Once that sinks in, your anger, resentment and contempt, which used to look so attractive and justified, suddenly feel petty and mean-spirited.

Or when you know that you're poor in spirit, you can face the murky waters of sexuality. At times your sex drive may feel baffling and uncontrollable. But because you're poor in spirit you know you can't fight this battle by yourself. In your own strength you are powerless against temptation. But you are hungry and thirsty for righteousness. So you surrender to God's power. You say, "Lord Jesus, I bring to you my little faith and my spiritual poverty. I bring to you my impure heart and ask you to make me pure in heart." The only way to keep the commandment is to trust the commander. In that way Matthew 5:27-28 won't crush us with shame and guilt for our many struggles, temptations and failures. By entering our spiritual poverty, we're liberated to accept God's grace. Once again, this exemplifies Jesus' accessible little way for little people.

Jesus wants us to pursue a pattern of righteousness that's even greater than the Pharisees' (Mt 5:20). The Pharisees' version of righteousness limited God's true intent behind the Old Testament. By his authority as the Son of David and Messiah, Jesus is correcting the Pharisee's faulty interpretation.

Jesus' vision of righteousness doesn't imply a lower standard that promotes moral complacency. In Matthew 5:30 Jesus tells us, "If your right hand causes you to stumble, cut it off and throw it away." It's one of Jesus' famous examples of hyperbole, but the point is serious: pursue a right life as Jesus has defined it. Hunger and thirst for it. Half-measures won't help you. Pay a price to get it. And if you're stuck and you can't help yourself, if you're trapped in your own anger or lust, then ask for help. What do beggars and children have in common? They ask for help when they need it. And they keep begging and keep asking. It's the only way to keep walking in Jesus' way.

YOU MUST DISPLAY MERCY . . . OR ELSE!
Matthew 5:38-48

After reading Matthew 5, the famous atheist Bertrand Russell once quipped, "The Christian principle 'Love your enemies' is good. . . . There is nothing to be said against it except that it is too difficult for most of us to practice sincerely."[31]

Many people would agree with Russell. At first glance (and if you read it out of context), it looks like Jesus is replacing the Old Testament laws with stricter, nearly impossible laws for showing mercy . . . or else. In other words, "Thou shalt be nice," Jesus seems to say, "and these are the exact rules for mercy-giving: (Rule A1)—If someone slaps you on the cheek, automatically offer him your other cheek; (Rule B2)—If someone asks for your shirt, give him your pants."

But, honestly, legislating mercy just isn't practical, possible or even beneficial. For instance, if someone breaks into my house, do I add (Rule C3)—If someone grabs your laptop, offer him your tropical fish collection? Do I really have to give to everyone who asks me for anything?

Unfortunately, we often fail to place this passage within the flow of the entire Gospel. Jesus has been interpreting portions of the Old Testament in light of life in the kingdom of heaven, life in and around Jesus himself. According to Jesus, this kingdom vision is so grand, beautiful and hopeful that it should crack our hearts wide open with wonder, praise and compassion. In contrast, our lives are constricted by our narrow, wounded, fragile egos. So, naturally, if you insult me, don't greet me or hate me, then I must insult, ignore and hate you back. In my insecurity and pettiness, my life looks very unlike Jesus.

And then we assume that God must be like us—small, fragile, petty and insecure. But Jesus declares that his heavenly Father is not like us. His love is broad and generous; "he causes his sun to rise on the evil and the good" (Mt 5:45). Out of his good and merciful heart the Father in heaven gives good things to those who ask him (Mt 7:9-11).

Given this context, we see that Jesus isn't laying down new regulations for mercy; he is offering the original intent for the Old Testament. "Just as my Father has surprised you with his radical goodness," Jesus is telling us, "just as I have surprised you with the good news of the kingdom, so you must live broad and generous lives, lives marked by surprising mercy and goodness. And don't limit your mercy to people you like or even to 'good people.' Let your mercy extend even to people you used to deem unpleasant, tainted and repugnant human beings. That's the way my Father loves; let his love (which is also my love) be the new standard of righteousness in the kingdom of heaven."

Then in Matthew 5:39-42 Jesus illustrates this new kingdom lifestyle with four vignettes of the Father's merciful heart. These are not laws; they are examples or case studies. For instance, in verse 39 Jesus tells us that if someone slaps you on your right cheek, you should offer your left cheek for another slap. Since like most people I am right-handed, if I slap you on your right cheek, I am back-handing you. I'm not punching you senseless—that would require a different response. It's my pathetic, insecure, small-hearted way to degrade you, to bring you down. But if you offer me your other cheek, you are saying, "No, sorry, but you can't bring me down: my Lord just called me the salt of the earth and the light of the world. I am blessed beyond measure. I don't need to play this little game of trading insults. Instead, let me give you a taste of new life in the kingdom of heaven: strike me on the other cheek. My Father's love is broad and generous. He never gets petty or mean-spirited; instead, he just keeps showing compassion even to evil people."[32]

In Matthew 5:41 Jesus instructs us to walk the extra mile with a Roman soldier. Jesus isn't giving us a law—i.e., you must be extra nice to soldiers even if they are torching your village. (Again, that would require a different response.) In Jesus' day, Roman soldiers had the right to force civilians to carry military gear one mile but no more.[33] It was a petty, mean-spirited way to say, "You do not matter; you are not important." So by gleefully offering to walk an extra mile, you would send a clear and surprising message: "First of all, you can't insult me because my life in the kingdom is broad and beautiful. Second, let me give you a taste of my Father's grace. Let's walk that extra mile, and as we walk I'll tell you what it feels like and what it looks like to live in the generous liberty of the kingdom of heaven."

After telling us to love and pray for our enemies (see Mt 5:43-44), Jesus provides one more practical, ordinary vignette of his Father's open heart of love. "If you only greet your brothers," he says, "what more are you doing than others? Do not even Gentiles to the same?" It's another example of our fragile, petty, insecure hearts. I go out of my way to greet nice, interesting people—people like me!—while I tend to avoid mean and dull people. But Jesus calls us to a new standard: the standard of the Father's heart.

Once we get this, once we start obeying Jesus' teaching in this passage, we will truly become world-changing salt and light. In 1990, a white South African Anglican priest named Michael Lapsley opened a letter that exploded in his face, blowing off his hand, ripping out an eyeball and shattering his eardrums. For years Lapsley had worked to bridge his country's racial divide; now the letter bomb was his "reward." But Lapsley chose the way of Jesus, the way of the Father's warm, generous, broad mercy even for evil people. Lapsley founded the Institute for the Healing of Memories in South Africa. Thousands of South Africans from all backgrounds have come together to heal the wounds of violence and separation.[34]

There was no law or regulation instructing Lapsley how to respond; there was only a new and living reality: the Father's heart as displayed in the life of Jesus. Lapsley took that path. For the follower of Jesus the gospel becomes the new standard of mercy. While we were lost in our sin, unpleasant and repugnant, sinners and even enemies of God (Rom 5:6-11), God sought us out and greeted us with love. At the cross, in the person of Jesus, God reconciled this unkind, cold, mean and petty world back to himself (2 Cor 5:21). How could we not greet the unpleasant and unkind with extravagant kindness and mercy?

Jesus concludes this section with a summary statement: "Be perfect, therefore, as your heavenly Father is perfect" (Mt 5:48). In the parallel passage in Luke's Gospel Jesus says, "Be merciful, just as your Father is merciful" (Lk 6:36). Jesus wasn't demanding a spot-free moral track record. Instead, he was calling us to a new standard of mercy: as God the Father and Jesus the Son constantly surprise us with mercy, shining on the good and the evil, the pleasant and the unpleasant, so his new community of people, kingdom people, should reflect the same surprising and generous mercy for the world.

STEALTHY SPIRITUALITY
Matthew 6:1-8, 16-18

According to an old Jewish tale titled "If Not Higher," there was once a beloved rabbi who disappeared every Friday.[35] Unable to find him anywhere, the devoted villagers boasted that their rabbi must ascend to heaven every Friday so he could talk with God. One day, however, a newcomer to their small village heard the stories and scoffed. "People don't ascend to heaven," he mocked. "I'll tell you where your rabbi really goes on Friday mornings."

So the next Friday morning the newcomer crept into the woods by the rabbi's house. He quietly watched the rabbi rise, say his prayers and, much to the onlooker's surprise, dress in the clothes of a common peasant. The rabbi walked into the woods, chopped down a small tree and cut it into firewood. Then the rabbi carried a bundle of wood to a shack in the poorest section of the village. An old woman and her sick son gladly received the bundle of wood for the coming week. They thanked the anonymous woodsman, unaware that it was the rabbi in disguise.

The skeptical newcomer, deeply moved by the rabbi's secret goodness, became the rabbi's disciple. Now whenever the villagers said, "On Friday mornings our rabbi ascends to heaven," he would quietly add, "If not higher."

This story illustrates a key aspect of how Matthew viewed Jesus' approach to the spiritual life. We could call it "secret righteousness" or "the stealth approach" to true spirituality. Throughout this Gospel Matthew ushers us into a quiet, unnoticed, unspectacular little way to follow and obey Jesus. In his typical systematic style, Matthew provides a clear and simple outline for Jesus' instruction found in chapter 6 verses 1-8 and 16-18:

- The command: "Be careful not to practice your righteousness in front of other to be seen by them" (Mt 6:1).[36]

- The warning: "If you do [practice your righteousness before others], you will have no reward from your Father in heaven" (Mt 6:1).

- The examples: How to live with true righteousness—how to give to the needy (Mt 6:2-4), how to pray (Mt 6:5-8, 9-15) and how to fast (Mt 6:16-18).

- The consequence of false spirituality: "Truly I tell you, they have their reward in full" (Mt 6:2, 5, 16).

- The promise for practicing authentic spirituality: "Then your Father, who sees what is done in secret, will reward you" (Mt 6:4, 6, 18).

In this passage Jesus is addressing a fundamental human need: the desire to be noticed, affirmed and blessed. In clear contrast to some worldviews that downplay or disregard human desires, Jesus acknowledges the reality and even the goodness of this basic human desire. For instance, when my three boys were younger, I could never sit beside a swimming pool without constantly hearing, "Dad, watch this. Watch this awesome cannonball dive—*ahhhhhh!*" "Watch me swim from one end of the pool to the other end." "Watch me get this stick." "Watch us play catch." "Watch me try to dunk my brother." Watching and then praising is a compulsory parental duty and delight. We just do it—instinctively and attentively. And I'm no different than my children because I crave affirmation and appreciation and—dare I say—applause.[37]

In this passage, Jesus basically tells the human race, "The desire for affirmation and even praise is within you. Don't deny or minimize it. But know that the need is too huge for a human solution. Your heart is like a leaky bucket: no matter how much you and others pour praise into the bucket, it never gets filled. It remains an empty, craving, gaping wound. First you have to heal your broken, leaky, needy heart, and there's only one thing that can fill the cracks: my Father's love."

That's the underlying vision in Matthew's account: Jesus keeps pointing us to his Father's healing, satisfying love. In Matthew 6:1-18, Jesus refers to God as "Father" nine times. In fact, this Gospel provides a star-tling picture of what constantly flows in the life of the triune God: God the Father affirms and delights in God the Son; God the Son praises the Father and "lives off" his love; the Spirit descends (see Mt 3:16), relish-ing and delighting in this dance of love.

As Matthew leads us through Jesus' teaching in chapter 6, we find Jesus offering two, and only two, divergent options for the spiritual life:

• Trust my (and now your) Father's infilling love; receive his reward.

• Find your "reward" right now through the admiration of fickle and fallible human beings.

Jesus had a name for people who perform good deeds "to be admired by others": hypocrites.[38] Hypocrites treat the world as their personal stage—primping, preening, puffing and performing with all their might. For them, spirituality becomes a theater to garner the praise of others rather than the backstage where we quietly and contentedly serve others and love God.

In three comical, exaggerated vignettes Jesus offers case studies of the second option, the path of hypocrisy. "If you really want it," Jesus seems to say, "you can probably get the praise of people. They will love and admire you. You will impress them with your fine, upstanding, righteous deeds. But be careful, because that's all you'll get." On three occasions Jesus tells us, "They have received their reward in full," a phrase that referred to a clean, crisp, complete business transaction.[39] In other words, Jesus made it clear that we can't live on the stage of life between two audiences: we have to choose to pursue the pleasure of God or the praise of others.

In the end, the path of hypocrisy and human praise does not satisfy our hearts; it can't heal the cracks at the bottom of our bucket. What we might call "front-stage theatrical righteousness" (look at me, notice me, pay attention to me) leads to bondage. When the applause doesn't come or when others give it sporadically or imperfectly, how do we respond? At best we're disappointed. At worst we demand it. And if the praise doesn't come, we begin to walk through life with a deep, soul-churning resentment: Why don't you notice me? Why don't you meet my needs? Why don't I receive the recognition I so clearly deserve?

Theatrical righteousness doesn't just lead to resentment; it also creates confusion and exhaustion. There are so many conflicting voices to heed, so many fickle people to please. Eventually the conflicting expectations of others almost always lead to exhaustion. Our lives become a frantic race—panting, running, sweating—to please the crowd of people in our lives. Real relationships with God and others become impossible because we can't stop and rest. We can't heed Christ's invitation to come (Mt 11:28-30) because we're too busy pleasing everybody else.

Fortunately Jesus invites us onto a better path: our identity and security as human beings must come from the Father's voice. In and through Christ, his life and death and resurrection, we can receive the same praise that Jesus received: "This is my son, whom I love; with him I am well pleased" (see also Eph 1:3-6).

In clear and practical terms, Jesus tells us to quit acting like hypocrites and pursue a life of secret, quiet righteousness. "When you give to the needy, do not let your left hand know what your right hand is doing" (Mt 6:3). "When you pray, go into your room, close the door and pray to your Father, who is unseen" (Mt 6:6). "When you fast, put oil on your head and wash your face" (Mt 6:17). Of course these three scenarios are merely examples of what our entire spiritual life should look like: a conspiracy of secret kindness, goodness, discipline and light rooted in the depths of the Father's delight in us.

This approach to the spiritual life frees us to remain deeply satisfied as we practice small, unnoticed deeds of goodness. Francis de Sales, a spiritual director from the 1600s, once cautioned, "Great opportunities to serve God rarely present themselves but little ones are frequent." So he urged all believers to "practice those little, humble virtues which grow like flowers at the foot of the cross: helping the poor, visiting the sick, and taking care of your family."[40]

My friend Jim is learning to find contentment in this little way of secret goodness. As an emergency room doctor, Jim's stressful and sometimes gruesome workload can leave him with a lingering resentment. Twelve-hour shifts grind down his body and mind, but Jim's work rarely

garners applause. Crisis after crisis, Jim patches up severely broken people only to get ready for the next wave of traumatized, bloody, messed-
up patients. Who could blame Jim for harboring some resentment?

But a few years ago, while participating in a Lenten Stations of the
Cross service, Jim had a profound encounter with Christ. Recalling that
Christ had suffered without receiving human applause, Jim sensed God
quietly say, "Just like my Son, you have the opportunity to receive true
approval. Practice the little way of following me even when others don't
notice you. Practice secret righteousness, and I will reward you. That's
much better than anything your patients or the hospital administration
could ever give you."

Jim's patients and his church family may never know that after that
routine service something shifted in his soul. On the other hand, perhaps they'll notice Jim doing his work and living his life with a little
more contentment. Why? Because every time Jim sews up a wound or
sets a broken arm, he's not doing it for his patients or for the hospital;
he's doing it for Christ. By joining that dance of triune love, God the
Father is slowly healing Jim's love-hungry heart. Accordingly, now Jesus
wants to whisper a secret to us: "Trust me, look to me, come away with
me, and I'll do that for you too.

A BIG PRAYER FOR LITTLE PEOPLE
Matthew 6:9-15

Our Father in heaven,
hallowed be your name,
your kingdom come,
your will be done,
    on earth as it is in heaven.
Give us today our daily bread.
And forgive us our debts,
    as we also have forgiven our debtors.
And lead us not into temptation,
but deliver us from the evil one. (Mt 6:9-13)

During my employment at a group home for developmentally disabled adults, I took Robert to Catholic Mass every Saturday afternoon. The liturgy of the Mass—the readings, hymns, homily and Eucharistic prayers—seemed to leave Robert a bit confused and dazed. But before Communion, everyone would grab a hand, hold it high and sing an a cappella version of the Lord's Prayer. I was always surprised to watch Robert straighten up and gustily sing every word by heart. He prayed with an intense, wild-eyed amazement. After a while, I looked forward to Mass so I could let Robert mentor me in the art of praying, believing and loving Jesus' prayer.

When I told this story to one of my friends, I mentioned, "It's touching to watch Robert sing the Lord's Prayer, but I don't know how much he understands." My friend responded, "Probably more than you and I combined." I think my friend was right.

Although this prayer is simple, it isn't shallow. Jesus packed it with doctrinal and theological depth. For instance, the opening words—"Our Father in heaven, hallowed be your name"—establish two profound truths about God's nature: his tender, father-like love and his awesome holiness.[41] On the one hand, Jesus is declaring that God is not just *like* a Father; God *is* our Father. This personal, warm heavenly Father draws us into his trinitarian dance of love and intimacy. Based on Jesus' authority and invitation, we can approach our heavenly Father with confidence, knowing that he will "give good gifts to those who ask him" (Mt 7:11).[42] We can come to God without "many words," because "[our] Father knows what [we] need before [we] ask him" (Mt 6:7-8). What a privilege and relief it is to come to God with our imperfect and raw prayers, even our groans (see Rom 8:26-27) and our anguished silence. Our Father knows what we need before the words are on our lips. Jesus' invitation to address God as "our Father" forms the first doctrinal truth—and joyful mystery—of prayer.[43]

But Jesus wants us to know and therefore pray another truth about God: his name is hallowed. Hallow means to "make holy" or to "make central" because God is utterly distinct in his awesome holiness. God's name refers to God as he is, not God as we want him to be. In Jesus' Bible, especially the words of the prophet Isaiah, God's holiness means that God is utterly distinct, set apart, unique (see Is 44:6-7). God alone is perfect in power, love, mercy and authority.

Notice that this statement about God's hallowedness isn't just a doctrine; it's also a prayer, a request, a petition. It is our request for God to do what only God can do—make his name holy, distinct and central in our lives and throughout all of creation. "The passive voice ('hallowed be') instead of the active ('hallow') preserves God's sovereignty and prevents the prayer from being a command." Our request specifically asks God, "Please make your real identity known so that others [and we ourselves] will recognize you as central and weighty."[44] Of course, this prayer could be seen as a threat to our safety and joy if we don't begin by knowing that this holy God is also "our Father."

These rich theological truths about the character of God shouldn't deter ordinary people from praying Jesus' prayer. After all, Jesus did keep it short—a mere sixty words in the New International Version. A child can memorize it. A developmentally disabled adult can sing it. Jesus wants us to know that real prayer isn't complicated; it isn't reserved for an elite corps of the spiritually advanced. Instead, it's reserved for those who know they need grace—the poor in spirit, the mourners, the mercy-needing and mercy-giving, the sinners and the sinned against, the beginners and non-experts. As Craig Keener observes, "This is a prayer for the desperate, who recognize that this world is not as it should be and that only God can set things right—the broken to whom Jesus promises the blessings of the kingdom (Mt 5:3-12)."[45]

Jesus invites these desperate people into an adventure of world-changing prayer. Matthew 6:10 captures its stunning miracle: "Your kingdom come, your will be done, on earth as it is in heaven." Once again, the kingdom implies the fulfillment of all God's promises when he will reign as king over the earth. When we pray along these lines we're saying, "God, by your name and in your character, by your holiness (which we do not share), in your perfect ways (which we can't duplicate), repair the world. Take all the broken things and fix them. Take every out-of-joint thing and set it in its proper place. Take all the ugly things and make them beautiful. Take every tragic tale and weave it into a redemption story, as you manifest your ultimate kingdom glory now." According to sixteenth-century writer John Calvin, we're asking

God to "restore to order at his will all that is lying waste upon the face of the earth."[46]

Notice that Jesus did not tell us to pray, "Your kingdom come into my heart." Obviously that's covered in the request, but Jesus was telling us to pray also for something bigger, grander and broader than personal transformation. He was inviting us to pray for the perfect, beautiful, restorative will of God to cover the earth—families, neighborhoods and nations; film festivals, universities and hospitals; cancer wards, slums and strip clubs; parks, forests and oceans. You can't pray this simple prayer without asking God and trusting God to change the world—and the way you look at the world.[47]

As a result, this isn't an easy or a safe prayer. It's not designed to reinforce the status quo. It's so bold and audacious that "big people," the self-sufficient and the comfortable, don't understand it. If they did, they wouldn't pray it—unless they wanted to subvert their petty kingdoms of power and privilege. Only the "little people," those who ache and yearn for a better world, those who hunger and thirst for righteousness and quickly display mercy, can truly pray this prayer.

That's why I was always stunned to watch Robert jubilantly sing this prayer. Week after week, day by day, Robert never asked for anything except an occasional second helping of chicken thighs or mashed potatoes. Five days a week he woke up at six, ate breakfast, got on a bus, worked at his "program," came home, ate dinner, did a few chores, watched movies and went to sleep. On weekends he may have participated in a dance, gone for a walk or attended church, but unlike most of the other residents, he hardly ever made demands. When he called his father and brother, they didn't respond. In almost every way, Robert did not have a say, a voice, a vote. But then every Saturday afternoon at approximately five forty-five, Robert lifted his eyes and arms and asked not just for chicken and potatoes but for the whole kingdom story—the lion and the lamb, the weapons of war into plowshares, the lame leaping for joy, the new heavens and the new earth. Week after week, Robert rose up with audacious boldness, asking God to repair the world until it radiated God's beauty and peace.

Unfortunately, without Robert's sense of spiritual poverty, we often approach God with a frenetic activism that sounds like, "Yeah, God, sure, may your kingdom come. But, really, it's up to us to fix the world, so would you give us a little help?" There's not a whiff of that attitude in Jesus' prayer. When we try to fix this world—or someone else's life—with our own power and cleverness, we often make a bigger mess. Of course this doesn't imply that we don't have our place in repairing the world. This prayer simply acknowledges the correct order: it begins with God's name, God's activity, God's character and God's initiative. God takes the lead and sets the agenda; we simply watch and try to do our part when we're called upon.

This prayer isn't saying that we should request only big, important things from God. Jesus also teaches us to pray for the small, seemingly insignificant things we face every day. First, there's the earthy, personal request in Matthew 6:11: "Give us today our daily bread." The Greek word for "daily" *(epiousios),* which occurs only here and in Luke 11:3, is tricky to translate. The best version is probably, "Give us today the food we need." With our colossal supermarkets and oversized refrigerator-freezers, it's difficult to empathize with a prayer for "daily" food. After all, we have enough food for the next six weeks. But for people of Jesus' day, and for billions of people on our planet today, food does come on a daily basis. So as we consistently pray this prayer, it trains us to walk with the underfed people of this world (and perhaps our unemployed neighbors) who wonder if they'll get a meal by nightfall. In our overfed but anxious culture, this prayer also trains us to trust our heavenly Father on a daily basis for all of our needs. I can't do much of anything—battle my addictions, confess my sin, help my neighbor, care for my children, trust God to care for loved ones—unless I do it one day at a time.[48]

In this simple prayer Jesus also invites us to give a few more "little things" to our heavenly Father: our ordinary struggles with failure ("forgive us our debts"), resentment ("as we also have forgiven our debtors") and temptation ("and lead us not into temptation"). It's tough to make it through a day without encountering at least one battle with failure, resentment or temptation. By telling us to pray about these utterly human struggles, Jesus walks with us in our daily lives. He even prays with us.

Remember, Jesus is the one who first invited us to pray this prayer.

During my work at the group home, Robert became my mentor, my spiritual guide for how to pray, love and even sing the Lord's Prayer. Based on Robert's example, I firmly believe it's best to pray the Lord's Prayer often, with your head up and, if possible, while holding someone's hand. How utterly like Jesus to make his richest, deepest, most challenging prayer accessible to "little people" like me and Robert.

FREEDOM FROM THE TRAP OF STUFF
Matthew 6:19-34; 7:7-12

Stuff. You name it—shoes, books, frying pans, necklaces, power tools, dresses, blue jeans, laptops and cars—we crave it. And once we get it, we hoard it. As a nation, we're masters of storing our stuff. The United States now has 2.3 billion square feet of self-storage space. According to an article in the *New York Times Magazine* and the Self Storage Association, it's now "physically possible that every American could stand—all at the same time—under the total canopy of self-storage roofing."[49]

Oh, how we crave more stuff. Rodney Clapp contends that this insatiability is the hallmark of the consumer. "The consumer is tutored that people basically consist of unmet needs that can be appeased by commodified goods and experiences. Accordingly, the consumer should think first and foremost of himself or herself and meeting his or her needs."[50]

So when we don't get the stuff we want, we churn with discontentment. When we do get the right stuff, we have to protect it. With or without stuff, we think about it, worry about it and end up trapped by it. In the end stuff possesses us, plunging us into a pit of anxiety and misery.

In the kingdom manifesto—or the Sermon on the Mount—Jesus offers a better way to live, a way of freedom and simplicity. In contrast to the insatiable nature of consumerism, this passage radiates joy and delight. It sparkles with Jesus' childlike trust, warmth, happiness and confidence. He invites us, urges us and even commands us: Do not worry. Do not worry about your stuff. Do not worry about your life. Do not even worry about where your next meal will come from. It's a waste of time: you can't add anything to your life by worrying (see Mt 6:27).[51]

But is Jesus being realistic here? Our fragile hearts, bent and warped by years of mistrust, rejection and disappointment, naturally cringe with cynicism. Was Jesus just singing a pre-modern version of Bobby McFerrin's eighties hit "Don't Worry, Be Happy"? It sure sounds nice, but someone has to bring home a paycheck, drive the kids to their dance lessons, mow the lawn and study for the next biochemistry final.

This passage isn't a manifesto against work; it isn't even primarily a denunciation of consumerism or anxiety. Instead, it's first and foremost a joyful declaration of God's goodness and our response to that goodness. In the previous passage (Mt 6:1-18) Jesus repeatedly referred to God as Father: his Father and our Father. Now he wants to free us from our insatiable bondage to consumerism—getting, storing and protecting more and more stuff. But this passage contains even better news. "If God really is your Father," Jesus seems to be saying, "if you aren't a cosmic orphan in a slowly fading universe, if the world really is bathed with God's fatherly love, then you can walk through it with joy and confidence and trust. No matter what happens to you—your job, your stuff, your wardrobe—no matter who loves you and supports you, you can walk through life with security and safety because your heavenly Father loves and provides for you."

In Matthew 1 we heard that God is with us. Now Jesus is telling us that God is for us. "So trust me," Jesus says. "Trust my Father and your Father. The triune God is for you, not against you." Based on this passage, here are few examples of how God is for us in Jesus:

• In Matthew 6:19-21 Jesus mentions "treasure" three times. Now, everyone has pleasures, things we value and prize. But sometimes Christians talk like we can't enjoy anything except spiritual things. We can't enjoy chocolate cake, a soccer match, a nice home or a beautiful shirt. But Jesus wasn't an ascetic who despised pleasure and desire. And this passage rings with Jesus' pleasure.[52] There is room in our hearts for a multitude of loves. However, there is room for only one treasure. Because Jesus is for us, he wants us to have the right treasure: God and his kingdom. If anything usurps God's rightful place as our true treasure, we're in trouble. Eventually we'll lose every lesser, phony treasure.

- In Matthew 6:24 Jesus warns us, "No one can serve two masters. . . . You cannot serve both God and money." Again, Jesus is for us here. He wants to save us from the pain of living with a divided heart. Money—or mammon, the spirit driving our nasty demand to hoard more money and more stuff—makes a lousy god. As Mark Buchanan states, "[Mammon] is surly and brutish, rarely lets you get a good night's sleep. . . . He brings with his gifts the sour aftertaste of ingratitude (it's not enough) or fear (it won't last) or insatiableness (I want more). . . . Mammon outshouts God. It's hard to hear what God has put in your heart with Mammon roaring."[53] Jesus wants to set us free from this lousy god. That's the motivation behind his blunt directive to choose our one master and Lord.

- In Matthew 6:25-26 Jesus uses a traditional rabbinic teaching technique to convey how much God is for us. If God provides food for birds, how much more will he care for us? If God clothes the flowers of the field, how much more will he clothe us? "Are you not much more valuable than they?" he asks (Mt 6:26). Jesus is telling us how much we matter to God the Father. Our lives matter. Our bodily needs matter. We matter. In verse 30 Jesus challenges us to believe this by calling us *oligopoistoi,* or "little faiths," a word that occurs four times in Matthew (see Mt 8:26; 14:31; 16:8). As John Nolland remarks, this word "is always used of the disciples and always points to their failure to believe that they will be taken care of."[54]

- In Matthew 6:25, 31 and 34, Jesus commands us, "Do not worry." Literally, the Greek word for "anxiety" means "choke" or "strangle." That's what anxiety feels like. While anxiety may sometimes have a biochemical basis requiring medical attention, for most of us it involves a choice: we don't want to trust God for our needs. Instead we seek our security in and give our worship to the spirit of consumerism. Jesus' point is that it doesn't help; it just leads to more anxiety than we can handle. Anxiety, the choice to not trust our heavenly Father, doesn't add anything to our lives. As a matter of fact, it subtracts.

- Finally, in Matthew 6:34, Jesus ends this section by telling us, "Do not worry about tomorrow, for tomorrow will worry about itself. Each day has enough trouble of its own." Initially, this tidbit of advice may seem anticlimactic, but again Jesus is trying to help us. This for-us Savior is practical, helpful and realistic. He's not asking for heroic feats of radical faith; he's asking for the most simple and childlike response: if you can't trust God for the next year, can you trust your heavenly Father for today? Can you live in this moment with simplicity of heart and childlike trust?

Of course Jesus didn't just command us in these things; he lived the life we should have lived. Consumerism and anxiety never gripped Jesus' heart. He lived a life of freedom, simplicity and trust. He also lived with joy and delight. He appreciated beauty, reveling in lilies and birds. More than any other human being, Jesus lived in and enjoyed the present moment as a gift from his Father's hand. He wants us to do the same, but Jesus lived it first—perfectly, gracefully, beautifully.

This may all sound good in theory. After all, it's easy for me to trust God as I'm sipping a fresh latte, the sun shining brightly, the sparrows singing and the rose bush blooming. As I take it all in with my twenty-twenty vision (thanks to my excellent health insurance plan), free of hunger and political oppression, Jesus' teaching sounds utterly believable. But what if my life unravels and I descend into a dark cloud of loss, doubt or confusion? What if I've failed and the consequences of my sin are bringing pain into my life and that of my loved ones? What if I'm unemployed and my children go to sleep with hunger pangs in their bellies? Is it enough to gaze at lilies and listen to birdsongs? Does Jesus really expect that his cheery "do not worry" will get us through those times of darkness and desolation?

According to this Gospel, Jesus is not only God for us, giving advice for a truly joyful life; he's also God with us. If just anyone told us not to be anxious, to trust God and to enjoy the birds and the lilies, we might gag with disgust. But Jesus wasn't merely the man of joy and delight; he was also the man of sorrows, the God who plunged into our deepest darkness, the one who walks with us through our pain and suffering, the one who was crucified between two sinners, the one who stood by his friend Peter during his most crushing personal failure. He is for us and he is with us. He shows us the Father's heart. He lived in loving, joyful, trust-filled union with the Father. And in our darkest and most anxious moments, he invites us to trust in his Father as well.

DISMANTLING THE SPIRIT OF JUDGMENT
Matthew 7:1-6

During my first year of graduate school in St. Paul, Minnesota, my wife and I were under enormous pressure. I was working thirty hours a week and taking a full load of courses. My scholarship was tied to my grades, so I had to maintain a B+ average. My wife was working over half-time as a waitress and also taking at least one graduate course. And we were both adjusting to life with a newborn baby. At times I nearly crumbled under the stress.

On one occasion, while my wife was working and I was struggling to learn New Testament Greek, our daughter wailed uncontrollably for two hours. I couldn't console her and as my stress level increased, she wailed all the more. I tried praying but then just gave up. I wanted to scream or cry or punch the wall. Although I was surrounded by support—seminary friends, a church community, my extended family, professors and mentors, nearby counselors—I realize how easily I could have snapped and done something evil.

Every once in a while I imagine this scenario with a different set of circumstances. Rather than a living in a cozy apartment in the suburbs, I'm struggling to hold down two jobs so I can afford rent in a high-rise complex near downtown Minneapolis. My child and I live alone, or perhaps I'm trying to end an abusive relationship. After a full day of cleaning hotel rooms, I'm exhausted, but now my baby, hungry and tired, starts screaming uncontrollably. Without support of any kind—no extended family, no church small group, no caring spouse—where do I turn? How do I deal with these raw feelings of anger and anxiety?

Based on these scenarios, I'm less likely to make quick and tidy moral judgments about parents who do snap under stress. I'm a little more open to Jesus' teaching in Matthew 7:1—"Do not judge, or you too will be judged." In this passage Jesus quietly dismantles an insidious cycle that operates in human hearts and communities: the cycle of condemnation and judgment. In this cycle I don't just judge moral behaviors; I judge you. And then based on my incomplete, hasty and harsh judgment, I devalue and then exclude you from my life or the life of our community.

This spirit of judgment poisons human relationships across marriages, families, churches, ethnic groups and nations.

But the sad truth is that we need this cycle. We know that something is wrong with the world and someone must pay, but it shouldn't be us. So we find a scapegoat—an individual or group of people to bear the brunt of our unhappiness. We still speak of people who are "beyond the pale," a reference to the ancient practice of forcing others to live beyond the communal fires that provided warmth and safety. If we can judge them, if we can remove them beyond the pale, then all shall be well with us.

With utter clarity and simplicity, Jesus frees the human race from this cycle. Notice his masterful technique: he uses humor to dismantle the spirit of judgment. In Matthew 7:3-4 he says, "Why do you look at the speck of sawdust in your brother's eye and pay no attention to the plank in your own eye? How can you say to your brother, 'Let me take the speck out of your eye,' when all the time there is a plank in your own eye?" In other words, imagine there's a man with a huge beam protruding from his eye attempting to perform delicate surgery on your eye. His beam keeps smashing into your face—and everyone else around him—but he's oblivious to his own problem. It's funny. And that's you, Jesus observes, when you perpetuate the cycle of judgment and condemnation. With this illustration Jesus tells us how idiotic we are, but he does it with warmth and humor. He could have shown contempt for the contemptuous and hated those who hate, but that would have accelerated our wretched pattern of judgment. Instead, Jesus threw the wrench of mercy into our hate-filled cycle, causing it to sputter and then grind to a halt.

Now, Jesus wasn't telling us to stop making moral judgments. But in our culture, many people assume that Jesus was rejecting absolute truth in favor of moral relativism. Rather, he was rejecting judgmentalism, a spirit of arrogant, self-righteous criticism of others without self-examination. Jesus did not reject moral absolutes.[55] As John Nolland comments:

> The call not to judge has made its way deeply into popular imagination: "Who am I to judge?" Unfortunately the applications peo-

ple often make (giving personal space to others; modesty about one's own capacity to discern what is right; the desire not to be faced with responsibility for decisions in complex or disputed matters) have little to do with the intention of either Jesus or the Gospel writers. In a postmodern context there can be a siren call to a radical pluralism. As popularly understood, the principle is soon set aside when the wrong done by the other person touches a place of deep personal investment.[56]

In Matthew 7:6 Jesus instructs us to live with a nonjudgmental moral discernment. Specifically, he tells us, "Do not give dogs what is sacred; do not throw your pearls to pigs."[57] Later in this Gospel Jesus warns us to beware of false prophets (Mt 7:15) and calls the religious leaders hypocrites and whitewashed tombs (Mt 23:27). Eventually, we must make moral judgments and tend to the speck in our neighbor's eye (see Mt 7:5). Commenting on Matthew 7:6, Dietrich Bonheoffer observes what happens when we ignore Jesus' words:

> The world upon whom grace is thrust as a bargain will grow tired of it, and it will not only trample upon the Holy, but also will tear apart those who force it on them. For its own sake, for the sake of the sinner, and for the sake of the community, the Holy is to be protected from cheap surrender. The Gospel is protected by the preaching of repentance which calls sin sin and declares the sinner guilty. . . . The preaching of grace can only be protected by the preaching of repentance.[58]

As followers of Jesus, we must make judgments—because it is impossible to live without making judgments. But we are also called to offer our judgments with a radically different spirit. Jesus calls us to avoid getting trapped in the cycle of self-righteous judgment and condemnation. We're called to dwell in the spirit of the Beatitudes—marked by spiritual poverty, meekness and mercy—as we live as salt and light.

As Jesus' followers, we are to be radically different, relating to others with profound humility in view of Jesus' call. Jesus is telling us here to stop playing God in our judgments of others. Specifically, Matthew 7 refers to our judging with a "future divine passive" verb tense; in other words, real and final judgments belong to God alone. None of us can make divine judgments about others. After all, what do I know about your life? Your pain and struggles, the direction of your life, the destination of your journey—all of these are a mystery to me. What is it like to be you? I have no idea. Your heart is a deep, mysterious universe to me.

So rather than attempt to make pronouncements about others, I need to begin by looking at myself. The root of the Latin word for "respect"—*respectare*—means "to look again." According to Matthew 7:3, we break the cycle of judgment whenever we look again at the logs in our own eye sockets. By looking at my own heart, practicing the art of self-reflection, I begin to undermine my personal cycle of judgment and condemnation.

Sadly, as one commentator has observed, "The darkness of compulsive judgmentalism distorts all my perceptions and poisons my heart like a noxious gas."[59] Jesus knows the law that operates in the heart of a fallen human being: I judge in my own favor. I take my own side. I'm an expert on your sins and flaws and, as a bonus, I know how to fix you. Unfortunately, I can't even see my own faults and have no idea how to fix them. In the words of novelist Walker Percy, "Why is it possible to learn more in ten minutes about the Crab Nebula in Taurus, which is 6,000 light-years away, than you presently know about yourself, even though you've been stuck with yourself all your life?"[60]

So Jesus begins with some simple advice: be humble by practicing the art of self-reflection. As a deeply blessed person (Mt 5:3-12), you can plumb the depths of your sin and weakness. Face your faults. In three clear but painful steps, Jesus invites you to "take a fearless moral inventory" on how you've betrayed God, others and yourself:[61]

- Start noticing the log in your eye (Mt 7:3).

- Spend less time and energy focusing on your neighbor's eye specks (Mt 7:4).

- Develop a plan to remove your own logs (Mt 7:5).

Also, Jesus is telling us to be different by relating to others with hope. For a follower of Jesus there can be only one goal for confrontation: the hope of restoration. I notice the log in your eye so that *you* can see more clearly. The operation is for your benefit. But typically, when we confront someone with their sin, we do it for our own benefit. We need to get something off our chest or set the record straight or make others pay for the pain they've caused us. I want you to see your "issues"—because they drive me crazy!

Jesus wants us to go deeper. The kingdom of God is about restoration, bringing wholeness out of wreckage. Whenever Jesus encountered brokenness—broken bodies, broken hearts, broken relationships—he brought his healing power. When I see my neighbor's brokenness, it's an opportunity not to cast judgment, to perpetuate the cycle of condemnation. Instead, in and through Jesus, it's a chance to offer the cold, clear water of mercy.

So when I see the speck in your eye, your sins and your flaws and your weakness, do I hunger and thirst for righteousness to take root and rise up in your heart? If I cannot give an emphatic yes to that question, I'm merely perpetuating the cycle of judgment and condemnation. I'm in no position to remove the speck from your eye. Instead, I need to live like the two blind beggars in Matthew 20, constantly and confidently crying out, "Lord, Son of David, have mercy on us!" (Mt 20:30).

MAKE A DECISION
Matthew 7:13-27

My neighbor, an older professor who sports a plush white goatee, is one of the nicest atheists I've ever met. As we were cordially chatting in his backyard one day, I noticed his shed and exclaimed, "Wow, that's a great-looking shed. Who built it for you?' Puffing out his chest a bit, he said, "Why, thank you. I built it myself—from scratch of course."

"That's amazing," I said. "How did you figure out how to do that?"

"It's pretty simple," he told me. "First, you read books on shed-building. And then, you build yourself a shed. But there's one very important step between those two steps: you make a decision. You have to decide that you will build the shed. That's the most important step: make a decision. There is no other way, my friend. Once you make that decision, the shed will get done."

Like my atheist friend, Jesus believed in making a decision. As Jesus concludes his powerful kingdom manifesto he delivers the same message: You have to decide to follow me—or you must decide not to follow me. After that, the rest of your life will get done.

It's not an easy message. Jesus calls for a clean-cut, uncompromising, life-altering, permanent, ongoing decision to follow him by listening to and then obeying his words. There is no other way. But after that, the life of discipleship will get done. Jesus wasn't soft about this need for an unyielding and ongoing decision. He started this sermon with an expansive tenderness; now he concludes it with an unqualified toughness and even narrowness.

In Matthew 7, Jesus frames the big decision of discipleship with four smaller pictures:

- Make a decision: the narrow way or the wide way (Mt 7:13-14).

- Make a decision: the good tree or the bad tree (Mt 7:15-20).

- Make a decision: authentic faith or phony faith (Mt 7:21-23).

- Make a decision: the rock-founded house or the sand-founded house (Mt 7:24-27).

Jesus emphasizes the same theme four times in a row: decide for me or against; decide to be with me or apart from me; decide to be my apprentice or someone else's apprentice. Or, as Bob Dylan railed, you "gotta serve somebody": it may be the devil, it may be the Lord, but it's gonna be somebody. You can't drift into following Jesus. It doesn't just sort of happen as you go with the flow. The spiritual path with Christ begins with grace and mercy, but that doesn't mean it's easy. As people in a twelve-step program repeat every week, "Half-measures availed us nothing." You can't follow Christ with half-measures either.

At first glance, the wide way, the false prophets, the phony faith and the sand-founded house all look good and feel right. After all, what's wrong with the profession in Matthew 7:22? By calling Jesus "Lord, Lord," these people seem to espouse doctrinal correctness. They could most likely sign the statement of faith that guides most evangelical churches. They've also engaged in successful and impressive ministries for Jesus—prophesying in his name, casting out demons and performing miracles.

So what's missing from their lives? Why does Jesus dismiss them in Matthew 7:23? The missing element appears to be the simple, ongoing decision to obey Jesus. As Dale Bruner soberly warns, "We learn from this story that it is possible to work for Jesus yet not work under him. We are intoxicated by the power of Christ's person and yet indifferent or even hostile to keeping his hard commands where they pinch us. . . . It is strangely possible to serve . . . Christ and yet in actual life not to obey him."[62]

In Matthew's Gospel, especially chapters 5-7, Jesus doesn't require remarkable, sensational exhibitions of raw spiritual power. Noticeable, inspiring, "anointed," successful, worldwide ministries do not impress Matthew's Jesus. Instead, Jesus commands us to follow him along a simple, humble path: embracing our spiritual poverty, hungering for righteousness, showing mercy to others, overcoming our contemptuous anger and sexual lust, speaking and standing by honest words, loving our enemies, greeting the unlikeable, trusting God for our daily needs, breaking the cycle of hatred and judgment. These are the quiet, simple, Jesus-ordained ways to please our Lord.

As he does so often in Matthew, Jesus echoes the great prophetic voice of God through Isaiah:

"The multitude of your sacrifices—
    what are they to me?" says the LORD.
I have more than enough of burnt offerings. . . .

Your hands are full of blood!
    Wash and make yourselves clean.
Take your evil deeds out of my sight;
    Stop doing wrong.
    Learn to do right; seek justice.
    Defend the oppressed.
Take up the cause of the fatherless,
    plead the case of the widow." (Is 1:11-17)

Matthew's Jesus and Isaiah's Almighty God have the same message for us: obedience is what really matters. That's the decision. That's the difference between the house that stands and the house that crashes.

Presumably both sets of people heard good information about Jesus, but only one set of people actually followed through and obeyed. Spiritual success, sensational deeds of faith and busy activity—these don't count if we don't obey Jesus in the little things of discipleship.

Matthew ends this section of Jesus' teaching—which also concludes the section that started in Matthew 5:1—with an observation: "When Jesus had finished saying these things, the crowds were amazed at his teaching, because he taught as one who had authority, and not as their teachers of the law" (Mt 7:28-29).[63] The entire section ends with Jesus' authority wowing the crowds. The so-called experts of the law, the Pharisees, didn't possess Jesus' authority. Jesus' teaching wasn't just ethical, nor was it merely prophetic (although it was both ethical and prophetic); it was also charged with messianic power. As D. A. Carson says, "He speaks in the first person and claims that his preaching fulfills the Old Testament; that he determines who enters the messianic kingdom; that as the Divine Judge he pronounces banishment; that the true heirs of the kingdom would be persecuted for their allegiance to him; and that he alone fully knows the will of his Father."[64]

In one sense, my atheist friend was as blunt as our Lord: make a decision. Will you build the shed of discipleship or not? And equally as important, Jesus asks us, "What kind of shed do you really want? Do you want the shoddy shed of big, important, impressive but ultimately shallow faith? Or do you want the quiet, hidden but God-pleasing shed of obedience? You can't have both, so choose one. It's time to make a decision."

THE BEAUTY OF BEING PRESENT
Matthew 8:1-17, 28-34

A few years ago I spent ten hours a week for thirty weeks visiting chronically sick patients in a large university hospital. After completing my three hundred hours of visitation, I concluded that our modern hospitals—efficient, bright and sterilized—qualify as one of the loneliest places on the planet. The long-term patients I visited were receiving exceptional medical care, but they were often lonely, scared and angry. Health care professionals could discuss diagnoses, prognoses, medications and treatment options, but they almost never engaged a patient's sense of agony or abandonment. I discovered that the worst thing about illness wasn't viruses or tumors or clogged arteries; it was fear and isolation and despair.

My friend "Bill" was in the hospital for 160 days. The doctors couldn't diagnose or cure him, so they made him meet with the psychiatrist. After testing and analyzing Bill, the psychiatrist concluded, "Well, Bill, you're not depressed, but you sure are hostile and withdrawn." Bill replied, "After lying in this bed for 160 days, having your leg amputated, listening to the doctors and residents endlessly discuss your case right in front of you without a cure or even a diagnosis, and watching thousands of stupid sitcoms and talk shows, wouldn't you be hostile and withdrawn?"

When Bill told me his story, it unearthed my own fears about sickness. I couldn't "fix" Bill or anyone else who was chronically ill. And what if someday I ended up like Bill—isolated, angry and powerless? That terrified me. For all of our disease-curing efficiency, we usually don't know how to provide healing presence. We cannot engage and cure the deepest wounds of abandonment, rage and fear.

But Jesus did. In the four healing stories found in Matthew 8, Jesus not only cured diseases, he also restored broken lives. He addressed wounds of the body and the gaping wounds of the human heart. He offered the ability to cure illness and be present to people in pain. These two forces in Jesus—his healing power and healing presence—usher us into the "new genesis" (Mt 1:1-17) and the kingdom wholeness (Mt 4:18-25) promised in Matthew's Gospel story.

The four healing stories in Matthew 8 (a leper in verses 1-4, the centurion's servant in verses 5-13, Peter's mother-in-law in verses 14-17 and the demoniacs in verses 28-34) reveal Immanuel in action, the with-us God walking beside us offering his healing presence and touch. In Matthew 8:3, "Jesus reached out his hand" and touched a marginalized, isolated leper. In verse 15 Jesus came into Peter's house and touched the hand of Peter's mother-in-law. Jesus didn't always touch the people he healed, but in 8:16 Matthew records that many who were demon-possessed "were brought to him." Jesus didn't merely focus on curing illnesses and treating symptoms. Instead he offered his personal presence and healing power, demonstrating that the long-awaited kingdom had arrived.[65]

Sick, suffering and traumatized people desperately crave this personal presence, especially the gift of touch. In a fascinating study of traumatized children, psychiatrist Dr. Bruce Perry reports, "Many of the traumatized children I've worked with who have made progress report having contact with at least one supportive adult. . . . Even the smallest gesture can sometimes make the difference to a child whose brain is hungry for affection. . . . In older children and adults massage has also been found to lower blood pressure, fight depression and cut stress by reducing the amount of stress hormones released in the brain."[66]

But Jesus didn't touch just cute babies and desirable adults; he touched despised and loathsome outcasts. In that day nobody touched lepers. A Jewish rabbi would never touch a woman unless she was his wife. Nobody maintained an open-door, open-heart policy for every demoniac in town. They were all "untouchables," but Jesus did the unthinkable: he touched them. In the case of the leper, Matthew records, "Jesus reached out his hand and touched the man. 'I am willing,' he said. 'Be clean!'" (Mt 8:3). That's the gospel in five words and one gesture of love. The living God approaches us in all of our shame and damage—all the hurt we've felt and all the pain we've caused others—and tells us, "I am willing. Be clean." And then he touches us.

According to Matthew 8:17, Jesus' ministry of personal presence was essential to his work. Matthew summarizes it by pointing back to Isaiah when he states, "He took up our infirmities and bore our diseases." The original passage in Isaiah 53 speaks about the "suffering servant," an individual who would enter into the suffering of God's people, identify with it, bear it and then remove it. In a startling claim, Matthew once again points to the fulfillment of God's story in Jesus: he is the suffering servant. Of course when he died on the cross Jesus identified with and bore away our sin and suffering. But Matthew also wants us to know that Jesus walks beside us every time we feel sick or forsaken. If the worst thing about suffering is the isolation and despair, then Immanuel will come near us and offer his personal presence and even his touch.

Not only did Jesus touch people with his personal presence but, as evidenced in the healing of the two demoniacs, he also offered power to restore sick and broken human beings. In Matthew 8:28 Jesus and his disciples arrive in the Gadarenes, an unfamiliar, pagan place marked by tombs, demons and unclean pigs. The demoniacs were so fierce that everyone just avoided them. These two broken men, distorted and disfigured, were in one sense not that different from Peter's mother-in-law or the centurion's servant. All were experiencing common human brokenness in a world bent and scarred by the Fall.

During my three hundred hours of visitation I also discovered that our bright, efficient, sophisticated hospitals contain people who are still haunted by demonic powers. In one of my pastoral visits at Stony Brook University Hospital I met a seventy-year-old patient who tried to shoo me away by saying, "Nice to see you, pastor, but you should really talk to my wife because she believes in God and I don't."

"Oh, really," I said. "Tell me why you don't believe in God."

"Okay, it's a very specific, quick story. I was serving in the United States army, stationed in Korea, when I came upon a sight that scarred me for life. A squad of North Korean soldiers had ambushed a busload of civilians, torching everything inside the bus—old men, young women, children, even infants in their mother's arms. I'll never forget the sight of charcoal babies and the stench of burnt human flesh. Something died in my heart on that day: God died, faith died, hope died. The memory still haunts me."

According to a biblical worldview, this man had encountered pure evil—both human and demonic.[67] But over and over again Matthew's Gospel story shows us that Jesus came to restore the kingdom even in the midst of evil's domain. Jesus came to heal our hatred and bitterness, our scars and nightmares, our trauma and addictions, the demonic things done to us and the demonic things done by us.

That's the point of the demon's frantic speech in Matthew 8:29: "What do you want with us, Son of God? . . . Have you come here to torture us before the appointed time?" The "appointed time" seems to mean the coming of God's kingdom power predicted in Matthew 4:17. When Jesus announced the inbreaking of God's kingdom it meant, "The time has come. The kingdom is here making all things new. This bent, broken, distorted world, this world haunted by demonic drives and evil nightmares, will become fully healed. It's not there yet, but in my presence and power the healing has started to break into this world." Jesus demonstrated that kingdom power by approaching and then healing two men broken and disfigured by demonic powers. And in his name and his power the church continues this ministry of healing presence.

In this vignette Jesus speaks only one word: "He said to them, 'Go!'" (Mt 8:32). Jesus stands there, utterly present to evil but even more present to the broken men before him. Like everyone else, Jesus saw the corrosive action of evil on their souls,[68] but unlike everyone else, he also saw the humanity, the image of God lying beneath the surface of ugliness and disfigurement. In spite of our brokenness and sickness and even our evil, Jesus sees our wholeness. And he has only to speak one word to begin this good work of restoration. Of course this healing never gets completed in this life, which is why we groan inwardly as we await "the redemption of our bodies" (Rom 8:23). In this life we will always yearn for the full restoration of Christ's good work in the cosmos, but in these four vignettes of Matthew 8 Jesus provides a foretaste of the world's full healing.

In the same way, when Jesus touched and healed the leper he was pointing to the full restoration of human brokenness. The Old Testament didn't reveal how to restore the broken lives of lepers, so lepers had to remain outside the camp. In fact, leprosy was nearly a hopeless cause—until Jesus showed up. By touching the leper Jesus was making a powerful visual statement: there is no one beyond the reach of God's redemptive power.[69] There is no one too broken, sinful, scarred, self-righteous, twisted, perverted or addicted to receive and be transformed by God's grace.

The utterly amazing good news is this: to start his restorative work in our souls, Jesus requires only that we believe—a little. Now, the centurion's confidence is so remarkable that even Jesus is stunned. In Matthew 8:10 he proclaims, "Truly I tell you, I have not found anyone in Israel with such great faith." And the leper also exudes confidence as he declares, "Lord, if you are willing, you can make me clean" (Mt 8:2). But the demoniacs spewing their rage certainly don't display heroic faith in Jesus. And despite this, Jesus hears and touches these broken people who cry out to him. Matthew 1 has set the tone for our spiritual journey: God is already seeking and approaching us (Mt 1:23). As Dale Bruner contends, "[For us] to approach Jesus . . . however well or badly we do it, is to get near help."[70]

This Gospel also wants us to know that being with Jesus, receiving his presence and his power, propels us to follow him by serving others in his name. As his followers we should constantly ask, "Who are the untouchables of my world?" Migrant workers, the addicted and traumatized, the lonely and angry, the convicted and condemned? How can we live our lives—individually and communally—so we serve as the presence of Jesus?

After his 160 days in the hospital Bill was released into a large nursing home on the other side of town. Sadly, the home offered even less personal presence and touch than the hospital. After walking through rows of old women slumped in wheelchairs, waiting for visitors who rarely came, I found Bill warehoused in a corner room without windows. His eyes brightened for a few minutes as we held hands and prayed. Then he fell asleep. He was dying and we both knew it would be my last visit. But I also knew that Bill would die with dignity and with faith in the risen Christ in whom he had come to believe.

As those who are connected to Jesus, trusting him in our spiritual poverty, we can offer others the personal presence of Jesus. By touching others we offer them the touch of Jesus. In our impersonal culture marked by deep loneliness, this ministry of presence—offering the presence of Christ, God with us, to others in their isolation and pain—is an amazing privilege and calling.

COUNTING THE COST
Matthew 8:18-27

My friend Emilio owns a tiny pizzeria that makes the best New York pizza on Long Island. Emilio hates "organized religion." Above the stove where he sticks the orders he also collects small newspaper clippings about flawed ministers. I call it his "rack of shame." Every time I come in for pizza he leans over the counter, slides a few clippings onto the counter and whispers, "Hey, look at this. This padre walked off with eighty thousand dollars. This pastor slept with three church members. This guy abused little boys for twenty years. Okay, do you get why I don't need your church?" Then with a triumphant flourish he replaces the articles on his rack of shame.

Naturally, over time I started to get defensive about these clergy-bashing conversations. I stared scouring the local papers for stories about nasty pizza guys, but unfortunately these individuals either live very clean lives—or nobody cares if they fail. One day Emilio struck at the heart of the issue by saying, "Look, my friend, here's my problem with ministers and all alleged Christians: I get sick of you talking about love, love, love and then acting like total frauds. You say, 'Oops, big screwup, my bad, but hey now—Jesus will forgive us.' You guys embezzle the funds and abuse little children and don't act like Jesus, and then you get immediate amnesty. That makes me puke. As far as I can tell, it costs you guys nothing to believe in Jesus. The more 'Christian' you get, the more nasty you act. Maybe you should act a little more un-Christian, like me, and you'd be nicer human beings!"

I finally admitted that Emilio had a point. In Matthew 8, sandwiched between four stories of tender, grace-filled, healing touch, we find three encounters with another side of Jesus—the challenging, uncompromising Master who calls us to a life of commitment and obedience. In this section Matthew wants us to know that Jesus doesn't just console and comfort broken sinners; he also calls us into a life of costly discipleship. In this section, Jesus' love is tender and tough, grace-filled and demanding.

The three vignettes in Matthew 8:18-27 focus on three flawed disciples with imperfect faith. And in each instance Jesus' love is expressed as a challenge. Verse 18 reports that great crowds were thronging around Jesus. Now, from a public relations standpoint, this would have been the perfect occasion to solidify Jesus' base by lowering the cost of discipleship, selling it at a discount. Instead, in all three encounters Jesus raises the bar of discipleship. It's as if he's saying, "Yes, I will accept you. Yes, I will heal your brokenness with my presence and my power. Yes, I will embrace you with your weak and faltering faith. But I also want you to count the cost, pay the price and follow me with your whole heart."

In Matthew 8:19 a scribe, or professional teacher of the law, approaches Jesus and says, "Teacher [or perhaps 'fellow teacher'], I will follow you wherever you go." Notice that he doesn't ask to follow Jesus nor does Jesus invite him to follow; instead, he announces that he *will* follow Jesus. By the scribe's own evaluation, he's ready and able to do this and his offer is a darn good deal—for Jesus, that is.

Jesus isn't impressed. Instead, he throws cold water on the scribe's offer by replying, "Foxes have dens and birds have nests, but the Son of Man has no place to lay his head" (Mt 8:20). It's a terse response, but underneath Jesus may have been implying something like this: "Do you really want to follow me wherever? We're on the road most of the time. I don't know where my next meal is coming from. I don't know where I'll sleep tomorrow night. We don't share the conveniences of middle-class existence. You have no idea what you're getting yourself into. We're going to marginal places of pain and abandonment. We'll touch lepers and howling demoniacs. Then we'll march into Jerusalem where I'll get murdered and all my disciples will scatter. It's a life marked by insecurity and vulnerability. That's what you're signing up for when you follow me. Is that the kind of 'teacher' you want to follow?"

Jesus' self-identification as the "the Son of Man" in this passage serves to define his authority as a teacher.[71] Deeply rooted in the Old Testament (see Dan 7), the Son of Man was a figure of awesome majesty and authority. And yet for Jesus, this title also conveys the idea of redemptive suffering (see Mt 20:28). In Matthew's Jesus, we find this strange combination: the glorious Son of Man who also suffers. And unlike the scribes, Jesus' authority as a teacher flows out of his wounds, not just his intellectual knowledge.

On one level, we'd like to assume that people with authority and power are exempt from suffering. But on another level, we know that true authority comes through suffering. For instance, if you're depressed, would you rather go to (a) someone with a cheerful disposition who can't fathom what it means to live with a mental illness, or (b) someone who knows about the agony of depression from firsthand experience? Who has more authority to speak into your life?[72] There is an authority, an experiential knowledge that flows from our wounds into the hearts of fellow sufferers. In the same way, we listen to Jesus the teacher not just because he's brilliant (although he is); we listen to him because he's suffered with us and for us.

Unfortunately, most contemporary, affluent churches don't understand this concept. Like the scribe in Matthew 8:18, we'd rather meet in cushy homes and lecture halls (modern sanctuaries) surrounded by interesting and well-groomed people (like us) and imbibe the latest and hippest teachings. But according to Jesus' life, discipleship doesn't happen in a classroom setting. Instead, believers become disciples by feeding the hungry, being exposed to trouble, dying to their old lives, losing almost everything and forgiving their enemies. We will speak with deeper authority for Jesus after we have walked with Jesus, obeyed Jesus and suffered with Jesus.[73]

In the second story of a would-be disciple (see Mt 8:21), a man approaches Jesus with what appears to be a reasonable request: he wants to go home and bury his father. Why does Jesus rough him up, especially since he clearly honored the care of parents (see Mt 15)? The request from this wannabe disciple may have implied one of two options:

• The man wanted to wait indefinitely until his father died so he could please his parents and put Jesus on hold.

• His father was already dead and buried but the man needed to wait until he could perform a traditional reburial. In Jesus' day the eldest son would return to his father's tomb a year later and "rebury" him by arranging the bones in a container and sliding it in a slot in the wall.

In either scenario, this "disciple" was trying to cut a deal with Jesus: "By golly, Jesus, someday I'll get really serious about following you." If this man were part of the contemporary American church, he might add, "It's complicated, Jesus: kids, job, sports, school. I promise that when _____ happens, I'll get serious about this discipleship thing. But right now my plate is just too full."

We might think Jesus would praise the initiative of this second potential disciple. At least he approached Jesus and offered something. Instead Jesus gives another blunt, one-line response: "Let the dead bury their own dead" (Mt 8:22). By saying this Jesus might have been providing a catchy way to say "let the spiritually dead take care of themselves," or he may have been implying that there's something even more important than waiting around until your father dies—following him. If this would-be disciple was using his father as an excuse to evade discipleship, Jesus cut through the excuse and challenged him to the core of his heart.

Finally, in the third story in this section, Jesus challenges an entire group of timid disciples into the joyful, challenging, costly adventure of following him. In the Greek text, the disciples' cry in the midst of the storm consists of three words: "Lord! Save! We-Perish!" The verb for "perish," used nineteen times in Matthew, has been translated as "we are sinking," "we are going down," "we are about to die" or "we are drowning." No matter how it's translated, the disciples were clearly in trouble. In Matthew 8:26 Jesus responds to their terrified cry by calling them "little-faiths" (see also Mt 6:30), a term of endearment and encouragement. At least Jesus saw some faith in his followers. And for him, a little faith is better than no faith—even a mustard-seed faith can move mountains. Grand heroics, sensational miracles and busy, loud, flashy, puffed-up "big-faith" disciples simply do not impress Jesus (see Mt 7:21-23).

While it may be startling to find such embarrassing stories about Jesus' followers sprinkled throughout the Gospel accounts, these little-faith incidents send a clear message about grace. "Look at our lives," they seem to say. "Look at our botched attempts to follow Jesus. Look at all of our spiritual belly flops. We were with Jesus; he was right there sleeping in our boat, and we still panicked. If there was hope for us, there's certainly hope for you, fellow little-faiths." In one sense we'll never outgrow our little-faith status. Jesus loves to move toward people who need his mercy.

Of course, none of this negates Emilio's point about his "rack of shame" collection. He was right about this: God expects us to grow up in Christ. Jesus expects our obedience. He's unhappy with people who call him "Lord" but who don't trust or obey. Who don't act like salt. Who don't love and forgive their enemies. Who refuse to touch lepers and outcasts. Clearly Jesus expects our raw faith to become perfected in love (see Mt 5:48).

But the slow transformation of little-faiths occurs in the context of grace. So Emilio was wrong about this: God's grace, rightly understood and truly experienced, will change the human heart. Finding an antidote to hypocrisy doesn't start with diluting our faith; it starts with diving deeper into the person of Jesus, the Son of Man, the one who looms large with authority, power and suffering love. If we begin the spiritual journey in poverty, knowing our dire need for grace, we will end up displaying gentleness and working for righteousness. Those who know and experience the Father's tender love cannot continue to treat others with cruelty or indifference. Once we taste the new wine of Jesus, we can't keep putting it back into those old wineskins of hypocrisy and disobedience.

EXTREME DESPERATION
Matthew 9:1-34

Walter and Tarek, the two main characters in the movie *The Visitor*, seem to be total opposites. Walter, an aging, white, upper-middle-class widower and economics professor in Connecticut, is a classic insider. From his position of wealth and privilege, Walter hovers above suffering and human entanglement, ignoring his students and recycling old syllabi and lectures. In contrast, Tarek, a young illegal immigrant from Syria, is a classic outsider. He subsists by playing the djembe at dank Manhattan jazz clubs while his Senegalese girlfriend sells handmade jewelry at flea markets. In contrast to Walter, who lives a life of safety and entitlement, Tarek dwells on the margins, constantly threatened by deportation.

When Walter travels to Manhattan he finds that Tarek and his girlfriend have occupied his rarely used apartment. Walter's initial annoyance gives way to compassion and he lets them stay. As their friendship grows and as Tarek introduces Walter into the vibrant drumming subculture, we see that the men actually have much in common. Tarek lives on the edge of poverty and exile; Walter flits on the edge of despair and emotional numbness. They both struggle against forces they can't control, yearning for connection and hope. In spite of their profound differences, they share one thing in common: they both need grace, love and rebirth. As a result, they both qualify for Jesus' marvelous open-door invitation: "Blessed are the poor in spirit, for theirs is the kingdom of heaven" (Mt 5:3).

Matthew 9 also introduces a cast of characters who, in spite of their vast differences, share the same human need for grace: the four men who need to get their friend healed (verses 1-8), spiritually "sick" sinners who need Jesus' healing (verses 9-13), a synagogue leader who needs a miracle for his sick daughter (verses 18 and 23-26), a desperately ill woman who needs healing (verses 19-22) and two blind men desperate to see again (verses 27-34).

The synagogue leader and the chronically ill woman couldn't have been more different. The synagogue leader was a respected male, moving at the center of power and influence. From all appearances he possessed a loving, intact nuclear family and a network of friends and financial resources. The woman, who had been "subject to bleeding for twelve years" (Mt 9:20), oozed neediness from the start. Her ailment had probably kept her from marriage and childbearing. Without a husband or adult children to care for her, she had depleted her resources as she gradually faded to the margins of the community.

Yet despite these differences, Matthew weaves them together in one story to make a point: they are both needy. When the ancient writers translated the Bible into Latin, they called these two stories the stories of *desperation in extremis*. Both characters had a need, and with their own resources they were powerless to meet that need. Also, both of them in their desperation turned to Jesus with bold and even audacious confidence that he would meet their need. Thus, they shared one all-consuming quest: to get to Jesus.

At one time, with his network of friends, family and social respect, the synagogue ruler probably soared above *desperation in extremis*, but then his twelve-year-old daughter died (Mk 5:42). Now, normally, respectable public leaders such as senators or doctors or executives or senior pastors don't show desperation. They speak calmly; they stand erect; they don't weep or beg in public. But this man was beyond all of that. His little girl was gone. As he stared death in the face, without fix-it-strategies, he descended into powerlessness. In his utter desperation he came to Jesus and begged, "My daughter has just died. But come and put your hand on her, and she will live" (Mt 9:18).

Both the respected synagogue ruler and the marginal woman seep with an open wound of human need. Money, power, influence, networks and family status—all of these resources may help us cover our need for a while, but eventually life will rip off our Band-Aids and expose our wounds. We are grace-hungry people. We all grow old and die, and we need hope. We create institutions that oppress others and we need justice. We face our inner loneliness and we need community. We battle internal forces of hate, greed and selfishness and we need the power to love.

Unfortunately, non-needy people—resource-rich, comfortable people with intact families and successful networks—often don't see their need for grace. But both *The Visitor* and Matthew's Gospel story combine the needy with the non-needy, the spiritually sick and the spiritually healthy, placing them on the same soil. This Gospel continually exposes our insatiable need for grace. By recounting his own call to discipleship (see Mt 9:9-11), Matthew reminds us of Jesus' claim that "good" people need grace just as much as anyone else. In the words of Isaiah, Jesus' favorite prophet in the Gospel of Matthew, our righteous deeds—not our awful deeds but our good deeds—are like a filthy rag (Is 64:6).

All of us—sinners and the "righteous," the sick and the "healthy"— hover on the edge of *desperation in extremis*. In the sobering words of Tim Keller, "When a Christian sees prostitutes, alcoholics, prisoners, drug addicts, unwed mothers, the homeless, refugees, he knows that he is looking in a mirror. Perhaps the Christian spent all of his life as a respectable middle-class person. No matter. He thinks, 'Spiritually I was just like these people, though physically and socially I never was where they are now. They are outcasts. I was an outcast.'"[74]

Sometimes I've found that people in twelve-step programs grasp this better than most good church people. As I've participated in a twelve-step program myself and as I've listened to the stories of other recovering addicts, I've reached this conclusion: it doesn't matter what you're hooked on—alcohol, heroin, sex, relationships, gambling, food, Christian service—you can't heal until you admit you're powerless to overcome your addiction. You begin with the first step of pure honesty about your situation (*desperation in extremis*) and you never outgrow this initial step of recovery. I've watched men and women enter recovery groups with Ph.D.s and GEDs, Armani suits and sweat suits, BMWs and Harleys because they have two things in common: (1) they're desperate, and (2) they're confident that this community and God can help them stay sober.

The two characters whose lives intersect in Matthew 9 display those same characteristics—desperation and confidence. And in both stories Jesus acts like he simply can't resist this combination of honest need and simple faith. After the desperate ("My daughter has just died") but confident ("But come . . . and she will live") plea of the synagogue ruler, Jesus "got up and went with him" (Mt 9:19), the same phrase used of the disciples who got up and followed Jesus. Jesus responds to this irresistible combination of desperation and confidence.

As Jesus was following the synagogue ruler, he encountered another desperate-confident individual. The woman had been suffering for twelve years and her resources were depleted. But in her desperation she turned to Jesus, approaching him from behind and touching the fringe of his garment as she said to herself, "If I only touch his cloak, I will be healed" (Mt 9:21).

Although some commentators argue that this act of touching Jesus' garment reveals a superstitious spirituality, we see only the results of her faith: Jesus responded positively to her desperation and confidence. Specifically, Matthew notes, "Jesus turned and saw her" (Mt 9:22). Seeing people was what Jesus did best. I wonder how often I truly see people. Usually I'm so busy, distracted and self-absorbed that I can't see the real you. I see a stereotype; I see the you who does not meet my needs; I see the you who has faults and flaws; I see the you who has wounded or disappointed me. Am I ever present to you, the real you with all your flaws and all your glorious beauty? Jesus was present.

After seeing her, Jesus verbally blessed the woman by saying, "Take heart, daughter. . . . Your faith has healed you" (Mt 9:22). It's hard for us to imagine the power of those simple words. For twelve years this woman had lived in sickness and isolation, without human touch or verbal blessing. And yet Jesus noticed her, gave her his full attention and verbally blessed her. When philosopher Josef Pieper tried to define the nature of love, he kept returning to Jesus' way of giving people his full attention and blessing them. According to Pieper, "Loving someone or something means finding him or it *probus*, the Latin word for good. It is a way of turning to [another human being] and saying, 'It's good that you exist; it's good that you are in this world!'"[75]

Jesus' pattern for responding to desperate people who confidently approach him seeking wholeness is this: he sees, he blesses and he heals. This pattern is repeated in each of the stories in Matthew 9. Desperate people—friends of a paralytic, a sinful tax collector and his buddies, a synagogue ruler, two blind men, a demoniac—come confidently to Jesus, and he sees, blesses and heals. He isn't repulsed by their raw and oozing wound of need; instead, he can't resist moving toward them in order to bring wholeness.

As flawed and prideful human beings, our tendency is to deny our own desperation. We're ashamed of our wounds, assuming that if others knew us—the real us with all our struggles and sins—they would flee. So we try hard to prove that we've moved beyond *desperation in extremis*.

Recently I attended a worship service at my son's church in Kansas City. I was moved by the sermon, a simple message about Jesus' words from the cross—"Father, into your hands I commit my spirit"—and the pastor's invitation to trust Jesus for our sins and our needs. At the close of the service, as we bowed our heads and prayed, he asked us to raise our hands if we were struggling to trust in the care of our heavenly Father. I knew I needed to raise my hand. I was living with a gaping wound of mistrust and anxiety, but for some reason I resisted. Yes, I'm needy, I argued with myself, but I'm not *that* needy. I don't want to admit to God and to this community that I'm powerless. I don't want others to see that I'm as desperate as a despised tax collector, a band of sinners, a grieving synagogue ruler, a chronically sick woman, two blind men or a mute demoniac.

So I didn't raise my hand. I refused to display my need for Jesus. I have a hunch that almost everyone else in that service did the same thing. But by being dishonest about our wounds, we cut ourselves off from the flow of Jesus' mercy. Rather than approaching Jesus with confidence we flee from him.

Sadly, we flee from community and mission as well. In Matthew 9 Jesus is demonstrating a clear pattern: as people gather around Jesus, approaching him with faith, he builds his church. As we place our confidence in him, he propels us outward in our love for other people. But it all starts with our desperation. In the words of Frodo Baggins we cry out, "I feel very small, and very uprooted, and well—desperate."[76] In this passage Jesus is inviting us into a Frodo-like experience of admitting our desperate need for God's grace. As we receive his mercy and healing, we are sent to bring good news to others in their places of desperation. As we repeat this pattern, *desperation in extremis* seems about as strange as a sick person visiting the doctor. And admitting our need and bringing it to Jesus is the only way to experience true healing.

UNLIKELY HEROES
Matthew 10:1-15

In his gripping novel *City of Thieves*, David Benioff weaves a tale about the Nazis' siege of Leningrad during World War II. Lev, a shy and scrawny petty thief, is thrown into the same jail cell as Kolya, an articulate and handsome deserter from the Russian army. Both of them should have faced execution, but instead they're offered a chance at freedom. They must fulfill a simple but dangerous assignment: secure a dozen eggs for a Russian colonel whose daughter needs a wedding cake. If they can't find the eggs in one week, the colonel will hunt them down and execute them. In a city suffering intense deprivation, finding a dozen eggs in less than a week becomes a ludicrous mission.

As they begin their quest, Lev, the hapless narrator of the story, recounts his lack of qualifications:

> This wasn't the way I had imagined my adventures, but reality ignored my wishes from the get-go, giving me a body best suited for stacking books in the library, injecting so much fear into my veins that I could only cower in the stairwell when the violence came. Maybe someday my arms and legs would thicken with muscle and fear would drain away like dirty bathwater. I wish I believed these things would happen, but I didn't. I was cursed with the pessi-

mism of both the Russians and the Jews, two of the gloomiest tribes in the world. Still, if there wasn't greatness in me, maybe I had the talent to recognize it in others.[77]

In the end, although he doesn't see any greatness in himself, and although he feels inadequate and even cursed, Lev outwits the German soldiers, wins the pretty girl's heart and returns to Leningrad with a dozen unbroken eggs. In this against-all-odds odyssey, Lev becomes an unspectacular and unlikely hero.

In chapter 10 Matthew recounts Jesus' selection of a band of unlikely heroes. There are only two remarkable things about these men: (1) they are utterly unspectacular in themselves, and (2) they become spectacular through their union with Jesus. Now, most lists of heroes in the ancient world contained short descriptions of the heroes' amazing exploits. For example, we read about the "much-traveled Odysseus, the man of many ways" or "Hector, the breaker of horses." But in this list of twelve disciples, the only descriptions are those of failure—for example, "Matthew the tax collector." By including these descriptions, this Gospel declares, "Look at the kinds of people Jesus will choose. Look what God can do in and through and with such imperfect people. Look at how Jesus transforms such unlikely heroes."

Up to this point in the Gospel of Matthew, Jesus has been doing everything as his disciples have watched. Jesus has healed the sick, stilled the storm, cast out demons, preached to the masses and called sinners into grace. But now Jesus does something unprecedented: "Jesus called his twelve disciples to him and gave them authority to drive out impure spirits and to heal every disease and sickness" (Mt 10:1). Just a few verses earlier Matthew recorded that Jesus went about "healing every disease and sickness" (9:35). With the same word construction, Matthew claims that this band of unlikely, unqualified disciples will perform Jesus' deeds.

In the context of the broader biblical story, this verse brings us back to the remarkable calling given to human beings in Genesis, when God created men and women and gave them authority to rule over "the fish of the sea and the birds of the air, over the livestock, over all the earth" (Gen 1:26 NIV 1984). Adam and Eve were called to live as bold, creative artists and coworkers with the living God. They were called to a life of dignity and honor. But through the fall into sin, our beautiful calling was marred and muddied. We no longer rule rightly; instead we oppress others, destroy God's good creation and are controlled by addictions, fear and shame. Our high and holy calling has devolved into a curse.

Now in Matthew 10:1 Jesus begins to reverse the curse by forming this community of unlikely heroes. Through the person and work of Jesus, God the Father is transforming us to an even higher level of authority and dignity. In Genesis 1, out of the nothingness of nonbeing, God created us and called us to be his coworkers. In this passage, out of the nothingness of human sinfulness and ordinariness, Jesus begins to recapitulate his fallen humanity. In the words of the fourth-century theologian Athanasius, when God's "noble works" (us) were "on the road to ruin," Christ intervened so that he "might turn again to incorruption men who had been turned back to corruption, and make them alive through death by the appropriation of his body and by the grace of his resurrection."[78]

But, surprisingly, at the start Jesus appears to restrict this beautiful plan of restoration. In fact, his words concern and even offend some people: "These twelve Jesus sent out with the following instructions: 'Do not go among the Gentiles or enter any town of the Samaritans. Go rather to the lost sheep of Israel'" (Mt 10:5-6). However, by the end of Matthew's Gospel Jesus tells his followers to make disciples from every nation. What are we to make of this confusing plan to restore the world by first narrowing its scope?

The Bible doesn't hide the fact that God chooses some people to be in a special relationship with him. God chose Abram, one man among millions, and said, "I will bless you" (Gen 12:2). To us this may seem unfair and exclusive. In the biblical story, however, being chosen implied a responsibility, not just a privilege. God kept telling his chosen people that they were chosen for a special purpose: to share God's love with the world. They were blessed in order to be a blessing to others. It's as if God's blessing always starts small and particular, like a single tiny seed, before it can spread out like a broad, beautiful and fruit-bearing tree.

Jesus' point here is that God hasn't abandoned Plan A to redeem the cosmos. He still wants to bless the world by working through his chosen people. But as he continues with Plan A, blessing the entire world through the blessed ones, Jesus also initiates the fulfillment of that plan, which was always aimed at including and blessing the Gentiles. So Jesus starts with a motley group of unlikely heroes who are sinners among sinners. The only thing that makes them different is this: Jesus has called them and given them his authority. This is the miracle of the new genesis in Jesus.

As Jesus authorizes his disciples, his theme remains consistent with earlier passages in Matthew: "Preach this message: 'The kingdom of heaven is near'" (Mt 10:7). God's reign, his transformation of broken human lives and pain-filled human institutions, has started now. The power of the kingdom is a present reality and a future hope.[79] The kingdom of heaven creates a new normal. Normal used to mean that brokenness stayed broken, injustice stayed unjust, addicts remained addicted, the resentful continued in their bitterness, the dead rotted in their graves, cowards never became brave, and the demon-possessed remained trapped. But Jesus changed all of that. In him the kingdom has come and God is reigning over and restoring his broken creation.

In fact, the actions Jesus lists in Matthew 10:8—healing the sick, raising the dead, cleansing the lepers and exorcising demons—are all acts of restoration. Disease destroys health. Death separates you from life. Leprosy disfigures your face and your connection to community. Demon possession ruptures your relationship with God. But now these enemies of human well-being are vanquished through Jesus. His power is available to restore and ultimately perfect humanity's dignity and glory. In Jesus, broken human beings can start flourishing in a transformed relationship with the pro-human God of life.

What's more, Jesus invites us, his unlikely and ordinary heroes, to join him in this new genesis of restoration. As one commentator claims, "The Lord makes his apostles confront every destructive force gnawing at man's being—physical and psychic evils, and then death itself."[80] This calling is an act of his election and not our qualification; he says, "freely you have received" (Mt 10:8). Jesus' work of transformation begins and continues through his grace and mercy, not through our merits or spiritual achievements.

Unfortunately, we usually can't fathom the pure freeness of grace. For instance, when I told someone that our son Mathew was attending medical school so he could become a medical missionary, she said, "Oh, you must have been a good parent. Good parents deserve good children. Maybe you should write a book on how to raise good kids." I nearly started choking. Frankly, I have a long list of mistakes I made as a parent—mistakes that make me cringe. And yet somehow I've received much more in my children than I deserve. "Freely you have received"— that's the message flowing from Jesus' call to his disciples. We're all unlikely, unqualified, unspectacular recruits for discipleship, but Jesus chooses us, changes us and uses us for his good purposes.

This section ends with some unexpected and lengthy instructions that we could title "How to Leave Unreceptive Places" (see Mt 10:11-15).[81] However, these verses aren't just random comments. They refer back to the beginning of the passage, where Jesus bestows his authority on this unlikely group. So now when the disciples enter a home, Jesus' blessing will enter that home through them. If the home is worthy of the disciples' blessing, the blessing will remain. But then, "If anyone will not welcome you or listen to your words, shake the dust off your feet when you leave that home or town" (Mt 10:14). In other words, the blessing of Jesus offered through the disciples won't stick to that unwelcoming home.

The twofold meaning is clear: First, people will resist the message. Second, this animosity shouldn't discourage Jesus' followers, because now they know who they are in him. Throughout this Gospel Jesus has been filling his disciples with a sense of destiny and importance. In chapter 4 he called an ordinary crew of fisherman and told them he would make them fishers of men. In chapter 5 he called his followers the salt of the earth and the light of the world. This unlikely bunch becomes fishers of men and salt and light only through the presence and power of Jesus.

Once again this is consistent with Matthew's theme of discipleship. Jesus doesn't call spectacular people to heroic deeds of glitzy faith. He calls the ordinary, the poor in spirit (Mt 5:3), those whose good deeds are hidden (Mt 6:1-18), the quietly obedient (Mt 7:21-27), the simple children (Mt 11:25), the bruised reeds and the smoldering wicks (Mt 12:20). God calls little and unspectacular people like Lev or Bilbo Baggins or you and me, the "things that are not" (1 Cor 1:28), so that no one will boast and everyone will know that it's God's power working through us to heal and transform this broken world. Of course, in the scope of Matthew's Gospel, this will happen only as Jesus' followers depend on him, trusting him and obeying his words.

MEAN PEOPLE
Matthew 10:16-42

We can now add "*Avatar* blues" to our list of postmodern ailments and disorders. Apparently that's what many fans experienced after watching the film. On one website, a topic thread popped up titled "Ways to cope with the depression of the dream of Pandora being intangible." After receiving over a thousand posts from depressed fans, the forum administrator opened another thread so people could continue to process their *Avatar*-related depression.

One fan wrote, "Ever since I went to see *Avatar* I have been depressed. Watching the wonderful world of Pandora and all the Na'vi made me want to be one of them. . . . I even contemplated suicide thinking that if I do I will be rebirthed in a world similar to Pandora." According to a CNN report, "Other fans have expressed feelings of disgust with the human race and disengagement with reality."[82]

On one hand, followers of Jesus might see the *Avatar* blues as a sign of our hunger for transformation and our longing for heaven's beauty. But then again, we could also see it as a disturbing trend in our culture: our inability to live in reality, especially a troubling reality that includes political turmoil, difficult people, interpersonal conflicts, and even rejections and betrayals. People are difficult. They can be mean and nasty, annoying, demanding and hurtful. It's so troubling that sometimes we'd like to strike back, grow cynical and bitter, or, unlike Jesus, withdraw completely.

But in Matthew 10 Jesus gives us two great truths about living on a fallen planet. First, people will hurt you. Second, you can love them anyway. In other words, unlike Pandora, the world really is screwed up. And unlike people with *Avatar* blues, you can live in this world with its mean and nasty people and not contemplate suicide or long to be reborn in fiction. In and through Jesus, you can continue living as salt and light despite the surrounding rottenness and darkness.

At this stage in Matthew's Gospel story, Jesus is running into opposition and he sees even more trouble looming on the horizon. He wants his followers to know that their association with him will get them in trouble too (see Mt 10:22). But rather than provide a free ride around relational conflict, Jesus promises to send them right into it, saying, "I am sending you out like sheep among wolves" (Mt 10:16). In real life sheep carefully avoid wolves. Wolves are mean, nasty things that maul sheep and then eat them alive. But Jesus was very clear: "I [the Greek is emphatic, as in 'I and I alone'] am sending you out like sheep among wolves." This impossible, dangerous mission is not a mistake. Jesus predicted it and planned it.

And then Jesus proceeds to outline in vivid detail what these wolves will do to the sheep. Notice the key verbs in this passage:

- "be handed over . . . and be flogged" (Mt 10:17)
- "brought before governors and kings" (Mt 10:18)
- "arrest you" (Mt 10:19)
- "betray . . . put to death" (Mt 10:21)
- "hated by everyone" (Mt 10:22)
- "When [not if, but when] you are persecuted" (Mt 10:23)

It's not a pretty list. But in the midst of this nasty wolf treatment Jesus expects his followers to keep acting like sheep. Sadly, throughout history, the church has often acted like a pack of wolves. Jesus' "sheep" have perpetrated all kinds of nasty acts of aggression. So when people look at the church and cry, "Wolves!" (e.g., crusaders, inquisitors, heresy hunters, colonialists, scientist punishers, slave traders, atheist haters, gay bashers and so on), we can simply confess, "You're right: at times we have failed miserably to follow and obey Jesus and I am horribly sorry." But we can also calmly, confidently and lovingly say, "But our Lord never wanted wolflike followers. It's our fault, not his."

Our first responsibility, according to these verses, is to act like sheep and doves: gentle, merciful, prayer-filled and pure in heart. Even in the midst of aggression we can control our response to others. We can choose to forgive and love our enemies.

So Jesus holds out high ideals of loving engagement with hostile people. But he also displays a remarkable realism when he tells us to be "as shrewd as snakes" (Mt 10:16). Sheep are innocent and gentle but they don't have to be stupid; Jesus' sheep can also be snakelike. Snakes are sneaky and wary. Snakes often use their natural camouflage to their advantage. Snakes stay low to the ground so you can't catch them. Snakes know when to head for cover. Jesus wants Christians to become strange sheep-hearted, snake-minded creatures.

At one point in my early twenties I tried to stop a street fight between two angry people from different cultures. Compelled to be like Jesus, I put my body between them and tried to bring peace. They didn't appreciate my involvement—as evidenced by a knockout punch to the face. My heart may have been in the right place (I wanted to bring Jesus' love into a nasty situation), but my mind certainly wasn't. First of all, I didn't even know their language. Second, I was a suburban do-gooder who represented the untrustworthy majority culture. No wonder they resented my presence. At the very least I could have called on more qualified people—like the police, for instance—who understood the neighborhood and handled these tense situations every day.

Of course this passage in Matthew troubles us (those of us in the affluent West, that is) because we don't expect persecution and danger. We expect people to like us because we're followers of Jesus, and then we resent them when they don't play fair and nice. We're surprised and enraged when Jesus' words actually come true and some people behave like wolves. We're shocked when people malign us and hurt us just because we're trying to be nice, Jesuslike people.

But based on this passage, we should really be asking why we don't we get into more trouble for following Jesus. As I see it, these are the most likely answers to that question:

• We are an exception, a historical and cultural anomaly. Historically, many Christians have been treated like sheep among wolves. In fact, many of Christ's followers are being persecuted around the world at this very moment. I have escaped this reality not because I'm better, smarter, nicer or more Christlike. Rather, I have escaped wolflike treatment because I'm an exception to Jesus' words in Matthew 10.

• My faith is defective so the wolves don't even notice me. I'm not very sheeplike. I am not poor in spirit, gentle, hungry for righteousness or merciful, and I don't hang out with lepers and tax collectors. In short, my faith is so weak, diluted and unsalty that no one notices me. I'm like an ineffective soccer player: the other teams never have to "mark" me because I'm not a threat to score a goal. I just take up space on the field.

Jesus never advocated dredging up persecution so we could feel more spiritual. Throughout Matthew we're told to listen to Jesus and build our lives on his words (see Mt 7:24-27). But based on this lifestyle, it's highly likely that eventually a wolf or two will threaten or perhaps even maul us. Eventually, as we keep acting like sheep-snakes, we will meet some disappointing and even mean and nasty wolves. We're not in Pandora; we live on planet earth, just like Jesus did.

But in the midst of all of this trouble, we don't have to slump into the "wolfy blues." As a matter of fact, although it's scary and painful, we don't have to stop acting like sheep. On four occasions in this passage Jesus commands us to not worry or be afraid (see Mt 10:19, 26, 28, 31). We've heard this command from Jesus before (see Mt 6:25). But apparently he has to keep repeating it because we are afraid. He even tells us not to be afraid when a wolf threatens to "kill the body" (Mt 10:28).

Once again, we don't develop this fearless posture by pumping up massive amounts of heroic, hyperspiritual faith. Our courage comes from something more ordinary and simple: trusting in our Father's care and protection, even in the midst of trouble.

On four occasions Jesus mentions either "my Father" (Mt 10:32-33) or "your Father" (Mt 10:20, 29). The word "God" does not even appear in this passage. Every time Jesus wants to tell us something about God he uses "Father." First of all, this name implies power, authority and majesty. God the Father can "destroy both soul and body in hell" (Mt 10:28).

And yet, for Jesus, "Father" also suggests personal love and care. This Father wants to help us. According to Jesus' words in Matthew 10:19-20, when people are mean and nasty to us, when they arrest us and haul us into court, our Father will give us the words to say "at that time." Based on the Father's daily, moment-by-moment care we can endure to the end (Mt 10:23). The Greek word for "endure" meant to "stay under," to "hang in there," to "keep going." Notice Jesus did not say that we have to be flashy, fanatical, successful or popular. Under my Father's care, he said, just hang in there.

Finally, the "Father" language for God means that we have value: "So don't be afraid; you are worth more than many sparrows" (Mt 10:31). In the immense complexity of the cosmos, filled with strange and awe-inspiring things—tidal waves, cheetahs, supernovas, peacocks, volcanoes and cobras—sparrows are tiny and plain, but God the Father values them. So, certainly, he will value you. You may feel puny and powerless and plain, but to God the Father you are not. In the eyes of the Father you matter.

These verses provide the basis for our commitment to the sanctity of human life. For all the political turmoil around that phrase, it still serves as our Jesus-ordained call to respect and honor every human being, to defend everyone's basic human rights. Unfortunately, we live in a culture that doesn't take this for granted anymore. According to philosopher Peter Singer, the sanctity of human life is an idea we need to jettison. Singer predicts that by 2040 "only a rump of hardcore, know-nothing religious fundamentalists will defend the view that every human being, from conception to death, is sacrosanct."[83]

Although we should reject the "hardcore fundamentalist" label, we should also gladly join the "rump" that honors the sanctity of every human being across the spectrum of life situations and cultures. Followers of Jesus constantly honor and protect the most vulnerable, inefficient or "useless" members of society: the unborn and aged, the defective and disabled, the marginalized and shoved-aside, the politically hated or despised, the victims of violence and genocide. We protect the vulnerable even if, like Jesus, people resent us, mock or try to tear us apart.

Jesus never promised us a Pandora-like easy life. In this passage from

Matthew 10 he promises that a life of faithfulness to Christ might be hard. At one point in *The Lord of the Rings*, Gandalf soberly tells Frodo, "All we have to decide is what to do with the time that is given to us. And already, Frodo, our time is beginning to look black. The Enemy is fast becoming strong. . . . We will be hard put to it. We should be very hard put to it, even if it were not for this deadly chance."[84] Ah, yes, adventures with Jesus often imply that "we will be hard put to it."

In this regard, I'm often challenged by our brothers and sisters around the globe who keep following Jesus and loving others in the midst of persecution. For instance, the Christians in Pakistan comprise only 2.5 percent of the total population, making them "'a fly on the wall' that can sometimes be treated as a nuisance" in this officially Islamic nation. On a recent visit to the U.S., the Reverend Munawar K. Rumalshah, a Christian leader in the northern city of Peshawar, reported on the government-endorsed "social and economic suffocation of the Christian community" in Pakistan. Pakistan's anti-blasphemy laws pose a constant threat for Christians. In addition, Rumalshah said that in his province alone, local mobs have publically urinated on Bibles and closed four churches.

However, despite this overt hatred toward Christians, Rumalshah isn't bitter. Instead, he works for better relationships with his Muslim neighbors and views the persecution as an opportunity to display Christ's love to others, even militant Muslims like al-Qaeda members. Rumalshah summarized how his church responds to persecution: "We clean the wounds of those who hate us and those who would kill us."[85]

Frankly, I'm dumbfounded by this kind of love and faithfulness. I would want to strike back or hide from my persecutors. But Jesus clearly told us to love those who hate us (see Mt 5:43-48). In this passage Jesus promises the presence of the triune God, even in the midst of profound persecution. In the very last words of this Gospel, Jesus proclaims, "And surely I am with you always, to the very end of the age" (Mt 28:20). Apparently, this small, hounded, harassed band of Christians in Pakistan believes these promises. They follow Jesus on the little way of discipleship. They are "hard put to it," but they also live in the presence of God, the Father who keeps loving, guiding and valuing his children.

THE VARYING RESPONSE TO JESUS

Matthew 11:1–16:12

Some people seem to attract trouble wherever they go. Jesus certainly fit that description—except he wasn't looking for it; the controversy just came with his identity and mission. Of course whenever someone walks around town making claims like Jesus did—Son of Man, Son of David, lord of the Sabbath, interpreter of the law, bearer of the kingdom—he's bound to provoke some strong reactions. In this section, the responses to Jesus start rolling in, and they're not always warm and fuzzy.

The first response comes from Jesus' baptizer, his cousin John the Baptist. At one point John's faith stood like a rock, but by Matthew 11 it's starting to crumble. Jesus treats John with remarkable gentleness and patience. But then Jesus starts denouncing his own stomping grounds, blasting them for their spiritual complacency. In chapter 12 Matthew begins to highlight the growing tension between Jesus and the Pharisees. It's a perfect chance for Jesus to back down and clarify these outlandish claims about his identify and mission. Instead, he ratchets them up. In chapter 12 alone Jesus claims that he's greater than the temple, Lord of the Sabbath, the suffering servant from Isaiah, greater than Jonah and greater than Solomon. It's little wonder that by the end of this section the Pharisees are trying to undermine his credibility.

As Matthew 13 opens, the crowds appear to love Jesus, although it's clear they don't grasp the big idea behind what it means to follow him. The disciples are starting to get it—well, sort of. Even when they receive special tutoring sessions with Jesus, they continue to regress in their journey of discipleship. But that doesn't stop Jesus from repeatedly exploring his main theme: the kingdom of heaven. He doesn't seem to care about mixing metaphors; he just wants something to sink in. In the end, he wants the disciples in particular to know the value of the kingdom, with its combination of over-the-top joy and go-for-broke urgency.

Along the path of disciple growth, there are a few glimmers of hopeful responses. For a brief moment, Peter dares to follow Jesus all the way out of the boat onto the raging waves. Of course he crashes and burns, but at least he got out of the boat. Then at the end of Matthew 15, a frantic pagan woman comes from out of nowhere and pleads with Jesus. For a brief moment, she also gets who Jesus is. It's not exactly an overwhelming reception for Jesus, but it's a start. And apparently, Jesus can produce some amazing results with tiny things like mustard seeds and lumps of dough.

JOHN THE BAPTIST MEETS
THE PROSPERITY GOSPEL
Matthew 11:1-15; 13:53-58; 14:1-11

According to a *New York Times* article, the prosperity gospel is thriving even in an economic downturn. In a recent gathering in Fort Worth, Texas, Kenneth and Gloria Copeland told their adoring fans that "God knows where the money is, and he knows how to get the money to you." They regaled a crowd of nine thousand followers with personal stories of God's provision: private airplanes and boats, vacations in Hawaii and cruises in Alaska, a motorcycle sent by an anonymous supporter, a ring of emeralds and diamonds.

Sitting up in section 316, a long-distance trucker named Stephen Biellier explained his loyalty to the Copelands and their ministry. Twenty-three years ago Copeland "rescued" Biellier from financial ruin. After buying his first truck at 22 percent interest, Biellier was floundering in debt. During this crisis he and his wife started donating to the Copelands and trusting for a miracle—and they got it. The Bielliers didn't go under like many of their peers. "We would have failed if Copeland hadn't been praying for us every day," Mrs. Biellier said. And although they're still over a hundred thousand dollars in debt, they believe that soon they will have an "overcoming year." According to one of Copeland's fellow preachers, "While everybody else is having a famine, his covenant people will be having the best of times."[1]

The prosperity gospel attracts believers because it promises unhindered financial success. Following Jesus will make you rich. God will give you good stuff—diamonds, designer handbags, fun vacations, nice cars, a fat bank account and business growth.

A more sophisticated version of the prosperity gospel appears among mainstream evangelicals: Jesus may not make you rich, but he will make your life better. If you give your heart to Jesus, problems will get resolved. Tensions and doubt will melt away. Dark nights of the soul, seasons of spiritual anguish and grief will last only until the next upbeat, bright and happy worship service. Wounded marriages will heal. Deep, aching longings—for sex or romance or a child or a good job—will be fulfilled. Faithful service to God will be rewarded on our timetable. Tragedies will be averted and happy endings will greet us around every corner. In short, we are almost always going up with Jesus. Jesus makes our lives complete.

Unfortunately, as optimistic and as American as this gospel appears, it is not Matthew's gospel, nor does it characterize the life of John the Baptist. In fact, John's story of following Jesus takes a sharp descent into violence and incompleteness. At one time adoring crowds trekked into the desert to hear John preach (Mt 3:1-12). They respected his teaching, which bore much fruit as mobs of followers plunged into the baptismal waters of repentance and new belief. John achieved spiritual success. Even the exciting new rabbi Jesus of Nazareth (could he be the Messiah?) came to John and everyone heard those heavenly words: "This is my Son, whom I love; with him I am well pleased" (Mt 3:17). John seemed to be on a spiritual journey marked by perpetual upward mobility.

But it didn't last. The "overcoming years" crashed. After this stunning success, we suddenly discover in Matthew 11 that John is in prison. He's no longer roaming about blasting religious leaders; instead, trapped in his dank prison cell ("arrested" and "bound" according to Mt 14:3), his mind swirls with doubt. So he sends an urgent question to Jesus: "Are you the one who is to come, or should we expect someone else?" (Mt 11:3).

It certainly wasn't John's best and brightest spiritual moment, but then his journey takes another turn for the worse. In Matthew 14, after John speaks out against Herod's marriage to Herodias, Herod's brother's wife, Herodias and her daughter concoct a plot to behead him (Mt 14:6-11). Surely God will intervene. Surely he won't allow this injustice. Surely Jesus will arrive in time to spring John from prison or raise him from the dead. But Matthew soberly reports, "His head was brought in on a platter and given to the girl, who carried it to her mother. John's disciples came and took his body and buried it. Then they went and told Jesus" (Mt 14:11-12).

Head cut off. John dies. Herodias laughs. Jesus grieves. The end.

It's not the story we wanted. It ends with the thud of incompleteness. On one hand, we should see the story for what it is: a journey of descent into suffering, sorrow and loss. Jesus boldly announced the coming of the kingdom (Mt 4:17), then he demonstrated the kingdom's power and presence by healing, delivering, preaching, saving and forgiving. But even in the midst of this overwhelming kingdom presence there remains a sense of incompleteness. In this life, all wounds do not get healed; all aches do not get fulfilled; all wrongs do not become right; all stories do not end in triumph.

In the words of the apostle Paul, we're suspended between the coming of the kingdom and the fulfillment of the kingdom. Jesus will eventually heal every wound and make every journey a redemption story, but it hasn't happened yet. So we groan as we await the fullness of the kingdom (Rom 8:18-25).

According to Catholic theologian Ronald Rolheiser, in this life all of our symphonies remain unfinished. Like John the Baptist we live lives marked by incompleteness. "We are built for the infinite," contends Rolheiser, "Grand Canyons without a bottom. Because of that we will, this side of eternity, always be lonely, restless, incomplete . . . living in the torment of the insufficiency of everything attainable." If we don't face the reality of our aching incompleteness, Rolheiser warns, "this incompleteness becomes a gnawing restlessness, a bitter center that robs us of all delight." Then we will start demanding that "someone or something—a marriage partner, a sexual partner, an ideal family, having children, an achievement, a vocational goal, a job—take all of our loneliness away."[2]

John's story stands as a corrective to every form of prosperity gospel, the expectation and demand that God give us a complete life now. In fact, John's journey of descent provides a living illustration of some of Jesus' key teachings in Matthew. In chapter 5 Jesus blesses those who are "persecuted because of righteousness" (Mt 5:10). He assumes that children of the Father, whose lives are marked by love and forgiveness, will still have real enemies (Mt 5:44). In chapter 10 Jesus promises that his followers will be dragged before governors and kings (Mt 10:18). At the end of chapter 13, even Jesus experiences temporary failure in his mission (see Mt 13:53-58).

In the middle of John's story Jesus proclaims, "From the days of John the Baptist until now, the kingdom of heaven has been subjected to violence, and violent people have been raiding it" (Mt 11:12). It's a strange and difficult verse, and translators have struggled with the Greek word *biazetai*. Should it be translated as "exercises violence" or as "suffers violence"? In other words, is violence done to the kingdom or by the kingdom? Given the context of this story—Jesus' sermon on persecution and John's experience in prison—Jesus seems to be saying that the kingdom must enter the world in the midst of violence and opposition.[3] Goodness will triumph, but it will be costly. Jesus, the vulnerable refugee king, will lead his children into victory, but they will suffer violence in the process. In fact, Jesus' own cross is the entry point for God the Father's ultimate triumph.

Frankly, after even a quick reading of Matthew's Gospel, it's hard to imagine how anyone could concoct a prosperity gospel of completeness,

success and pure ascent in this life. Jesus never guaranteed uninter-
rupted health, wealth or even safety. And yet I routinely meet followers
of Jesus who experience hardship, persecution or the ache of incompleteness and assume God has betrayed them. "I didn't sign up for this," we
sometimes tell God and others. Oh, but we did. If Jesus, our Lord and
Master, would experience betrayal and suffering, how can we expect
complete fulfillment in this life?

It's important to remember that incompleteness doesn't ultimately
spell tragedy. For one thing, in the midst of John's doubts and even his
beheading, he remains faithful to Jesus. Jesus tells his disciples, "The
one who stands firm to the end will be saved" (Mt 10:22). He then says
to John, "Blessed is anyone who does not stumble on account of me" (Mt
11:6). Once again, Jesus offers mercy to little-faiths. He does not say,
"Shame on you, John, for not displaying mighty, overcoming faith." Instead, he makes faith accessible to ordinary, flawed people like John and
like us.

Second, Jesus knows something John doesn't yet: the resurrection is
coming. When everything seems lost and dead, swallowed by sin and
cruelty, the disciples will hear the angels proclaim, "He is not here; he
has risen, just as he said" (Mt 28:6). All things will be reconciled and
transformed in Christ (Eph 1:10). From this point on in Matthew, Jesus
will start dropping hints about his death and resurrection. Through
veiled references such as the "sign of Jonah," he will proclaim that glory
unimaginable is on the way. All of our incomplete stories and unfinished
symphonies will one day find completeness in and through Christ.

My friends Bill and Janine are living in the hope of Jesus' resurrection. After faithfully serving on a church staff for ten years, they were
suddenly fired. Rumors circulated about inappropriate and even sinful
behavior. Without warning, without even a chance to address the issues,
they were asked to leave the church. In one day they lost their jobs and
their church family. Their world shattered.

When Bill talked to me he said, "It feels like a crucifixion. Does that
sound too dramatic?" I imagine that John the Baptist would have felt the
same way. "No," I said, "that doesn't sound too dramatic. But, Bill, with
Jesus if there's a crucifixion, there's always a resurrection. It won't be

easy. The scars may remain, and it might not happen in this life. You may ache until Jesus comes, but resurrection will come."

Bill was silent for a long time before he finally said, "I like that. I still don't like what happened. I'm angry and sad, but I can still start looking for Jesus' resurrection power."

Like Bill, like John the Baptist, our lives are marked by incompleteness. We won't always experience prosperity or upward ascent. We won't overcome everything right away; sometimes we'll yearn and hurt and wait, even for a lifetime. However, this shouldn't surprise us because it's the life Jesus promised.

But Jesus also promised resurrection. In Tolkien's *Lord of the Rings*, Samwise asks the right question: "Will all of our sad stories become untrue?" In other words, will God finish all of our incomplete stories? Will Jesus the Son bring goodness out of evil, truth out of doubt, light out of darkness? Will God heal the wounds of abuse, addictions, unfulfilled desires, grief, divorce and trauma? Will our stories end well? The answer is an emphatic *yes*, an empty-tombed, death-defeating, Christ-is-risen yes! John the Baptist knows it now. Our aching, longing, yearning lives will know it too. In this life we'll get glimpses and foretastes of our full glory with Christ. One day, when his kingdom comes in fullness, we'll experience full transformation.

WOE TO THOSE ON THE INSIDE TRACK
Matthew 11:20-30

While I was trying to visit a hospitalized church member, I wandered into the wrong room and started chatting with a middle-aged man with only a few teeth, a tangled beard and wild hair. I didn't see any signs of visitors—no cards or flowers—so he was thrilled to tell me the tale of his injury and surgery. Apparently he had fallen off a ladder and shattered most of the tiny bones in his left foot. It required hours of delicate reconstructive surgery. When I asked him if the accident happened at home or at work he launched into the following story:

> Nah, I lost my job, and then I lost my home too. I used to have a home, but I lost it. Then I used to live in the woods until some

vigilantes came with torches and burned our little tent village to the ground. Then I used to get around on my bicycle until a rich lady in her huge SUV ran into me, dragging me and my bike for over a hundred feet. She never apologized or offered to buy a new bike. Ya know, while we waited for the police to come, she chatted on her cell phone about her recent shopping trip.

So when I get out of here I guess I'll try to find a place to stay for awhile, but then I'll move back into the woods. Ya know, it really isn't that bad. As long as I have my health and a roof or at least a tent over my head I'm happy as a clam. I do have a lot of faith in the Lord, ya know. He always comes through for me. I never have to worry about where my next meal will come from. I just have to keep it simple, living one day at a time, trusting God and staying content. Ya know, the Lord will provide for me.

The utter sincerity and simplicity of his story unnerved me. The week before I had preached an eloquent sermon on trusting in God and living with contentment. But for the most part, my life is riddled with anxiety and a churning discontentment. After someone burnt this man's tent to the ground and crushed his bicycle, he owned nothing. I have three cars, a master's degree in theology, a nice home, a retirement account, a great insurance plan and a wonderful network of support. I have studied the Gospels in their original language; I've sat through hundreds of deep Bible studies; I've read thousands of good Christian books. But my new friend seemed to have more contentment and less anxiety than I did. In a few major areas of life he seemed to have more faith than me. For some reason he gets it as I struggle to get it.

I don't mention this story to glorify homelessness or to defend the automatic "innocence" of every homeless man. However, it does reflect the message Jesus was trying to send at the end of Matthew 11: be careful about your approach to the spiritual life. Sometimes the people with the most knowledge and privilege and power, the people who should be on the inside track, are only wading in the shallow end of the faith pool. In their arrogance and smugness, they squander their spiritual resources and opportunities. On the other hand, sometimes the unlikely people, those who seem to be on the outside track, the little children and the poor in spirit and the meek and the hungry, are swimming in the deep end.

When we read the Gospels, it can seem like Jesus has two personalities: the ticked-off Jesus and the sweet Jesus. Up to this point in Matthew we've seen mostly the sweet Jesus. He touches lepers and heals the sick. He eats with sinners and restores the brokenhearted. He is the Lord of compassion and grace. But in Matthew 11:20 Jesus doesn't act gentle; he threatens with words of woe. "Woe to you, Chorazin! Woe to you, Bethsaida! . . . And you, Capernaum, will you be lifted to the heavens? No, you will go down to Hades." Now he becomes the Lord of judgment and threats.

Of course, this wasn't an angry, immature tirade against random towns and people. First of all, Jesus' woes, like Yahweh's in the Old Testament, were always laced with love. They were like the "threats" of a heartsick lover who discovers his wife's unfaithfulness (see Jer 2:1-13). Second, Jesus' threats were directed at specific places: his hometowns. These were Jesus' stomping grounds, the places where he bought bread and worshiped and attended funerals and weddings. These were also the places where Jesus performed most of his miracles. In other words, these towns had the inside track. They had spiritual privilege and power, but they wasted it. So Jesus blasted them for their smug arrogance and elitism. Tyre and Sidon were wicked pagan cities that would receive more leniency than Jesus' hometowns.

Jesus' judgments and threats always start with the most spiritually advanced people, the people who know much but practice little. He doesn't warn those who need conversion; he warns those who think they already have it. These people have Jesus' presence and power right in front of them but it doesn't change them. They don't repent. They don't obey him or even take him seriously.

This passage serves as a sober warning to privileged believers in all times and from all places. "Woe to you," Jesus says, "when you know so much about me but practice so little of that knowledge." These woes are designed to break our hearts wide open with humility and longing. I think Jesus wants to say something like, "When it comes to spiritual growth opportunities, you have the inside track. You have more Bibles and spiritual growth resources than all the people in Cairo and Mexico City and Shanghai and Lagos, but has the Word really changed your hearts? Has it made you recognize who I am? Has it moved you to repent of your self-righteousness?"

These threatening questions aren't meant to make us hang our heads with shame. Instead, in the midst of Jesus' demolition of our pride, our attempts to justify ourselves with our knowledge and privilege, he offers an invitation: "Come to me, all you who are weary and burdened, and I will give you rest" (Mt 11:28). This invitation isn't for those stuck in their smug sense of privilege; it's for a group of unlikely, underprivileged infants. All of this causes Jesus to burst into prayer and thanksgiving: "I praise you, Father, Lord of heaven and earth, because you have hidden these things from the wise and learned, and revealed them to little children" (Mt 11:25).

In Jesus' day achieving a deep relationship with God was like becoming a brain surgeon: it was reserved for an elite cadre of specialists. Knowledge of God required intellectual brilliance. Stupid people, slow people, sinful people and even ordinary people were on the outside track. Jesus sliced through this approach to the spiritual life, offering his invitation instead to the spiritually poor, those who know they're sick and need a doctor. In a bold and surprising twist, Jesus drives us all to the urgency and simplicity of intimacy with the Father.

This does not mean smart people cannot follow Jesus. Throughout the centuries Jesus has sought and found many brilliant disciples. Jesus isn't opposed to scholarship; actually, the church needs more scientists, economists, doctors, mathematicians and physicists. Jesus' point is that our brilliance will not make us more acceptable to God the Father. In his prayer, the "wise and learned" are the best of human achievers: the intellectuals who trust in their brilliance, the beautiful who trust in their beauty, the rich who trust in their wealth, the religiously devoted who trust in their morality, the mighty who trust in their power. Jesus is addressing our temptation to trust in our resources without humbly following Jesus' little way of faith and obedience.

Jesus warns us that it's the little children who really get it. And God the Father arranged the spiritual life this way because it delighted him—

"this is what you were pleased to do" (Mt 11:26). This arrangement was and is and always will be alive in God's trinitarian life: "All things have been committed to me by my Father. No one knows the Son except the Father, and no one knows the Father except the Son and those to whom the Son chooses to reveal him" (Mt 11:27). Jesus is making an amazing claim about himself here: everything of God has been revealed through and in him. God has a name—"Father"—and Jesus reveals the Father to us. We can't get anything from God unless it's a gift from Jesus. That's why infants and the poor in spirit get it: they live with a spiritual posture of receptivity and openness.

This truth has profound implications for how we approach God the Father. Jesus' big, open-hearted invitation—"Come to me, all you who are weary and burdened, and I will give you rest" (Mt 11:28)—hinges on one basic qualification: we come as spiritual infants. In the past perhaps we've tried to join the wise and the learned, the spiritually advanced, the morally upright (at least more upright than most), the healthy who don't need a doctor, but it's made us weary and heavy-laden. It's too much pressure; the yoke is too heavy and it's ground us into the dirt. We're tired of playing the super-nice-efficient-productive-perfect-mature-moral Christian man or woman. Attempting to justify ourselves and create our own salvation programs hasn't worked.

Then we wake up and hear Jesus' stirring words. First are words of warning: "Woe to you when you think you have the inside track but really know nothing. Woe to you when you think you're going up when you're really going down. Woe to you when you think you're an adult when you're really a child." Then after he demolishes our pride and self-salvation projects, he whispers, "Blessings to you when you're an infant. Blessings to you when my words cause you to repent, grow, love, trust and obey. My blessings to you if you receive everything as a gift from my Father's hands." We realize that Jesus makes one and only one offer: "Come just as you are; come as the flawed, sinful, spiritual struggler that you truly are. That's my final offer."

This approach to the spiritual life also has a profound impact on how we relate to others. It changes how we create and sustain Christian community. In these simple, unassuming, comforting verses Jesus has once and for all abolished any basis for elitism. In the kingdom, human standards of wealth, intelligence, power, privilege, Christian activity, race, gender and ethnicity are unreliable guides to who's on the inside track. The underprivileged, the poor, the uneducated and the infants—these people are our heroes and mothers and fathers of the faith. Christians around the world and immigrant groups in America are already showing the alleged inside-trackers how to dive into the deep end of faith. After all, basing our lives on a Savior who dies on a cross for our sins certainly levels the playing field. Inside and outside tracks no longer exist. There is no longer any room for boasting, only gratitude, wonder and—best of all—childlike rest.

FIGHTING FOR REDEMPTION
Matthew 12:1-21

Last year a friend asked me to pray before the annual banquet for the varsity football team at a major university. Before the prayer we were invited to stand and sing the National Anthem. So we all dutifully stood—about five hundred young men, family members, girlfriends, cheerleaders, coaches, administrators, boosters and fans. As we started to sing, I was shocked that everyone around me continued casually chatting.

I was deeply offended by the lack of respect and dignity. I thought about all the American veterans I've known, men and women who risked their lives and shed their blood so we could stand in this beautiful banquet hall and celebrate the success of a college football team. I thought about veterans who watched their buddies get blown to bits or shot in the head. I thought about soldiers who descended into posttraumatic stress or addiction.

It doesn't mean that I like war or think every war is justified just because America fights it. Certainly not. But that night I started to realize that loving God and loving life also compels us to love particular finite, imperfect things like people and nations and churches and communities. By its nature love implies a willingness to fight for people, for their health and wholeness, even to the point of giving our lives.

So, naturally, when God with us appears in the person of Jesus, we expect him to fight for certain things. And indeed he fights with passion.

In Matthew 12 we find Jesus willing to fight for something that's close to his heart: the transformation of his broken creation, especially the transformation of human beings.

That's the essence of Jesus' conflict over the Sabbath in this passage. Some Christians read this story and conclude that Jesus was abolishing the Sabbath. But that misses the point entirely. The Sabbath was God's gift to human beings, a beautiful gift that symbolized his desire to restore his tired and tattered creation. Once a week, God set aside a twenty-four-hour period for us to focus on one thing: enjoying God's good creation and receiving his gift of restoration. Unfortunately, in Jesus' day this gift had degenerated into a spiritual burden. So Jesus fought not just for the integrity of the Sabbath but for the transformation of the human beings for whom the Sabbath was made.[4]

All the trouble started when Jesus walked through some cornfields and allowed his disciples to eat from it. It's a simple process: get hungry, eat food, hunger problem solved—even on the Sabbath. But for the Pharisees it wasn't that simple. Many years earlier, as they fretted how to define "work," they had systematized thirty-nine categories of forbidden activity. Those thirty-nine activities were further broken down and defined. For instance, the rules said you couldn't carry a burden on the Sabbath, but what is a "burden"? Well, a burden is anything that weighs more than two dried figs. God's beautiful gift had become a quagmire of rules and restrictions.[5]

Jesus fights for the Sabbath because he's fighting to transform us. He refers to Scripture three times ("Haven't you read . . . ?") as he builds a case for the Sabbath and those who need constant Sabbath restoration:

- King David (Mt 12:3-4, based on 1 Sam 21:1-6). Living in the wilderness, chased by King Saul, on the brink of starvation, David and his men found the bread in the house of God in Shiloh and ate it. God allowed David to live because God cares about hungry people. He would rather have people live than starve, even on the Sabbath.

- Israel's priests (Mt 12:5). Temple worship always required that someone had to work so others could worship. No one could work on the Sabbath except for the priests. In their case, worship offered to God took precedence over Sabbath regulations. Thus, Jesus pointed them back to their own Scripture and said, "Haven't you read in the Law that the priests on Sabbath duty in the temple desecrate the Sabbath and yet are innocent?"

- The prophets (Mt 12:7). For the second time in the Gospel of Matthew (see also Mt 9:11) Jesus reaches into the heart of the Bible and quotes Hosea 6:6, in which God says, "I desire mercy, not sacrifice." Sacrifice includes all the fine things we do for God, all the things that cause us to say, "Look, God (and everyone else), see how serious I am about my faith. I give, I pray, I serve, I work, I study." But God would rather have attitudes and actions of mercy than impressive sacrifices. Mercy leads to action, but for Jesus mercy always flows from a radically transformed heart.

So in three quick jabs Jesus tells us who he is: he's greater than David; he's greater than the temple; he is the king with the big, merciful heart for his people. But he is also the king who has complete authority over the Sabbath (see Mt 12:8).[6]

In the next little scene Jesus demonstrates his willingness to fight for our transformation (Mt 12:9-14). Matthew begins the story like this: "Going up from that place, he went into their synagogue." Jesus shows up at the synagogue on the Sabbath and sees a man whose hand is "withered," which in that culture probably meant he couldn't work. The religious leaders have trailed Jesus like a pack of reporters hounds a pesky politician, waiting to expose him. "Is it lawful to heal on the Sabbath?" they ask. Everyone knows the "correct" answer: no. Technically, according to the Pharisees' complicated Sabbath rule book, Jesus could only offer healing if the man's life was in danger. Since the man's hand has been withered from birth, Jesus should wait and restore it tomorrow, on a non-Sabbath day. By waiting just one day, Jesus could have avoided the conflict and still healed the man. But Jesus couldn't drop the issue because he's too passionate about our transformation. In verse 13 Matthew reports, "So [the man] stretched it out and it was completely restored, just as sound as the other."

This little incident conveys the essence of the gospel: Jesus doesn't just identify our brokenness; he offers to transform us and all of his broken creation. Whenever or wherever a human life is distorted, broken, bent, confused or perverted, Jesus sees it and moves toward that need with compassion and power. Jesus has an irrepressible drive toward wholeness; he wants to see broken lives transformed into their God-ordained beauty and glory.

Notice what Jesus does not do: he doesn't pick a fight just for the sake of fighting—even if he's on the right side of an issue. Once again Matthew reaches back into Isaiah's picture of the suffering servant, the nonviolent fighter who brings transformation and who will bring "justice through to victory" (Mt 12:20).[7] Jesus' passionate quest for victory involves his own style of justice: "He will not quarrel or cry out; no one will hear his voice in the streets. A bruised reed he will not break, and a smoldering wick he will not snuff out" (Mt 12:19-20).

Unfortunately, as the history of the church shows so clearly, we want to be on Jesus' side but sometimes we lack Jesus' character. We long for the days when the lion will lay down with the lamb, when the hungry will go to bed without stomach pains, when the tear-drenched eyes will be wiped clean, when the enslaved will find freedom, when those who are far from the Father's love will come to Jesus; we want Jesus' program and we have Jesus' passion, but we lack Jesus' process for transforming lives.

In our haste and our pride, we often forsake Jesus' merciful style. Lashing out with angry words, we blame and judge. We get so consumed in our causes—our right and good and just causes—that we do violence to our own bodies and souls and then do violence to others. We may adopt Jesus' agenda but we retain our impatient, pushy, intimidating, overbearing personalities. We're busy doing things for Jesus, but we've lost touch with his presence and style. In contrast, Jesus protected vulnerable people, the bruised reeds and smoldering wicks.

A few years ago my friend James, an American serviceman stationed in Iraq, helped me understand Jesus' passion for restoration in the midst of a violent world. James could clearly articulate his brokenness—a distant relationship with his immigrant father, an addiction to online pornography, fears about his future, insecurities that ruptured his connection to community—but he had no language for Christ's power to change his life. Finally, it dawned on him that Jesus was fighting for him, fighting for his transformation, that at the cross Jesus even laid down his life as a ransom so James and other human beings could find freedom. With a new grasp on the gospel, James sent me the following e-mail:

> Lately, redemption has been on my mind. I was reading the best car magazine ever, *Sport Compact Car.* I have an obsession with rice rockets, little import cars with insanely large turbos and modified engines. Flipping through my magazines I am filled with hope and dreams of my own project car. But my favorite stories are ones where the cars have been salvaged from rust and ruin and made into show-winning tuners. It reminds me of Jesus. Where others see a rusty, broken vehicle, a true tuner will see hidden potential. And when Jesus sees me, does he see a broken-down man or something more? Redemption is like working on a project car. Jesus is the mechanic and I am the busted junker that needs repairing.

Ah, yes, Jesus sees in us the beautiful, powerful, glorious "project car." James captured the essence of Jesus' work of transformation: in Christ we are slowly changed into our true selves, our better-than-ourself selves. Jesus not only salvages us from the junkyard; Jesus not only sees our hidden potential; Jesus not only repairs us and fixes us up; best of all, Jesus transforms us into a show-winning tuner.

According to Jesus, that's a battle worth fighting for.

THE ONE UNFORGIVABLE SIN
Matthew 12:22-50

My friend Martha, a completely unchurched, anxiety-riddled, intimacy-deprived young woman, constantly tells me how much she admires Jesus. After reading the Gospels, she's convinced that Jesus is the best friend she could ever have. So although she mistrusts every form of institutional religion, she keeps telling me that she'd love to spend her afternoons "chillin' with Jesus."

Up to this point in Matthew's Gospel, we'd have to agree that "chillin' with Jesus" would make any sinner feel safe and secure. But then, as soon as we have Jesus analyzed and systematized, he says or does something unpredictable. In this section of Matthew 12, Jesus mentions a sin that cannot and will not be forgiven. The idea of Jesus refusing to forgive anyone for anything doesn't seem to square with Matthew's encounter with Jesus in chapter 9. Is it possible to wander beyond the reach of God's grace? Is it really possible that the infinitely tolerant, gentle Jesus would lock the door and leave some poor sinner out in the cold?

The topic of "the unforgivable sin" is raised after Jesus encounters a blind and mute demoniac. Now, I've often heard people cope with their troubles by saying something like, "Yeah, it's bad, but I know someone who's worse off than me." Well, here's one person who can't say that. He's at the bottom of the barrel. In baseball lingo, he's stepped up to the plate with three strikes against him. Demon-possessed, blind and mute—life has already pronounced him "out."

Fortunately, Jesus specializes in hard-to-fix cases. It takes only half a verse to record the healing; the rest of the chapter recounts the controversy spurred by it. (We have to wonder why beautiful acts of restoration produce such controversy.) One group of eyewitnesses respond with awe and wonder (Mt 12:23). But the Pharisees respond with cynicism, muttering, "It is only by Beelzebul, the prince of demons, that this fellow drives out demons" (Mt 12:24). "Beelzebul" was a slang term meaning "lord of the flies," "lord of garbage" or "lord of the dung pile." The Pharisees are saying that Jesus is in cahoots with Satan. Concluding that he is the Messiah acting in the Spirit's power is intolerable to them, so they have to prove he's a crackpot, a wacko, a few peas shy of a casserole.

In the next few verses Jesus reveals his intellectual brilliance. As the one who lived the life we should have lived, Jesus possessed the perfect, fully human mind-heart integration. He felt deeply, but these verses show how deeply he also thought. He acts like a logician, making two concise and tidy arguments:

1. "Every kingdom divided against itself will be ruined, and every city or household divided against itself will not stand" (Mt 12:25). In other words, Satan wouldn't fight against himself. No one is that stupid. If I've just finished remodeling my house, I won't take a sledgehammer and destroy the rooms I've just remodeled.

2. "And if I drive out demons by Beelzebul, by whom do your people drive them out?" (Mt 12:27). Here Jesus is pointing out a logical inconsistency. The Pharisees' argument means that they are also in cahoots with Satan.

It's a brilliant, two-point, knockout counter-argument.

Then Jesus offers one more twist to his line of thought: "Or again, how can anyone enter a strong man's house and carry off his possessions unless he first ties up the strong man?" (Mt 12:29). Jesus compares Satan to a powerful individual who has his possessions safe and secure. In order to rob the strong man, a burglar would have to first tie him up. The demoniac in verse 22 was one of the strong man's possessions; by healing him, Jesus entered Satan's house and repossessed the man. It's a daring metaphor: Jesus is the burglar who barges into Satan's house and ties him up, ransacking the place and letting Satan's possessions go free.

And then Jesus draws a line in the sand: "Whoever is not with me is against me, and whoever does not gather with me scatters" (Mt 12:30). That's why it's so dangerous to insinuate that Jesus is in league with Satan. Nothing could be further from the truth: Jesus is at war with Beelzebul; Jesus is trying to enter, burglarize, ransack Satan's house and haul away his most precious possession—human souls. Satan wants to cripple, enslave and destroy human beings. Jesus wants to set them free through his power. There is no neutrality in these two agendas.

At this point Jesus introduces the concept of the unforgiveable sin. The first thing to notice is his sweeping statement in the first half of Matthew 12:31: "Every kind of sin and slander can be forgiven." What an astounding statement. There are no exceptions, no hard cases, no loopholes. David committed adultery and God forgave him. Peter denied Jesus three times—when Jesus needed him the most—and God forgave him. Paul was a blasphemer and a murderer and God forgave him.

Yet some people assume they're beyond God's forgiveness. They've done something so awful, disgusting, perverted or ugly that God couldn't possibly forgive it—at least not all of it. In this verse, Jesus takes his place as our Redeemer and says that every blasphemy will be forgiven. Reflecting back on Jesus' work on the cross, the writer of the book of Hebrews would declare, "He is able to save completely those who come to God through him, because he always lives to intercede for them" (Heb 7:25).

That's the amazing good news. But then Jesus continues with the potential bad news: "But blasphemy against the Spirit will not be forgiven" (Mt 12:31). Jesus has just said that every sin and blasphemy can be forgiven. Jesus has just healed the worst-case-scenario guy. However, the Pharisees basically say, "Nah, it can't be. He can't be the God of restoration. There has to be some other explanation. Hey, how about this one: Jesus gets his power from the lord of filth and dung?" The Pharisees' problem isn't their bad behavior; it's their hardened hearts. They'll do anything to discredit and therefore avoid Jesus as Savior, forgiver and transformer.

That's the point behind Jesus' indictment in Matthew 12:39-42. When the Pharisees and teachers of the law ask Jesus for a sign, he shoots back, "A wicked and adulterous generation asks for a sign!" (Mt 12:39). Then he offers them one—the resurrection: "For as Jonah was three days and three nights in the belly of a huge fish, so the Son of Man will be three days and three nights in the heart of the earth" (Mt 12:40). In these resurrection stories, both Jonah and Jesus are dead and gone. Both of them are beyond hope. Both of them are at a complete dead end.[8] But God raises both of them after three days and three nights of despair. The people of Nineveh, those wicked and cruel outsiders, listened to Jonah—unlike the prideful spiritual leaders of Jesus' day.

What have these leaders done? They've cut themselves off from forgiveness. It's not that they *can't* be forgiven; it's that they *won't* be forgiven. Imagine that you have survived a plane crash but your leg has become horribly infected and you are raging with fever. The only doctor from on board the plane offers to help you. You just have to admit that you can't heal yourself. You must become a patient, submitting to the doctor's care and taking his advice and the medication he offers. If you trust the doctor, you will be healed. If you refuse to admit your need, if you refuse to trust the doctor, if you spit back the medicine, you will not get healthy. Eventually you will die. At some point you have to make a choice: go to the doctor or avoid the doctor. If you keep saying things like, "That worthless doctor—he's just a quack and money-monger. I don't need him. I'll cure myself," you will not heal.

In the same way the Christian story says some very explicit things about our spiritual condition:

• We are in trouble. We have all survived a horrible spiritual plane crash and now we're spiritually sick, although we constantly deny, minimize or blame others for our sickness.

• Help is available. That's why Jesus compared himself to a doctor (see Mt 9:9-11). That's why Jesus says, "Every kind of sin and slander can be forgiven." He can do that.

• Help is not automatic. We can turn down the offer. We take our injuries and wounds and infections and hide them. We can keep saying, "I got it; I can do it myself." That's what Jesus calls the "blasphemy against the Spirit."[9]

• We have to come the whole way for healing. We can't say, "I need a little help with my anger or my lust or my fears. I need a better love life and a better job." No, healing doesn't start until we surrender the care of our lives to Jesus.

• Healing and forgiveness lead to a life of obedience, which Jesus defines as doing "the will of my Father in heaven" (Mt 12:50). For Jesus, there's a direct link between grace and forgiveness and listening and obeying. Trusting Jesus leads to spiritual transformation and thus obedience to Jesus. According to Jesus, this is what makes us his brothers and sisters.

I often talk to people who understand all of this but then say, "It's too easy. You mean I just believe in Jesus and he restores me to health?" I respond, "No, it's the hardest thing you'll ever do in your life. It will take a miracle to pull it off. You can't even surrender by yourself. Due to our hardened, Pharisee-like hearts, we have to tell God, 'Help me! I keep running away from you. I'm so stubborn and selfish that I can't even take the first step.' Then you fall into God's hands of mercy, and he catches you. 'Come to me and rest,' Jesus said, so you come and rest in him alone."

The only people who won't receive healing and the restoration are those who are just too damned stubborn or self-righteous to admit they need it. The word *damned* means just that: in the end they bear their own curse and they wind up in hell; they refuse forgiveness; they refuse the radical healing treatment because they're convinced either they don't need it or Jesus can't supply it.

That's what Jesus is trying to tell the Pharisees—and all of us who share the Pharisees' spiritual self-sufficiency and pride: "I am the Lord of impossible cases. I can restore the brokenhearted and the burnt out, the molested and the bitter, the traumatized, the divorced and the HIV-positive, the herpes-ridden, the obese and the barren, the sick and the dying, the lonely and the shoved-aside, the porn addicts and the adulterers, the children who live on the street and the parents whose children are addicted or gay. I can even save and transform hardhearted, self-righteous, morally upright Pharisees. Come to me—all of you—and I will give you rest. Learn life from me. Surrender your life to me. Fall into my hands of mercy. Let me heal your brokenness and give you a new life."

THE UNLIKELY JOURNEY OF THE LITTLE SEED
Matthew 13:1-20

In her book *Distracted*, Maggie Johnson contends that our contemporary problem with paying attention runs deep. We can access 50 million websites, 2.5 million books in print, new technologies and scientific gains, but "we are nurturing a culture of social diffusion, intellectual fragmentation, and sensory detachment. In this new world, something is amiss. And that something is attention."[10]

According to the Bible and the teachings of Jesus, our struggle to pay attention isn't new. When it comes to following Christ, we've always had a short or nonexistent attention span. That's why in this parable and interpretation Jesus gives us one key word: *listen*. In Matthew 12 the Pharisees utterly failed to listen to Jesus. Now in chapter 13 Jesus tells us to "listen" or "hear" on fourteen occasions. He starts a parable with "Listen" (Mt 13:3 NRSV) and concludes it with "Let anyone with ears listen!" (Mt 13:9 NRSV).

In the end, for Jesus there are only two kinds of people: listeners and nonlisteners, those who hear and those who don't. Those who quit or never get started on the spiritual journey with Christ—the Pharisees from Matthew 12:31, for instance—fail because they won't listen. Those who endure and bear good fruit do so because they listen and keep listening. Ultimately, our life with Jesus begins and continues through our receptivity to his words.

This parable in the first part of Matthew 13 isn't just a little morality tale. Jesus' essential message isn't, "Okay, gang, try real hard to listen to me. If you don't listen well, you'll get in trouble. If you do listen well, you'll get bonus points. In the end, it all depends on your effort to succeed at listening."

But for years that was how I read the parable—on a simplistic, moralistic level. And at first blush it seems easy to grasp. There are four types of soil, three of them bad and one good. Don't be the bad soils; do be the good soil. But before any of this, the parable focuses on the work of Jesus, the sower: "A farmer went out to sow his seed" (Mt 13:3). We had nothing to do with this prior work. That's how Jesus operates: he flings good seed all over the place. He's the prodigal God with us, generously throwing the seed with wild abandon.[11]

The parable also reminds us of God's power to sustain our frail and fragile faith. In Jesus' story only one of four seeds becomes fruitful. Twenty-five percent of the seeds never get started, twenty-five percent wilt under pressure, and twenty-five percent get choked to death. Faced with hard soil, the burning sun and deadly weeds, most of the seeds cannot survive because the odds are stacked against them. But then, look, a miracle: a small part of the scattered seed not only makes it but flourishes and produces a huge harvest. In Jesus' day a good crop would yield a tenfold harvest, so a yield of thirty-, sixty- or a hundredfold was miraculous.

In one sense, Jesus' entire life and ministry was like the little seed: small, exposed, vulnerable—and yet brimming with fruitfulness. At the beginning of Matthew 13, Jesus has to borrow a boat so people can hear him speak. His followers consist of ordinary and even undesirable people. He has nowhere to lay his head and his hometown disowns him. In spite of failures, threats, dangers and opposition, Jesus is not discouraged and he trusts his Father. By God's grace and power, there will be a harvest and it will be grand.[12]

In another sense, we are like the little seed, too. Our faith is a weak and fragile thing. How can we possibly get the process started and how can we ever keep it alive? Left to ourselves, our hearts will receive God's Word like hard, shallow, cluttered soil receives a life-bearing seed. We will see but not perceive; we will hear but not listen or understand. We don't just need a boost to get up and running on the spiritual path; we need a miracle—one to get started and one to keep our faith growing. And that's what this parable promises: a miracle. Jesus says, "By flinging the seed so generously, my prodigal Father will start the process. By making that seed grow into a healthy plant, my Father will continue the process. By sustaining you through dangers and snares, my Father will bring you to an incredible harvest."

The parable begins and ends with grace. Jesus says it this way: "The knowledge of the secrets of the kingdom of heaven has been given to you" (Mt 13:11). The original word for "secrets" in this verse signified something that people couldn't figure out for themselves.[13] In contrast to the Pharisees' approach to spiritual life, in our journey we can only say, "We didn't deserve it; we didn't earn it; God shared his secrets with us based on total grace." In other words, our faith is a sheer gift. That's why Jesus could turn to the disciples and say, "Blessed are your eyes because they see, and your ears because they hear" (Mt 13:16). It is our responsibility to respond to this generous sower, but we didn't start the process and we don't sustain it by ourselves. Jesus chose to reveal the truth to us (see also Mt 11:27; 16:17). Jesus disparages the spiritual pride that takes God's grace for granted and then looks with smugness and contempt on others.

But there's another side to the good news of God's undeserved blessing on unlikely people. As N. T. Wright observes, "The really troubling thing about this passage . . . is that [the coming of Jesus' kingdom] is bringing both judgment and mercy. And part of the judgment is that people will look and look and not see what God is doing."[14] In the words of Jesus (who was quoting Isaiah), "Though seeing, they do not see; though hearing, they do not hear or understand. . . . You will be ever hearing but never understanding; you will be ever seeing but never perceiving" (Mt 13:13-14). In other words, people will stare at the beautiful colors of God's kingdom, but their colorblindness will prevent them from seeing the pattern of grace; they just see a confusing mash of random colors and shapes.[15]

This work of grace and judgment doesn't lead to fatalism—that is, we either have faith or we don't and there's nothing we can do about it. Jesus expects us to respond for or against this intrusive offer of grace. As we respond and continue to respond to his grace, we start to reflect the character of our heavenly Father. According to Jesus, the offer of grace is free but it's never cheap or easy. It requires our wholehearted involvement and participation. In this parable, Jesus summarizes the process of discipleship with one word: listen. He didn't mean listen and then do whatever you want. He meant listen and then obey what I say; listen and then build your lives on my words; listen like your whole life depends on it.

For genuine disciples of Jesus, listening is life. The two times God the Father speaks in this Gospel, he basically says the same thing: "This is my son, whom I love; listen to him" (Mt 3:17; 17:5). In a sense, following Jesus consists of one lifelong, growing act of listening to our Lord. We listen as an act of obedience. We listen because our heavenly Father is good (Mt 7:9-11). We listen because of Jesus' authority (Mt 7:28-29). We listen to words of warning and comfort (Mt 11). We listen even when it propels us into a difficult journey of loss, danger and suffering (Mt 10). We listen in good times and bad. We listen to Jesus more than the surrounding distractions and temptations. But more than anything, we listen because Jesus has captured our hearts with his beauty and glory.

The storyteller J. R. R. Tolkien understood the way true treasure will capture our hearts with wonder, attention and love. Tolkien called it "staggerment." For instance, in *The Hobbit* when Bilbo finds the incredible treasure trove lying under Smaug the dragon, "There [were] no words left to express [Bilbo's] staggerment. . . . His heart was filled and pierced with enchantment and with the desire of dwarves; and he gazed motionless, almost forgetting the frightful guardian, at the gold beyond price and count."[16] No one had to tell Bilbo to act or feel pierced by enchantment or desire. He didn't need ten lessons on paying attention to the piles of gold. In the presence of such beauty and glory, he couldn't help gazing at the treasure, and he couldn't help almost forgetting about the ugly, dangerous dragon.

In the same way, Jesus has already told us (Mt 6:21) and will tell us again shortly (Mt 13:44-46) that when he captures our heart with true treasure, we will pay attention to him. In the presence of Jesus' glory and authority, our hearts fill with staggerment for him, the truest and deepest treasure our hearts could ever find. Captivated by his goodness and power, our hearts will be pierced with enchantment and desire. But unlike Bilbo, we're not enchanted with a shallow earthly treasure; we're gazing on the real treasure.

In this sense, we don't listen because Jesus—or some other religious authority—is screaming in our ears. We listen because we're in love with the one who loves us. We listen because God the Father loves God the Son and continually calls him his beloved. We listen because this God of love invites us into his love, calling us his beloved daughters and sons. We listen because he chose to bless us beyond our wildest dreams, even when our hearts were calloused and our ears were dull. His love broke through and reached us. And, finally, we listen because God's love compels us to love others; God's offer of mercy compels us to share his mercy (Mt 5:7, 43-48). As we listen to Jesus we also long for others to hear his voice and respond to his love.[17]

WOULD YOU HURRY UP AND DO SOMETHING!
Matthew 13:24-43, 47-50

My friend Rich runs a ministry through our church that reaches out to the family members of inmates. In our culture, convicts rank near or at the bottom of the social respect scale, and by association, their family members don't rank much higher. So Rich and his team of volunteers visit the inmates' family members not just at Christmas (which might be expected) but throughout the year. As far as ministries go, it isn't exactly big, flashy and exciting. No major newspapers or websites have highlighted the wonderful work among inmates and their families. Civic leaders and even most of our church leaders don't know it exists. It's a small, hidden, quiet way to share the love of Christ with some forgotten people.

In one sense, this under-the-radar ministry epitomizes Jesus' mission in the Gospel of Matthew. In Jesus' day (much like in our own), people based their spirituality on a simple expectation: if God was working to deliver his people from bondage, if the real Messiah had actually come to earth, things better start shaping up in a hurry. The evil, oppressive people needed to get vacuumed up like clods of cat hair; the good, faithful, righteous people needed freedom and revenge. If any Messiah wanted to earn our respect, he had to hurry up and make some drastic changes.

Instead they got Jesus, the God with us who acts like my friend Rich and his team of volunteers—building a community of diverse people, then binding up the broken people on the margins of society rather than wooing the powerful and the righteous. At this point in Matthew Jesus doesn't have a lot to show for his efforts—a minor following, maybe, but even that consists of a mixed bag of faithful and faithless. Back in chapter 4, amid much excitement and confidence, Jesus announced the coming reign of God, but now, a few years later, his ministry bears the marks of imperfection.

Not one to ignore serious questions and issues, Jesus begins to address the people's assumptions about the coming kingdom. In a series of three parables and images, Jesus in essence admits that his results often appear slow and tedious. But despite this, he still declares his hope-filled vision for the kingdom of heaven.

In the first story, generally called the parable of "the wheat and the tares," Jesus compares the kingdom of heaven to a "man who sowed good seed in his field" (Mt 13:24). Jesus and God the Father are like the farmer in this story—generously flinging good seed and making good things grow (see Mt 5:45; 7:9-11).

Unfortunately, there's something sinister at work as well: "But while everyone was sleeping, his enemies came and sowed weeds among the wheat, and went away" (Mt 13:25). According to Jesus, there is a dark, twisted figure in the universe who constantly opposes God's good work (in verse 39 he will tell us this figure is the devil). From the beginning of his ministry, Jesus has made it clear that he came to battle and defeat these forces of anti-creation and person-destruction (see Mt 4:1-11, 24; 8:16-17, 33).[18]

To make matters worse, this enemy sows not on the periphery but right in the middle of God's field. Confused by the presence of the tares, the servants ask, "Sir, didn't you sow good seed in your field? Where then did the weeds come from? . . . Do you want us to go and pull them up?" (Mt 13:27-28). As good, conscientious and impatient servants they want to help their master with his problem. They want to help him hurry up and straighten out the mess in the field.

In case we miss the point of the parable, Jesus himself offers the interpretive key. He's the farmer who flings the good seed. "The field is the world, and the good seed stands for the people of the kingdom. The weeds are the people of the evil one" (Mt 13:37-39). The wheat and the tares, the sons of the kingdom and the sons of the evil one, will remain intertwined until the end of time. The real believers and the phony believers are bound together, sharing the same field as well as the same sunshine, soil and nutrients.

Surprisingly, in this parable Jesus acknowledges the temporary imperfection of his good work. After all, those nasty tares aren't just outside the church; they're inside Jesus' field mixing in with the wheat. Throughout history this has been a tough truth to accept. For many people it's still shocking—or at least disappointing—to find such dreadful people and behaviors not just in the world but right in the church. It's tempting to ask—or even demand—that Jesus hurry up and fix this messy situation. And if he can't fix it on our timetable, we'll help him move faster by identifying (with our self-made infallible tare detectors) and uprooting all those evil tares.

Instead, Jesus instructs us to remain patient and keep our nose out of his business. Notice that when his judgment day finally arrives, the promised separation between wheat and tares will be complete and thorough: "The Son of Man will send out his angels, and they will weed out of his kingdom everything that causes sin and all who do evil" (Mt 13:41).[19] A few verses later in another parable Jesus will repeat this theme of coming separation (Mt 13:49).

But in the meantime, as we live in this imperfect community called the church, Jesus asks us to practice patience with others. As John Calvin said regarding this parable, "So long as the church is on pilgrimage in this world, the good and the sincere will be mixed in with the bad and hypocrites. So the children of God must arm themselves with patience and maintain an unbroken constancy of faith among all the offenses which can trouble them."[20]

The next two parables also focus on the slow, inefficient progress of Jesus' kingdom. In many ways Jesus' entire kingdom movement, including his followers, looked as insignificant, vulnerable and imperfect as a tiny brown mustard seed. Everybody knew that mustard seeds produced unruly, scraggly bushes. Everybody also knew that leaven, an ugly little lump that was kneaded into the bread dough, couldn't penetrate a half-bushel of dough.[21] In Jewish tradition, yeast was usually a symbol of an unwanted or even evil influence. How could God possibly take symbols of imperfection and brokenness and turn them into something good and glorious? It would take a miracle.

But that's what happens in the kingdom of heaven. The tiny mustard seed will become a world-sheltering tree; the ugly blob of leaven will produce a world-nourishing loaf of bread—just as a barbaric cross will produce hope for the world. Once again, Jesus speaks about the kingdom of heaven, and those who have embraced that kingdom, with an irrepressible and exuberant hope.

That's the point of the birds coming to the mighty tree. Jesus' first hearers would have known this picture. According to a promise in Ezekiel 17:23, God would plant a small shoot that would "produce branches and bear fruit and become a splendid cedar. Birds of every kind will nest in it; they will find shelter in the shade of its branches." The lowly mustard shrub pales in comparison with the splendid cedar tree. The contrast emphasizes that it's God's power at work, even in the midst of our littleness and imperfection. The birds of the air represent people from every nation, racial and ethnic group coming to know and rest in the living God (see Ezek 31:6). Jesus gives his little band of disciples the confidence that in and through their union with him they can become the healing force that acts like a sheltering tree and a nourishing loaf for the whole world.

But this world-sheltering tree and this world-nourishing loaf don't come crashing into the world with pomp and power and pageantry.

We don't become a mighty and splendid cedar tree that cries out, "Look at me. You can't resist me." Instead, God's powerful love hides and grows within the daily acts of mercy offered by ordinary and even powerless people.

While I worked at the group home for developmentally disabled adults, I witnessed many incidents of the power of Jesus' kingdom alive and growing in the midst of ordinary people. One Saturday afternoon "Robert" wanted to attend Mass because his buddy and fellow resident "Billy" was serving as a Eucharistic minister. One of the most moving worship experiences I've ever had involved walking to the front of the church to receive Communion from Billy. As he handed me the bread and joyfully proclaimed, "The body of Christ," it struck me that this was mustard seed stuff. God's powerful grace reaches down and changes my life through ordinary places and simple people. Jesus' kingdom is alive and well, growing in the midst of wheat and tares, thriving in places of insignificance. In ways that we can never control or make happen, the little mustard seed will grow into a beautiful tree; the little lump of dough will grow into a nourishing loaf. Jesus will make it happen.

JOY HAPPENS
Matthew 13:44-46

The Christian writer and activist Wendell Berry was once asked, "Do you often find it hard to be joyful?" Berry responded:

> Sure. But it's an obligation. What a horrible thing if you give up on joy just because of facts. . . . You never know when joy is going to hit. People have been joyful in the bitterest of circumstances. . . . Some of the best parties I've ever been to have taken place when we were [working in a barn] in miserable conditions, and all of a sudden everybody gets a big joke going, and everybody is laughing and happy right in the midst of what the modern world would consider the most miserable conditions: sweaty, hot, no air conditioning, no rest, everybody tired and smelling bad. So [joy] happens.[22]

In the two potent little parables found in Matthew 13:44-46 Jesus wants us to know that joy happens. We've already heard plenty about hardship (see Mt 10), and as Jesus heads toward the cross we'll hear more about suffering. But Jesus also wants us to know about joy. He doesn't mean that joy happens through random, quirky, roll-of-the-dice events that take God by surprise. For Jesus joy is always connected to treasure, or that which makes life worthwhile and fulfilling. When you know and possess real treasure, real joy will also happen—even when, as Berry says, we're in miserable conditions. In Matthew 6:21 Jesus said, "For where your treasure is, there your heart will be also." In other words, your heart follows your treasure. In these two parables Jesus adds a twist and basically says, "Your joy will also follow the real treasure."

All of the parables in Matthew 13 focus on a specific treasure that, according to Jesus, makes life worthwhile: the kingdom of heaven. In the parable found in Matthew 13:44-46 Jesus says, "The kingdom of heaven is like treasure hidden in a field. When a man found it, he hid it again, and then in his joy went and sold all he had and bought that field." In case we didn't get it the first time, Jesus tells us the same thing with a different image: "Again, the kingdom of heaven is like a merchant looking for fine pearls. When he found one of great value, he went away and sold everything he had and bought it" (Mt 13:45-46).

With these two earthy metaphors Jesus is telling us two things: first, the kingdom of heaven—which is intimately connected with the in-breaking and ongoing presence of Jesus, God with us—is the one great treasure. Second, it's worth any price to get and keep this treasure. In other words, the joy of having the treasure swells and grows larger than the reality of sacrifice and suffering.

This must have struck a chord with the disciples, because they gave up a lot to follow Jesus. They were starting to understand that the world would often respond to Jesus' presence with opposition and even hostility and hatred. They were also starting to understand that following Jesus leads to a process of deep personal transformation—facing our sin, repenting, learning new patterns of life and joining a new community with flawed people. In short, in the words of Gandalf to Bilbo in *The Hobbit*, following Jesus means that "there are no safe paths" anymore.[23]

At some point the disciples probably started to ask, "What are we doing? Is this really worth it?" Based on his authority and true identity, Jesus wants to assure them, "Yes, I tell you, it's worth it. I'm offering you real treasure that leads to real joy. No human suffering can tarnish the value of this treasure."

There is nothing better than spending your life for the kingdom of heaven, Jesus says. Ultimately, it is the only treasure that brings true joy. It's worth living for and it's worth dying for, and God wants to give it to us. Two times in this story Jesus tells us that his heavenly Father wants us to have treasure and joy. Many people assume that God is anti-joy, anti-fun, anti-delight, anti-passion, anti-creation, anti-treasure—just plain anti-everything in the universe. In contrast, over and over again, Jesus shows us that he is utterly and passionately pro-human. In these two tiny stories Jesus gives us two different pictures of God's good heart: God wants to give us life's ultimate treasure, the treasure that gives us real joy.

In neither of these stories do we actually find the treasure; instead it finds us. In both of the stories the finders seem surprised by their treasures. One guy sticks his shovel in the ground, trying to plow up some dirt and—voilà!—his blade hits the treasure chest. Just as he's done thousands of times before, a pearl diver strips down and plunges into the blue-green water, going down and down until he catches a glint of an ordinary oyster shell, grabs it and begins his frantic ascent, his lungs nearly bursting for air. He breaks through the surface, gasping and heaving as he struggles into the boat. He cracks open the oyster and—will you look at that!—it's an enormous, perfect pearl.

Some people think this grace is too easy. Actually, receiving God's grace is difficult because we must admit that we can't get the treasure and find real joy by ourselves. We are utterly powerless to obtain the ultimate treasure. God has it and it's ours for the taking, but we have to ask for it. But we do have a role to play in receiving the treasure. First, we have to believe that Jesus has it; he is the owner of the one treasure and the one pearl of great price. Second, Jesus also called for a passionate and personal response. We can say yes or no; we can accept it or reject it; but we can't straddle the fence forever. The kingdom is here, Jesus keeps saying—now decide.

Making this decision, trusting Jesus and then following through, will not make our lives easier. Just as the disciples experienced hardship in Matthew's Gospel, our lives may get harder. Friends may reject us. Our sins and bad habits, once safely tucked into our subconscious, may start to rise to our awareness, and now we actually have to deal with them. We may meet lots of unholy people—many of them right in the church.

None of this should surprise us or unnerve us. Throughout this Gospel Jesus promises us tears, persecutions and even our own cross. But he also promises us the joy of finding the one and only treasure. And treasure finding—or, more accurately, treasure *receiving*—makes everything bearable.

Perhaps this is the greatest lesson we in the affluent West can learn from our brothers and sisters living in the global South. On many occasions I've been moved and challenged by their grasp of the two truths in these parables: Jesus and his kingdom are the real treasure, and the presence of Jesus makes joy happen. For instance, after the Haiti earthquake, I listened to an NPR story from Florida about four American doctors who went to Port au Prince to bind up the wounded. When they arrived they quickly immersed themselves in meeting the needs of 125 patients with horrific conditions: crushed pelvises, open and oozing sores, broken femurs and cracked skulls. It was a scene of overwhelming loss, pain and trauma.

But suddenly, the doctors reported, something happened that changed everything. A Haitian man with a guitar entered the makeshift trauma ward, sat down in the corner of the large tent and started playing a simple, quiet song. Without any coaxing or commanding, one by one the patients started singing with the lone guitarist. The voices became louder and more joyful. Then the patients with broken bones and open sores spontaneously stood up and started dancing. Some of the healthier patients helped those who were unable to stand.

At first the doctors couldn't understand the words, although they heard the name "Jesus." Finally, a translator gave them the words to the simple chorus: "Jesus, thank you for loving us." The American doctors were utterly stunned. They didn't have a category to explain this sudden outpouring of joy and praise.

These parables provide the explanation: our suffering brothers and sisters are clinging to the real treasure of Jesus and his kingdom. They know that nothing in life can tarnish that treasure. Of course I'm not implying that we don't need to help suffering people with their raw, physical needs.[24] That would be counter to what Jesus does and says elsewhere in this Gospel (see Mt 25:31-46). However, we in the affluent West need these dear brothers and sisters to be our leaders and mentors. They should be teaching us about clinging to the real treasure. They can tell us that when the treasure captures our hearts, once Jesus fills us with the "staggerment" of his value, beauty and authority, we will cling to Jesus. And once that happens, joy will happen too. No one can take that joy away from us.

BEAUTIFUL FLOPS
Matthew 14:22-33

R. O. Blechman is often hailed as the most famous illustrator in the world. His drawings, cartoons and animations have appeared in movies, television shows, magazines and graphic novels. But for every successful work, Blechman claims that most people would be shocked by his string of failures. In a series of letters to a young protégé, Blechman shared his ongoing struggle with artistic flops:

> Preliminary drawings and sketches often are discouraging things, pale shadows of one's bold intentions. Seemingly nonsense, they're especially dispiriting for beginners. . . . "Is that what I did," the novice might ask, "and I consider myself an artist?!" . . . Speaking for myself (but also for other illustrators, I'm sure), my trash basket is full of false starts and failed drawings. . . . There should be a Museum of Failed Art. It would exhibit all the terrible art that would have ended up in trash bins and garbage cans, lost and unknown to the public life.[25]

Surprisingly, the Bible contains a Museum of Failed Discipleship. Over and over again the Gospels record the stories of the disciples' spiritual failures. If anyone were trying to write a fictional, legendary account of the life of Jesus, this would not be the way to do it. We tend to cover up our heroes' faults, and we're even more likely to gloss over our own colossal flops. Instead, the Gospels allow us to see the disciples' failures—and most of those stories came from the disciples themselves. This not only adds to the historical reliability of the Gospel accounts; it also encourages us in our own faltering attempts to follow Jesus.

Matthew 14 records a failure by Peter, the leader of Jesus' band of followers. Since it's only found in Matthew and is an unusual account (walking on water wasn't an everyday occurrence), some Bible scholars doubt the historicity of this story. But it's highly unlikely that the early church, founded on Peter's leadership, would have concocted it—it's too unimpressive, too great a flop. In Blechman's words, this story would serve as Exhibit A in the Museum of Failed Faith. It would forever remind Peter, "Is that what I did, and I consider myself a disciple?!"

On the other hand, we have to credit Peter with getting out of the boat. Obviously he's been paying attention to Jesus' lessons. In Matthew 9 and 10 Jesus handed the disciples his authority to heal. So Peter probably imagines that if he can heal, why can't he also walk on water? So when Jesus gives that one-word command, "Come" (or, literally, "start coming"), Peter takes a few cautious steps toward him.

In fact, in the midst of the storm, all the disciples hear Jesus' clear and reassuring words: "Take courage. It is I. Don't be afraid." These words appear in almost exactly the middle of this story: there are about ninety words before them and about ninety words after. They aren't just a friendly greeting, either. They are the same majestic, awe-inspiring words spoken by Yahweh to Moses back in Exodus. They carry the same authority as God's words to the people when they were returning from exile:

> Do not fear, for I have redeemed you;
>   I have summoned you by name; you are mine.
> When you pass through the waters,
>   I will be with you. . . .
> For I am the LORD your God,
>   the Holy One of Israel, your Savior. (Is 43:1-3)[26]

When Peter hears Jesus' words, he believes—sort of. Perhaps he is trying to take Jesus' lesson on listening to heart (see Mt 13:1-23). So he listens and pays attention to Jesus—for a few seconds. As long as he stays focused on Jesus all is well; as soon as he starts looking around and listening to the waves and wind, he crashes.

As our mentor and leader, Peter has a valuable lesson to teach about discipleship: we will fail. Our failures may sound like a belly flop or a cannonball—or just like slipping overboard—but we will fail. But Jesus' response to Peter shows us another lesson about discipleship: our failures don't have to define us.

In the end, this story focuses on Jesus, not Peter. Jesus is the Lord of our storms and the master of our failures. He doesn't maneuver our lives around the tempests, nor does he talk us out of our flops. Actually, Matthew 14:22 says that Jesus "made the disciples get into the boat." The little boat is heading right into the storm, and Peter is heading right into his colossal failure. And yet, Matthew records that in the midst of Peter's plunge, "Immediately Jesus reached out his hand and caught him" (Mt 14:31).

Throughout this Gospel we've seen Jesus' readiness to stand in solidarity with sinners and flops like us. Like Blechman, there will be days when we'll ask ourselves, "Is that what I did, and I consider myself a follower of Jesus? Did I really fail him that much? Was I that selfish? Did I ignore the cry of the poor and needy that often? Did I fail to encourage you when you needed it?"

Our failures could easily sink us in sin and shame; instead, we're offered a Savior. We don't have to hang our heads in shame and regret. Instead of replaying the lowlights of our failures, we can replay the highlights of Christ's forgiveness.

Practically, this means that I don't have to allow the fear of failure to control my life. As someone has said, "Don't be afraid of fear. All of the best things in life are frightening."[27] Learning to walk was scary. Riding a bicycle for the first time was scary. Getting married was scary. Admitting I had addictive behaviors was scary. Sharing my dreams and fears with a friend was scary. It's scary to come out of the womb and it's scary to die. It's all scary because we might fail and the failure might crush us.

But in the midst of this failure aversion, in the heart of Matthew's Gospel, we find a story about Peter's failure, and it doesn't sink him. Jesus grabs him. Peter and all the disciples even learn some valuable lessons from Peter's failed attempt to walk on water. They learn that failure happens, that it isn't fatal and that Jesus can handle our failures. In the midst of failure they also learn another remarkable lesson: Jesus is worthy of worship. Actually, the entire story ends in a mini worship service.

Based on all the lessons Peter learned from failure, I wonder why I'm still afraid to fail. For a moment Peter listened to Jesus and lived without fear. As I write these sentences, I wonder what I'd try to do for Jesus' sake if I was a little more foolish and a little less controlled by fear.

MISSING THE POINT OF IT ALL
Matthew 15:1-20

In her novel *The Poisonwood Bible*, author Barbara Kingsolver tells the story of a man named Nathan Price, a determined missionary in the Belgian Congo during the early 1960s. Nathan is a serious Christian whose actions seldom reflect the spirit of Jesus. Instead, he is a harsh, arrogant, uncompassionate man. When the new believers in his church hesitate to baptize their children in the river, Nathan refuses to listen to the reason for their objection: crocodiles. On another occasion, his church members tell him that a certain native term means "glorious" when pronounced one way and "poisonwood tree" when pronounced a different way. Nathan refuses to change, ending every sermon shouting "Jesus is poisonwood" instead of "Jesus is glorious." At the end of the story, Nathan's daughter records, "I am born of a man who believed he could tell nothing but the truth, while he set down for all time the Poisonwood Bible."[28]

Kingsolver provides followers of Jesus with a serious challenge: does our way of following Jesus truly change us? Are we becoming more like Jesus? Do we engage in spiritual activities and make wordy pronouncements without becoming poor in spirit, little children who desperately need Jesus' grace? In short, are we missing the point of it all?

In Matthew 15 this challenge comes directly from Jesus. The Pharisees, the "true believers" of Jesus' day, were missing the point of it all. Later in this Gospel, Jesus will give us the main points of our spiritual journey with him: love the Lord your God with all your heart, soul and mind, then love your neighbor as yourself (Mt 22:37-39). For the Pharisees, outward forms of religious activity and spiritual busyness did not lead to a transformed heart. Like Nathan Price, these religious leaders had a distorted spirituality that, although supposedly brimming with spiritual activities for God, did not really connect to God. They didn't embrace spiritual poverty; they didn't know their need for mercy; they didn't have a pure heart. Therefore their spiritual lives didn't lead to love for God and their neighbors.

Jesus uses two case studies to help his disciples get to the point of it all: ritual hand washing and the kosher food laws. For Jesus, neither practice was bad in itself. Many people read this passage and think, "Hand washing and food laws? How silly! What a bunch of nonsense!" Then they rush to dispose of every kind of ritual or formality in the spiritual life. Out with hand washing, dietary food laws, corporate prayers of confession, following the yearly church calendar, wearing robes, kneeling during worship and so on. But that also misses the point. Jesus' argument with the Pharisees was that they practiced these rituals without a transformed heart. For Jesus, transformation always starts from the inside out. In Matthew 6:21 he says it this way: "For where your treasure is, there your heart will be also." In other words, our treasure determines the direction of our heart; our heart sets the pattern for our behavior. The Pharisees wanted to obey God, or at least do religious things for God, without experiencing a transformed heart. As a result, they didn't grow in God love (obedience) or neighbor love (mercy).

The first case study involved the ritual of hand washing. In Matthew 15:2 the Pharisees complained that Jesus' disciples did not follow the proper ritualistic procedure (note that Jesus probably did wash his hands but didn't force his disciples to do it). In the Old Testament, God prescribed a rule for his people: if you touched something unclean, say a dead body, you had to remove the uncleanness by washing your hands. Because you could easily become unclean without knowing it, the Pharisees instituted a safeguard system of washing their hands before every meal. They extended this ritual by taking a full-body bath every morning and evening after entering public life.

Jesus objected to this colossal missing of the point. While the Pharisees scrupulously followed hand washing regulations, going even beyond what God required, they didn't practice neighborly love toward their own parents. Instead, in their heightened sense of duty, they advocated that children who made vows to God didn't have to fulfill their vows to their parents. For the Pharisees, a "God vow" completely absolved them from fulfilling a "neighbor vow." Jesus viewed this as a distortion of true spirituality. The tradition may have had roots in the Bible (see Num 30:2), but it led to a rupture with the fifth commandment, "Honor your father and mother"—and part of honoring parents meant providing for them. Jesus never severed love for God from love for others. In Dale Bruner's words, "If the God of the Ten Commandments orders the care of parents, then any teaching that even subtly seeks to divert this care, even in the name of God, is deviant, not divine."[29]

The second test case involved dietary food laws. In our culture of fast food and Hot Pockets, it's hard to imagine anyone squabbling about food laws. But the ancient Jewish believers viewed their diet as essential to their spiritual and communal health. Food laws mattered; they weren't a trivial issue. Leviticus 11 carefully delineated what foods did and did not go into the mouths of the Jewish people. What they ate and who they ate with defined the community. The message was clear: Don't mess with God's menu.

Thus, throughout history, despite differences in culture and cuisine, Jewish kitchens around the world have shared a commitment to *kashrut*, or keeping a kosher kitchen. Today, some Christians value these food laws for their health benefits, but the Bible says nothing about that. Instead, Leviticus 11:44-47 clearly states the main purpose for the food laws: "I am the LORD your God; consecrate yourselves and be holy, because I am holy. Do not make yourselves unclean by any creature that moves along the ground. I am the LORD, who brought you up out of Egypt to be your God. . . . You must distinguish between the unclean and the clean, between living creatures that may be eaten and those that may not be eaten." Based on these verses, a contemporary rabbi summarizes the purpose of keeping kosher as "a daily lifestyle that expresses Israel's chosenness. . . . No other nation, the world will say, insists on expressing one's connection to the divine through so mundane an act as eating." In his words, abolishing the dietary laws would abolish the distinction between Gentile and Jew.[30] Maintaining a kosher diet reminded a devout Jew every day that he or she was chosen and special before God.

Once again, Jesus attacked missing the point. Although the food laws reminded devout Jewish people that they were special and chosen, they also excluded everyone who couldn't practice them—Gentiles, unclean Jewish sinners and many ordinary Jews who didn't have the opportunity to keep the Pharisees' rigorous outward observance of the law. Based on the food laws, Jesus shouldn't have eaten with sinners. But if he couldn't eat with sinners, how could he reach them? How could he have been born into an unclean world? How could he die on the cross bearing the uncleanness of our sins? How could the kingdom spread to all nations?

For Jesus, the central issue is this: what transforms the human heart? What causes us to grow in love for God and neighbor? And on the other hand, what defiles the heart? What causes us to become impure in our love for God and our concern for neighbors? In Jesus' words, food goes into our mouth and passes into the sewer. The real point is what flows from our heart. The Pharisees kept the food laws, but according to Jesus' searing indictment, "These people honor me with their lips [or their religious activities, we might add], but their hearts are far from me" (Mt 15:8). Based on this, it's not surprising that Jesus' disciples came and told him, "Do you know that the Pharisees were offended when they heard this?" (Mt 15:12).

Once again, Jesus was not abolishing all external rites and rituals. He was merely stating the order: transformation starts with God's work deep in our heart, producing an overflow of trust in God's fatherly goodness, which results in obedience to God and concern for one's neighbor.

Some people argue that Jesus cares only about our heart, but that also misses the point of this passage. A transformed heart also implies changes in our outward behavior. In 15:19 Matthew intentionally organizes Jesus' words to point us back to the Ten Commandments. Notice how Jesus puts it: "For out of the heart come evil thoughts [the tenth commandment]—murder [the sixth commandment], adultery, sexual immorality [the seventh commandment], theft [the eighth commandment], false testimony, slander [the ninth commandment]."[31] Earlier Jesus said that a healthy tree will produce fruit (Mt 7:16-20). In other words, obedience and mercy always flow from a transformed heart.

Of course this isn't just a first-century problem for those obtuse Pharisees. We know they missed the point, but do we know how we miss the point? Like the dedicated missionary Nathan Price, we can fulfill our duties—engaging in Bible studies, serving on committees, sharing our faith, attending small groups and the best worship services in town—while our hearts remain unfazed and untransformed. Our approach to the spiritual life can be a lot like moving deck chairs around on the Titanic: we're still going down, but we sure look busy and impressive in the meantime.

The deceptive thing about certain outward behaviors—from ritual hand washings to attending Bible studies—is that I can use them to "master" my spiritual life. Like a modern-day Pharisee, if I spend thirty minutes a day in prayer and meditation (which I should), or avoid inappropriate Internet sites (which I should), then I believe I am controlling the transformation of my own heart.

Jesus offers a deeper vision for spiritual transformation. It begins with his gateway invitation: "Blessed are the poor in spirit" (Mt 5:3). We never get beyond this. We can never transform our own hearts. God does the work. And we keep receiving his mercy and surrendering to his power. As my friend Bob, a recovering addict, recently told me, "If I try to fight this thing on my own, if I try to gain control of it and master it, I'm doomed to failure. It masters me. I've tried to change my own heart—thousands of times—but now I have to continually acknowledge my powerlessness. Or, as I'm used to saying, I can't do it; God can; so I'll let him do it."

As we continue to surrender, trusting in and receiving his mercy, we will slowly grow in God love (obedience) and neighbor love (mercy). Living in poverty of spirit, we will become less like Nathan Price. Instead, with our mustard seed of little faith, with slow and faltering steps—sometimes walking on the water and sometimes sinking into the water—we will build our lives on the rock of Jesus' words, and we will reflect the Father's heart of mercy to others. That is real transformation.

GETTING IN THE HOUSE
Matthew 15:21-28

In one of his classic children's stories Dr. Seuss introduces the Sneetches: tall, yellow creatures who live on beaches. A select group of Sneetches with green stars on their bellies boast, "We're the best kind of Sneetch on the beaches." So "with their snoots in the air, they would sniff and they'd snort, 'We'll have nothing to do with the Plain-Belly sort!'"

Then one day a stranger, "a fix-it-up-chappie named Sylvester Mc-Monkey McBean," zips up in his strange "Star-On machine." For a mere three dollars his machine will put a green star on anyone who wants it. So the non-star Sneetches line up for the procedure. Now they're no longer excluded; they have the same bragging rights. This disturbs the former in-group, but for a mere ten dollars, McBean takes stars off with another machine. Now this former in-group and then not-so-in group become the new in-group. So McBean brings out a new Star-On machine. According to the narrator, this escalates "until neither the plain or star-bellies knew whether this one was that one or that one was this one or which one was what one . . . or what one was who."[32]

Obviously, this is a sophisticated tale about inclusion and exclusion—the joy of joining the insiders group and the agony of being left out in the cold. Throughout Matthew's very Jewish Gospel we've seen hints—the foreign women in the genealogy (Mt 1:2-17), the appearance of the Magi (Mt 2:1-12), John the Baptist's move away from the temple (Mt 3:1-4), the healing of the centurion's servant (Mt 8:5-13), the abolition of the dietary laws (Mt 15:1-20)—that Jesus' kingdom will reflect his diverse creation. But does Jesus really mean it? Can any outsider and foreigner get "in" with God the Father through Jesus, God the Son? If so, when and how will the shift be made, the doors be flung open?

In this passage Jesus invites an outsider in—although at first it doesn't seem to present a great way to launch a multiethnic ministry. A woman with a need, raw and vulnerable, approaches Jesus and starts shouting (the Greek word *krazo* is an intense, high-decibel word). The disciples and every other Jewish male would have labeled her a hysterical foreigner. Of course, from her perspective she's just a mom who needs help for her sick daughter. Surprisingly, Jesus appears to give her the star-bellied Sneetch treatment, replying, "We'll have nothing to do with the Plain-Belly sort of Gentile foreigners." However, she keeps pressing, and finally Jesus relents and grants her request.

What are the clues that help us interpret Jesus' response to this woman? First, Matthew tells us up front that she's from the land of Tyre and Sidon, two code words for "foreigner land." She's a Canaanite, not only from outside the nation of Israel but also part of a long history of conflict and ethnic hatred. The Canaanites weren't just victims; they were often perpetrators of exclusion, violence and cruelty against their neighbors.[33] On many levels, she's a classic outsider, a starless Sneetch in a world of green-bellied Sneetches. Clearly, she does not "belong" in this story.

In every human culture and group there's a powerful urge to bring some people in and keep others out. C. S. Lewis called it the lure of "the inner ring."[34] We include or exclude people because they don't meet our standards of excellence, intelligence, racial or ethnic purity, moral goodness, family background, religious practice and so on.

However, it's important to note that Jesus and his disciples respond in very different ways to her cry for help. Jesus displays deep compassion—he never wants to send her away—but he wrestles with the timing of the request. Thus, in Matthew 15:24 he says matter-of-factly, "I was sent only to the lost sheep of Israel." This isn't just a flippant remark; it cuts to the heart of his understanding of history and his mission.

The story of the Bible is very simple: God loves and desires to bless the whole world—every person and every ethnic group. However, the God of the Bible has a very specific plan. By blessing and then working through one family and one nation, God will spread his love to the whole earth. This is his strategy for worldwide blessing and salvation, and Jesus believes in it—after all, it's his plan too! He's already stated his commitment to this plan (see Mt 10:5-6). But so far in Matthew his forays into Gentile evangelism have been small and isolated. Will Jesus use this opportunity to open the doors to every nation and tribe and tongue? We shall see.

The disciples just want this woman to get lost. She's a pain in the neck. In Matthew 15:23 they say (notice their commanding tone), "Send her away, for she keeps crying out after us." In other words, "Get rid of her. She's loud and annoying. She's bothering us."

If we were in the disciples' place, no doubt it would be easy for us to judge this woman too. Slapping a label on others allows us to easily exclude them from our lives. After all, this woman is from Canaan—why doesn't she get her own people to help her? Apparently she's a single mother—where's her husband? Her daughter is demon-possessed—can't she control her own children and household? The disciples have her sized up, labeled, categorized, judged.

We're not much better. It's just as easy for us to label and judge other people: "You're black," "You're white," "Those Chinese young men," "He's drunk," "She's bipolar," "They're illegal immigrants." Recently I spent a Saturday evening at the Kansas City Rescue Mission with about a hundred men. Sadly, I lumped them all into one category: the homeless. But after an evening talking and playing table games, I discovered that their stories of brokenness and failure, along with their stories of redemption, were unique. There is no "homeless man" category: there's only Johnny, Seth, Jerome and Patrick.

Much to everyone's surprise, the foreign woman in Matthew 15 displays a gutsy, vibrant and theologically correct faith in Jesus in spite of her pagan background and questionable history. First, she addresses Jesus as Lord and Son of David (Mt 15:22), two deeply biblical messianic titles.[35] Second, she cries for "mercy." Somehow she knows that Jesus can't resist a genuine plea for mercy. Third, she doesn't pick up on Jesus' reluctance; she clings only to the fact that he never says "no." Unlike the disciples, Jesus doesn't want to get rid of her. So she hangs around unfazed, unable to leave or give up the fight for her daughter's sanity and freedom.

This remarkable woman shows us how to get "in" with God's mercy: through faith in Jesus' mercy. Everything seems stacked against her— her ethnicity, her gender, her problems, the disciples' animosity, even Jesus' slowness to act. But she hangs on to Jesus; she clings to his ability to display mercy and heal.

In a sense, this outsider receives salvation because she demonstrates faith that the Pharisees refuse to and the disciples don't always show. She models the Beatitudes, the values and traits of Jesus' kingdom society.

She's poor in spirit; she mourns; she hungers and thirsts for righteousness. We've seen this kind of faith before in an unclean leper and a foreign centurion. These people all receive remarkable things from Jesus, not because of their background, ethnicity or moral excellence. They receive because they cling (or chomp like a bulldog!) to Jesus' words of hope and healing.

Without abandoning his original strategy to bless the world through "the lost sheep of the house of Israel," Jesus opens the door to a new community of men and women, centered on Jesus, representing every tribe and nation and tongue. Up till now the Canaanites have been hopeless outsiders, a pack of wild dogs roaming the streets and scrounging for food. Now through Jesus this Canaanite woman is in the house, under the table, receiving scraps from the master's hand. That's shocking enough. Before you know it, she and every outsider, every oppressed and excluded ethnic group, will be sitting at the family table as daughters and sons, kings and queens, partaking of the Father's lavish feast.

Indeed, that's exactly what we see happen in Matthew. As soon as Jesus lets the Canaanite woman in the door, his kingdom community starts to become a beautiful mosaic of men and women from every ethnicity. Although we sometimes fail to reflect God's diverse creation, we live in an age that's rediscovering his plan for every ethnic group, family background, gender, economic status and education level. Soon after Jesus' ascension, the apostle Paul will declare, "There is no longer Greek and Jew, circumcised and uncircumcised, barbarian, Scythian, slave and free; but Christ is all and in all" (Col 3:11). The kingdom startles us with its beauty in Jesus. "Look who's in the house now!" we exclaim. "I'm in the house! That's a miracle. You're in the house. And look at them—they're in the house too. We're all here. We're all feasting from the table of Jesus, the king, because he invited us in. At last we belong to him and we're living life with him."

FAITH IS "IMPOSSIBLE"
Matthew 15:29–16:12

Francis Collins, the brilliant scientist and former director of the Human Genome Project, took a quirky path to faith in Jesus Christ. Early in life he concluded that he was an agnostic, a position he held through medical school, his Ph.D. studies and his initial scientific research. But certain factors—the complexity of the genome, the historicity of Christ, the authentic faith of believers—kept pointing him to faith in a personal God. Eventually he knew he had to make a decision about Christ, but he hesitated, as he said, "afraid of the consequences, and afflicted with doubts." Here's how he describes the event that finally led to his conversion:

> A full year had passed since I decided to believe in some sort of God, and now I was being called to account. On a beautiful fall day, as I was hiking in the Cascade Mountains during my first trip west of the Mississippi, the majesty and beauty of God's creation overwhelmed my resistance. As I rounded a corner and saw a beautiful and unexpected frozen waterfall, hundreds of feet high, I knew the search was over. The next morning, I knelt in the dewy grass as the sun rose and surrendered to Jesus Christ.[36]

This story demonstrates something I've noticed about faith. First, faith involves more than facts. For all of Collins' commitment to rational inquiry and the scientific method (tools he still respects and utilizes), his final push toward faith was a miraculous, unexpected, even mystical encounter with beauty. Second, faith is seldom predictable, simple or even easy. Jesus says as much in his parable of the sower (Mt 13:1-23). In that story, only one of four seeds survives the perilous journey along the path of faith. The journey is fraught with unplanned twists and turns, unforeseen dangers and even uncontrollable destruction. In many ways faith requires a miracle—or, perhaps, faith is a miracle.

Sometimes Christians assume and then communicate to others that faith should be easy. For instance, in heated debates with contemporary atheists such as Christopher Hitchens, Sam Harris and Richard Dawkins, I've rarely heard a follower of Jesus honestly say, "You guys are right about one point: faith isn't easy. Sometimes I have a hard time believing. Sometimes I just can't. Honestly, in certain respects my faith is hanging by a thread. It took a miracle to start me on the path with Jesus and it takes a miracle to keep me going."

In the stories in this portion of Matthew, we find almost everyone struggling to "find" faith.[37] In fact, nearly everyone muffs it. Chapters 8 through 15 contain clear indicators of God's power and presence in Jesus. So we would assume that after watching Jesus perform miraculous feedings and healings, anyone could look at the evidence, sift it and analyze it, then decide to follow Jesus. But the Pharisees and the Sadducees come to Jesus and test him "by asking him to show them a sign from heaven" (Mt 16:1). The evidence isn't enough. The religious leaders have seen the facts but spin a different interpretation: Jesus, the untrained, sinner-loving, non-temple-endorsed teacher from lowly Nazareth, can't possibly be the Messiah. For them it's just easier not to believe.

And Jesus doesn't offer them much help—in fact, Matthew records that he "left them and went away" (Mt 16:4). With this action Jesus is basically saying, "This conversation is over. You will always see exactly what you've decided to see." The main issue here isn't the presence or absence of evidence; for Jesus, the issue is the religious leaders' hardness of heart. Continuing a conversation based on logic or evidence, or providing another spectacular sign from God, won't change a closed heart or mind. Breaking a hardened heart fundamentally requires a miraculous intervention. God must transform the heart and mind through an encounter with Jesus, God with us.

Surprisingly, the disciples also display a need for a miraculous intervention. By this point in the story, they've watched Jesus heal the sick, raise a paralytic, cure the blind, restore demoniacs, feed the masses with a few loaves of bread, even walk on water, but when they find themselves without food (Mt 16:5), they still lack faith. After the first miraculous feeding (Mt 14), they should be responding with a big, eager statement like, "Wow, Jesus, we've already seen your power, so tell us what to do and we'll do it." Instead, they cynically mumble among themselves. They're no better than the Pharisees and Sadducees: without divine intervention, without a supernatural work of grace, no one "finds" faith.

Jesus makes the same point about Peter's declaration, "You are the Messiah, the Son of the living God" (Mt 16:15). Jesus agrees with Peter but then says, "This was not revealed to you by flesh and blood, but by my Father in heaven" (Mt 16:17). Our rational minds and our moral effort, our "flesh and blood," won't lead us to faith. The problem isn't the absence or presence of facts; the problem is our heart condition. Left to ourselves, riddled with self-absorption and fear, we display a remarkable aversion to God. As C. S. Lewis has said, in our quest for God we often act like a mouse searching for a cat: we enjoy the hunt as long as we don't actually find the cat.[38] God must intervene or we're lost. Faith isn't our work; from start to finish it's God's gift.

So how do we "get" faith? First and foremost, Matthew's Jesus wants us to ask for it (see Mt 7:7). Like children who trust their papa, we ask for it. Like those who are spiritually poor and can't buy it, we ask for it. Like sick people who need healing, we ask for it. For Jesus, faith (and even the ability to ask for faith) isn't an achievement of the spiritually elite; it's a gift for little-faiths, for beginners and strugglers, even for the spiritually dense and hardhearted. Jesus reminds us that our Father loves to give good gifts to his children, so we ask and then keep asking (Mt 7:7-11). We even ask for the faith to have faith. Following Jesus implies one long journey of asking for faith.

Second, Jesus also wants us to look for it. That was his point back in Matthew 7 when he gave us the threefold pattern for our prayer life: ask, seek, knock (or, literally, "ask and keep asking," "seek and keep seeking," "knock and keep knocking"). Like the Pharisees, Sadducees and even Jesus' closest followers, we often look for faith's "evidence" in the wrong places or with the wrong instruments. Francis Collins tells a parable about a man who set out to study deep-sea life by using a net with a mesh size of three inches. After catching many wonderful creatures, the man concluded that there are no deep-sea fish smaller than three inches.[39]

Collins uses this illustration to show that science isn't the only valid "net" for finding truth; however, it equally applies to how we approach the spiritual life. Sometimes we look for big, flashy, exciting, noisy displays of faith when God just wants our quiet, humble obedience flowing from a spiritually bankrupt heart.

In this Gospel Jesus wants us to use a different net, to look for faith's evidence in other places. He finds evidence for faith in ordinary, hidden and even "godforsaken" places and people. From the irregular people in his genealogy to his scandalous birth, from the calling of fisherman and tax collectors to the blessing of infants and the poor in spirit, Jesus' power appears in unusual places. If we're going to find evidence for faith, we'll have to look in the places and among the people where Jesus often shows up.

My friends Saul and Pilar Cruz run a ministry in Mexico City called Armonia. There they minister to the poorest of the poor—not with big, flashy programs or handouts, but by walking beside the people, befriending them and mentoring them, even being changed themselves through the give and take of friendship. When I was with the Cruzes, we visited a young single woman who was struggling to raise her two small children. She was devastated and alone, recently abandoned by her husband. Armonia didn't give her a handout. Instead they mentored her, guiding her as a mother, feeding her children once a day, showing her practical skills like how to use a slow cooker, teaching her how to read and study the Bible, providing job training and helping her grow in Christ. Now this young woman is starting to mentor other young mothers.

This is kingdom work—ordinary, quiet acts of love that change the world. There are many "signs" that faith is real, but in effect Jesus says, "Do you really want a sign? I've already shown you many: the hungry are fed, the blind see and the little people have good news. Later I'll show you another sign: I'll be in the tomb for three days and then rise again. But the problem isn't with my signs; the problem is with your sign-detecting equipment—the human heart. Let me perform surgery on your sin-corroded arteries. Then, as your heart heals, look for my signs in quiet and hidden places among little and broken people. Then you'll suddenly live in a sign-charged world."

4

THE GROWING CONFLICT WITH JESUS

Matthew 16:13–25:46

We tend to remember all the warm, cozy stories about a fuzzy and nice Jesus. But as we move into the fourth section of Matthew's Gospel, we find a lot of people who are trying to manage or "handle" Jesus, and Jesus acts very "unnice." These people want to define what kind of Messiah Jesus should be. Peter takes the first crack at handling Jesus, and poor Peter doesn't fare well—Jesus blasts him and calls him "Satan."

In this section, Jesus continues to clarify and defend his vision for his role and mission. Despite the pressure to conform to everyone else's messianic expectations, Jesus knows he's a Messiah who must head to the cross and serve as a ransom for our sins. And that's what he'll do. He doesn't let anybody handle or control his identity and mission, which he has received from his heavenly Father (see Mt 17:1-13).

After teaching some more on forgiveness, marriage, wealth and grace, Jesus enters Jerusalem as the man in charge (Mt 21). It's an exuberant entrance, filled with children shouting, "Hosanna to the Son of David." That doesn't sit well with the Pharisees, who demand to know where he's getting his authority. From that point on, Jesus' relationship with the

Pharisees permanently unravels. He refuses to shower them with warm fuzzies. As a matter of fact, after a protracted debating session, Jesus spends an entire section blasting them for their hypocrisy. Of course he's not just warning *those* people—the phony, shallow religious leaders. Jesus is indicting all of us. And he warns all of us to wake up, pay attention, get ready and start showing mercy before it's too late.

But then, surprisingly, in the midst of these heated arguments and passionate warnings, Jesus almost breaks down—according to Luke he starts weeping—and says, "How often I have longed to gather your children together, as a hen gathers her chicks under her wings, and you were not willing" (Mt 23:37). It's Jesus' heartrending love song for his wayward people. It's exactly unlike us and exactly like Jesus. We don't treat our enemies this way. We just want to get rid of them. But together with God the Father, God the Son seeks to be with us. He longs to heal the sick and unrighteous. But how can this holy and glorious God permanently dwell with such sinful people? That story is revealed fully in the final section of Matthew.

SPIRITUAL BUT NOT RELIGIOUS
Matthew 16:13-28

I meet many people who say they love Jesus or believe in God, but then they're quick to add, "I guess I'm spiritual but not religious." Before the twentieth century we used the words "spiritual" and "religious" almost interchangeably, but now many people prefer the "spiritual but not religious" (or SNR) label. *New York Times* columnist Charles M. Blow recounts his conversation with a young woman who had just returned from a monthlong vacation in Costa Rica. After transitioning from "religious" to "nonbeliever" to "spiritual," she was now "awakened." According to Blow:

> Putting aside the fact that most young people probably couldn't afford to take a monthlong vacation in a foreign country, and the fact that her spiritual awakening was admittedly spiked by copious amounts of Costa Rican rum, her story struck me as increasingly normative. Many young adults seem to be moving away from orga-

nized religion while simultaneously trying desperately to connect
with their spirituality.[1]

He's right. Researcher Robert C. Fuller contends that one in five
American adults now claims the SNR label.[2] There might be some up-
sides to this trend, but there's also a noticeable downside: it's often linked
with the assumption that church is bad, irrelevant or at best optional to
one's spiritual journey. According to Jesus, this penchant for "church-
free" or "church-lite" discipleship (let's call it JNC, or "Jesus but no
church") isn't just an innocent difference of opinion; it's a colossal rejection of Jesus' plan for a new genesis. Jesus restores the world through a
new community, a specific, concrete group of real human beings—
amazing, gifted and fabulous, as well as difficult, annoying and flawed—
who live with him.

The story in Matthew 16:13-28 begins in the region of Caesarea
Philippi, on the northernmost border of Israel, "as pagan a territory as
one could find."[3] It's here that Peter, directed "not by flesh and blood,"
makes the clear and concise declaration about Jesus' true identity: "You
are the Messiah, the Son of the living God" (Mt 16:16). Messiah was
everything to God's people. Messiah meant the fulfillment of every
promise, the satisfaction of every longing and the answer to every prayer.
According to a beautiful Hawaiian pidgin version of the Gospels, Peter
declares, "You da Christ Guy, da Spesho Guy God Wen Send. Da God
who alive for real kine, you his Boy."[4]

Jesus doesn't deny or dilute Peter's declaration of faith; instead, he
honors the confession and blesses Peter. He even pronounces, "And I tell
you that you are Peter, and on this rock I will build my church, and the
gates of Hades will not overcome it" (Mt 16:18). This is perhaps the most
contested verse in the entire New Testament. The controversy hinges on
a single question: Is the rock Peter (the Roman Catholic view), or is the
rock Peter's confession (the Protestant view)? Perhaps the best answer is
"yes" and "yes." But as Craig Keener observes, it's a specific Peter who
makes a specific confession, the Christ-pointing and Jesus-exalting Peter, who becomes the rock of Jesus' church.

Jesus gives this new community incredible worth and respect. First,
he gives them an amazing promise: "I will build my church, and the

gates of Hades will not overcome it." As Matthew emphasizes often throughout this Gospel, Jesus' followers will go through suffering and persecution—at times often—but ultimately nothing can destroy their little faith, not even death itself.[5] Then Jesus gives them a confidence-boosting (and perhaps slightly terrifying) challenge: "I will give you the keys of the kingdom" (Mt 16:19). Keys are given to those who have authority. Keys command respect and dignity and even power. The religious leaders had keys, but they used their keys to lock the front door and keep people out (Mt 23:13). Now Jesus declares that the real keys belong to Peter and his fellow Christ-followers.

Apparently Jesus says this without laughing, cringing or crying. We often fail to grasp how preposterous this must have seemed to everyone except Jesus. Here they are, a tiny band of ordinary people who constantly display little faith (or at times no faith), wandering in a pagan land far from the centers of religious power, blessed for admitting their spiritual poverty, blessed for their mourning-merciful hearts, promised persecution and hatred, gaining momentum by adding lepers and demoniacs and sinners to their ranks, and yet the Messiah tells them, "I will give you the keys of the kingdom." It's like handing a six-year-old the keys to the family's new Mercedes and telling him, "Take it for a spin on the freeway, son; you're in charge."

Why did he hand the keys to such a questionable group of people? Is it any wonder that now, over two thousand years later, people claim, "I'm spiritual but not religious" or "I want Jesus but not the church"? In one sense, by offering his keys to the disciples Jesus created his own problem with the church.[6]

But according to this passage, Jesus knew about this "problem" from the beginning. He knows how often we'll bungle our key-bearing responsibilities. It all started with Peter. Right after Peter's marvelous declaration about Jesus, his faith implodes. Peter has it half right: Jesus is the Christ. But he also has it half wrong: Jesus is also the suffering Christ. So after Jesus keeps telling his disciples that he will suffer and die (Mt 16:21), Peter performs an intervention on Jesus. The Greek word for "took aside" refers to a wealthier, stronger person condescending to help a poorer, weaker person. Peter's advice is simple: "Stop this nonsense about suffering and dying. Get your act together and behave like a real Messiah."

Unfortunately, for all his helpful intentions, Peter is pulling a page from Satan's playbook (see Mt 4:1-11). Wheeling around, Jesus faces Peter and says, "Get behind me, Satan!" (Mt 16:23). Within minutes Peter the Rock becomes Peter the Chump. The hero chokes. A man exuding the sweet aroma of spiritual insight now reeks with the backed-up sewer of demonic self-interest.

It's as if this story is announcing, "Welcome to the church, the most beautiful-hideous, holy-depraved, lovely-ragged group of people on the face of the earth. Welcome to the place of exalted spiritual insight and degraded self-interest. You'll find saints and sinners here, but mostly you'll just find saintly sinners and sinning saints. Hopefully, we're all slowly becoming more saint than sinner, but if you're looking for undiluted holiness, if you're searching for a perfect, pain-free, totally consistent community living around Jesus, forget it. It doesn't exist. It never did. Get over it."[7]

And yet Jesus emphatically declares, "I will build my church, and the gates of Hades will not prevail against it." It's as if Jesus stands with his imperfect church and says, "Despite its flaws, despite its shallowness and self-interest, despite its collection of slow-changing saints, it is *my* church, and I will build it up and never tear it down." Like all the individuals Jesus has encountered in this Gospel—a leper, a chronically sick woman, a howling demoniac, a noisy blind man—Jesus treats the church with mercy: he knows our oozing wounds but he still comes to us, embraces us, challenges us, teaches us and walks beside us until we become healthy and obedient.

Jesus never tires of rehabilitating his church. One of the miracles in this Gospel is that Jesus actually calls Peter back into discipleship. Peter fails so often. He steps out of the boat and then starts to sink. He makes a bold declaration of faith and then acts like Satan. But Jesus keeps saying, "If anyone would come after me . . . " It's not just a challenge; it's an invitation. He will rebuke us, but he never stops building his church. In this passage Jesus reveals his plan to restore the world: it's through and sometimes in spite of but never apart from his church.

Loving, working for and living within his church isn't easy. At times it feels like carrying a cross. Throughout the history of Christian spirituality much has been written about cross-bearing and self-denial, but in the in the context of this story, carrying our cross includes a call to enter and remain in Jesus' broken church.

It will cost us. There will be pain. I will discover things about you that shock me: you are selfish, petty, controlling and mean. You may gossip about me. You are opinionated and boring. You have poor taste in music and politics. You are uneducated or overeducated. These disappointing discoveries are a cross to bear.

Worse, I discover things about myself. I am selfish, petty, controlling and mean. Out of my pain I can wound ten other people. I want my way just as much as you want yours. I despise and judge all those judgmental people. I narrowly dismiss all those narrow and dismissive people. I see my own heart. I see that I am like Peter: a little devil who needs to get in line behind Jesus again. Fantasies about myself, my righteousness, my goodness and my Christlikeness get blown to bits. This is also a heavy cross to bear.

What should I do? I can throw my hands up in disgust and walk away. I can say, "I didn't sign up for this burden" and exit the church for good. Or I can stay put, commit to community, bear my cross, deny myself and lose my life for Jesus' sake. In other words, while being fully human just like Jesus, honestly expressing my pain and disappointment, I make a choice to follow Jesus by walking the path of love. Like John of the Cross, who was wounded and betrayed by his own community, I can declare, "If I put love into a community I will always have love to draw out of that community." So I choose to put love into the community even when I don't feel love from the community.

Ronald Rolheiser offers the following analogy for the church's call to stay together around Jesus:

> [Imagine that] the family is home for Christmas, but your spouse is in a sulk, you are fighting tiredness and anger, your seventeen year old son is pathologically restless and doesn't want to be there, your aging mother isn't well and you are anxious about her, your uncle Charlie is batty as an owl . . . and everyone is too lazy or selfish to

help you prepare the dinner. You are readying to celebrate but . . . your family is not the holy family, nor a Hallmark card for that matter. Its hurts, pathologies, and Achilles heels lie open not very far from the surface . . . but you are celebrating Christmas and, underneath it all, there is joy present. A human version of the messianic banquet is taking place and a human family is meeting around Jesus' birth.[8]

In the same way, we the unholy family, the snarled mix of sinner-saints gather in our imperfect way, but we gather around and in and through and because of Jesus—and that makes all the difference. There is a reason we're all here, a reason that's bigger than all of our dysfunctions and pathologies. Jesus is building his church and he will keep the project going and he will get it done all the way through the resurrection and life in the kingdom. So stay put, fellow saints and sinners; he isn't finished with you yet—and he isn't finished with him or her or them either.

WHAT A WONDERFUL WORLD
Matthew 17:1-23

According to my favorite Søren Kierkegaard parable, once upon a time a prince fell in love with a peasant maid. The prince desired to marry the peasant maiden, but he also wanted her to respond in joyful love. Although the king knew he could overwhelm her with power and glory, terrifying her into submission, that wouldn't result in true love. At last he decided he had only one option: he must become a peasant, but this transformation couldn't be an act or a mere disguise. Forgoing his kingly pomp and power, he must become a peasant in every respect—wearing peasant clothes, performing peasant labor, eating peasant food and sharing peasant joys and sorrows. In this way, he could woo and win her heart with genuine love.[9]

Throughout most of Matthew's Gospel, Jesus' glory remains hidden beneath peasant garb. From his genealogy to his flight as a political refugee, from his baptism in the Jordan River to his mingling with sinners and his travels with failure-prone disciples, Jesus entered into our world and became one of us. In response, the political powers ignored him and the religious authorities wanted to eliminate him. God came to us and it was underwhelming, but Jesus appeared to want it that way.

Now, however, in an incredible encounter on a mountain, Jesus' peasant garb is suddenly removed and his hidden but true identity is revealed: he is the world's glorious king. In Matthew 16 Peter confessed the glory of Jesus by proclaiming, "You are the Messiah, the Son of the living God." In chapter 17 Jesus confesses and displays his own glory. At this point in the story, it almost startles us. The numerous references to Jesus' earthy humanity could lull us into forgetting that he's also the thunderous God of Israel who has come to save his people and heal this sick world.

Everything about this encounter shouts, "Glory!" Starting with "After six days" and "led them up a high mountain," Matthew seems to grab his readers and say, "Are you listening here? Exactly six days after Jesus predicted his own suffering and death he ascended the mountain and displayed his power and glory." The six days would have reminded Matthew's Jewish readers of Moses' awe-inspiring meeting with God (Ex 24:16). The mountain imagery indicates an upcoming, overwhelming encounter with the living God.[10]

Through the theme of brilliant light, Jesus displays his glory in a unique way. Matthew records, "His face shone like the sun, and his clothes became as white as the light. . . . While he was still speaking, a bright cloud covered them" (Mt 17:2-5). At times the hidden glory of a king must shine forth through his peasant garb. Something similar happened to Moses when he stepped down from the mountain and his face shone with the glory of God. But Moses' brightness was a reflected glory; Jesus' glory shone forth from his union with the Father (see Mt 11:27). Unlike any human being before or since, Jesus as the living God was the source of true glory, not a creaturely object of glory.

This display of Jesus' glory carried tremendous symbolic weight, both for those first Christ-followers and for us. First, the transfiguration causes us to focus all of our attention on Jesus. As Peter scrambled to do something impressive for Jesus (Mt 17:4), the Father's voice rebuked and stilled his frantic activism. "This is my Son," the Father said, "whom I love; with him I am well pleased. Listen to him!" (Mt 17:5). When the story ends, the disciples have no choice except to focus on Jesus: "They saw no one except Jesus" (Mt 17:8). In the synoptic Gospels—Matthew, Mark and Luke—God the Father talks directly to earth on only two occasions and says the same thing: "Listen to Jesus." As Dale Bruner points out, "Jesus does not eclipse the Father; he reveals him."[11]

Jesus' stunning brightness, along with the power of his true identity as the ruler of everything, overwhelmed his disciples. Matthew records that they "fell on their faces," which is the same Greek word used of the epileptic boy who kept falling into the fire in Matthew 17:15. When we truly see Jesus' glory, we simply fall flat on our faces in awe and wonder.

Second, the appearance of Moses and Elijah unified what we know today as the Old and New Testaments. The Bible contains only one story, not two stories; one God, not two Gods. Over and over I hear well-educated, responsible church members who routinely rupture the Bible into two stories: the story of the mean Old Testament God of law and judgment versus the story of the nice New Testament God of grace and mercy. Matthew doesn't want us to make that mistake,[12] urging us to value the entire story of creation-Jews-exodus-Law-Prophets-Jesus-kingdom-cross-resurrection-heaven. The story hangs together as one unit. Jesus fulfills and completes but never obliterates the single storyline.

Third, by revealing Jesus' true identity and glory, the transfiguration provided a "sneak preview" of his coming resurrection. The transfiguration meant that Jesus could and would display his glory. Matthew's Gospel often emphasizes the suffering of Jesus and his followers, but this passage reminds us that suffering isn't the only promise. Throughout the centuries, Jesus' followers have held two truths in dynamic tension: Jesus' (and our) descent into suffering, and Jesus' (and our) ascent into glory. In this passage, Matthew wants us to know that there's a glorious ascent for Jesus and for us. There's a powerful king who's ushering in a new world and it's better than anything we could ever imagine.

In this Gospel, encounters with Jesus' overwhelming glory sometimes come with power and force. For instance, after Jesus calms the waves during the violent storm, his disciples gasp, "Truly you are the Son of God" (Mt 14:33). But in line with Matthew's emphasis on the little way of discipleship, transfiguration-like moments also come to us through unspectacular, ordinary places and people. Sometimes, like Peter, James and John, we feel Jesus' glorious presence in our spiritual poverty and ignorance. Notice Peter's pathetic attempt to do something "nice" for Jesus: "Lord, . . . if you wish, I will put up three shelters—one for you, one for Moses and one for Elijah" (Mt 17:4). The Father's reply in verse 5 rebukes Peter's mistaken notion that Jesus is on a par with Moses and Elijah. After facing their inadequacies and sins, the disciples fall on the ground, broken by shame, unraveled by their unworthiness. Then Jesus surprises them with his gentle touch and healing words: "Get up. . . . Don't be afraid" (Mt 17:7). Without any dramatic faith or heroic efforts on the disciples' part, Jesus transforms them at the point of their deepest shame, fear and spiritual dullness.

Matthew often tells us, "Don't look for Jesus' glory over there, with all those sensational, loud, impressive, dramatic people and events. Come over here where it's quiet and simple. Walk with the poor and the suffering. Be faithful to Jesus with your small acts of obedience among little people. Open your eyes to ordinary moments charged with the glory of Jesus' presence."

A few months ago, I climbed a hill on the outskirts of Cabo San Lucas, Mexico, to attend a simple but beautiful Spanish-English worship service. From the liturgy to the open-air architecture, from a short but profound message on the prodigal son story in Luke 15 to the beauty of the Eucharist, everything about the service revealed Christ's radiant glory. But the most brilliant moment came at the end of the service. After the priest proclaimed, "The service is ended; go in peace," the musicians broke into Louis Armstrong's "What a Wonderful World." Nobody moved. Mexicans and Americans, rich and poor, young and old, men and women—we all lingered until the song was over before erupting into applause and praise. After the worship service, in the light of Christ's death and resurrection and coming glory, that song had become utterly believable.

Unfortunately, like Peter we try to grab these glimpses of glory and build tents for them, demanding that they become the routine stuff of life. Instead, Jesus touches and raises us, leading us back down the mountain so we can offer his healing touch to the broken world we left behind.[13] Later in Matthew 17 Jesus walks down into the misery of a brokenhearted father ("Lord, have mercy on my son," Mt 7:15) and the disappointment of his faithless disciples ("You unbelieving and perverse generation. . . . How long shall I stay with you? How long shall I put up with you?" Mt 17:17). By his example, Jesus outlines for us the threefold movement of life with him:

- Jesus invites us up the mountain to see his glory.
- Jesus transforms our spiritual dullness on the mountaintop.[14]
- Jesus calls us down into the world's brokenness.

Most of us like it when Jesus invites us up and then heals us on the mountaintop; we resist or even resent the call to come down into the world's ugliness and pain. After my beautiful mountaintop experience in Cabo San Lucas, I sauntered back down the hill where I met hordes of loud and drunk American college students, elderly peasant women hawking tiny painted turtles and young women inviting me into "massage parlors." I wanted to walk back up the hill to another beautiful church service. The noise and squalor of downtown Cabo didn't match the lyrics of "What a Wonderful World." Instead I heard a clanging song of drunkenness, pain and lust.

But as the church of Jesus Christ we will train our ears and our eyes to hear and see both songs: songs of Christ's glory and songs of the world's brokenness. The Japanese film director Akira Kurosawa once said that the "artist is the one who does not look away."[15] In this sense, followers of Jesus are also artists. First, we will not look away from Jesus' glory. In corporate worship and personal times of silent prayer, we will yearn for a true glimpse. We will spend time doing nothing else except listening to the Father who tells us to listen to Jesus. But, secondly, as artists of the spiritual life, we also won't look away from the world's pain and agony. With Jesus, we'll descend the mountain of glory and walk among the anguished and the imperfect people around us.

A PERSON'S A PERSON, NO MATTER HOW SMALL
Matthew 17:24–18:20

In Dr. Seuss's classic book *Horton Hears a Who*, a bewildered but kind-hearted elephant named Horton hears a tiny voice crying out from an ordinary flower. Much to his surprise, Horton discovers an entire society, "Who-ville," of little creatures who need his help. The other jungle animals mock Horton—"He talks to a dust speck! He's out of his head!"—but Horton is determined to protect this village of little people. He can't abandon Who-ville because, in Horton's words, "After all, a person's a person, no matter how small."[16]

More than just a cute children's fable, this book is an eloquent statement about human rights and the dignity of each person. Jesus makes a similar statement in Matthew 17:24–18:20. Little people matter to him and his Father, Jesus declares, and they should matter to Jesus' followers too. They deserve respect, dignity and care. Neglecting, disrespecting or dehumanizing even one little person will make us accountable to king Jesus, lord and protector of little people.

Jesus often mingled with little people—children, women without rights, social misfits such as lepers, the chronically ill, religious outsiders, tax collectors and prostitutes, and even spiritual wanderers (see Mt 18:12-13). Our contemporary world is filled with similar groups of people: angry adolescents, unwanted babies, old folks crammed into nursing homes, the mentally ill, moral failures, immigrants and the vast substrata of the world's poor, or what one author calls "the bottom billion."[17] At times in our haste we walk right past them. They are insubstantial, insignificant and even invisible to us. Sadly, in the words of an ancient prayer of confession, "We have not heard the cry of the poor and needy"—and sometimes that includes the poor and needy in our own church, neighborhood or home.

In this passage Jesus envisions a new community that starts to see, honor and protect little people. This doesn't always mean that the big people help the little people, as in the "spiritually competent" help the "spiritually incompetent," or the rich assist "those poor people." Jesus begins with a simple premise: in God's sight, we're all little people. Or, as he says elsewhere, "Truly I tell you, unless you change and be-

come like little children, you will never enter the kingdom of heaven"
(Mt 18:3).

For Jesus, this was a matter of life or death: become little children—
all of you—or you'll have no part in the kingdom. In one way or another,
Jesus has said this before in Matthew's Gospel: "Blessed are the poor in
spirit" (Mt 5:3), "It is not the healthy who need a doctor, but the sick"
(Mt 9:12), "You have hidden these things from the wise and learned, and
revealed them to little children" (Mt 11:25). It's as though he has posted
a sign over the doorway leading into the kingdom of heaven: "For children only." We enter through that door by receiving Christ, but we must
reenter the same door every day for the rest of our life.[18]

Of course Jesus wasn't advocating an immature, ignorant or passive
approach to life. Rather, he was emphasizing that children aren't grown-
ups yet. Someday they'll get bigger and smarter, but for now they're still
growing and learning. They are still *homo viators*, people "on the way,"
people on a journey. As Thomas Merton once said, "We do not want to
be beginners. But let us be convinced of the fact that we will never be
anything but beginners, all our life!"[19]

Our poor in spirit, childlike beginner status has a profound impact on
our relationships: it leads to a commitment to care for the "little ones" all
around us. Notice how often Jesus refers to each *one:*

- "If anyone causes *one* of these little ones—those who believe in me—
  to stumble . . ." (Mt 18:6).

- "See that you do not despise *one* of these little ones" (Mt 18:10).

- "If a man owns a hundred sheep, and one of them wanders away, will
  he not leave the ninety-nine on the hills and go to look for the *one* that
  wandered off? . . . In the same way your Father in heaven is not willing
  that any of these little ones should perish" (Mt 18:12-14).

The Greek word for "one"—literally, "the micron"—refers to the marginalized, insignificant, invisible people we tend to ignore or even step
on as we ascend the ladder of success, comfort and privilege.[20]

More mafioso than gentle shepherd in this passage, Jesus warns, "You
mess with one of my little ones and you'll wind up at the bottom of the
river." That's the thrust of Matthew 18:6: "If anyone causes one of these

little ones—those who believe in me—to stumble, it would be better for them to have a large millstone hung around their neck and to be drowned in the depths of the sea." Even the angels kick into high alert to protect Jesus' little ones: "See that you do not despise one of these little ones. For I tell you that their angels in heaven always see the face of my Father in heaven" (Mt 18:10).[21] Jesus' warning covers anything from torture to abuse to emotional cruelty.

The word Jesus uses for "despise" in verse 10 means to treat with disdain, implying a wounding act of contempt. This kind of contempt occurs often in our society. When I was staying in Mexico, every morning I traveled with a different group of tourists into Cabo San Lucas. On one particular morning, the shuttle van driver was a timid, overweight Mexican man with a deformed left ear. Four of the American tourists wanted to pay the man with a hundred pesos rather than ten American dollars, a difference of roughly two dollars per person. With his broken English, the driver tried to explain the written policy: American dollars only. The tourists became loud, rude and pushy until the driver finally relented and agreed to their terms. When the driver stepped away from the van for a minute, one of the tourists spewed, "Wow, what a f****** grump! That guy was so cheap!" Another tourist laughed and chimed in, "Yeah, why don't you ask him about his ear. Maybe a wild dog bit it off."

How this must break the heart of our heavenly Father! Jesus' warning was clear: don't mess with the people he cares about. Once again we see his gritty commitment to respect and dignify even the "micro-people," those we deem unimportant, alien, deformed, slow, costly or inferior. Pope John Paul II spoke for every follower of Jesus when he wrote, "The protection and defense of the human person—every person and the whole person, especially those who are vulnerable and most helpless: this is the task which the Catholic Church, in the name of Jesus Christ, cannot and will not forsake."[22] In other words, as those who belong to Jesus, as those who share our Father's heart of mercy and goodness, we should be vigilant to reflect his tender and protective care for vulnerable people.

This protection extends even to spiritual wanderers. Many religious

people tend to dismiss those who "wander off" (see Mt 18:12-13).[23]
The message is often all too clear: if you can't get your life together, if
you keep living with such spiritual incompetence, if you keep getting
lost in your sin and addiction, then you deserve our disrespect and
contempt. Fortunately Jesus doesn't treat us or anyone else that way.
Rather than shame us with cold disdain, Jesus lavishes us with warm
dignity. Again we see his heart beating in unison with the heart of his
Father, the one who "is not willing that any of these little ones should
be lost" (Mt 18:14).

But it's also important to note that lavishing people with respect
doesn't lead only to gentleness and compassion. It also means that because I respect you, because of your inherent dignity in God's eyes, I
will speak the painful truth that helps you grow. Jesus demonstrates
this willingness when he warns us about being "thrown into eternal
fire" (Mt 18:8) and "thrown into the fire of hell" (Mt 18:9). It's astounding that Jesus, the most loving person in history, spoke so often about
hell, but it's consistent with his big-hearted, merciful approach to every
person he met.

As a contemporary example, let's say you discover that your grandma
confuses rat poison with creamer and routinely scoops it into her coffee.
If you say nothing, you really don't love your grandmother. If your
neighbor plays Russian roulette while you watch *Seinfeld* reruns and
drink a cold Sam Adams, you really don't love your neighbor. Spiritually speaking, living without Christ is like ingesting a poison or playing
Russian roulette. Jesus can't love us and then allow us to keep choosing
the path of eternal separation from his personal presence (i.e., hell). In
his love Jesus fights for our full restoration, even if he must say hard
truths to us.[24]

The same tough love informs Matthew 18:15-20. In chapter 7 Jesus
told us, "Do not judge"; now he says, "If your brother or sister sins, go
and point out their fault" (Mt 18:15). The first command addresses our
tendency to dismiss people through our hasty conclusions; the second
speaks to our tendency to dismiss them by ignoring their destructive
behaviors and attitudes. Since we live in a tolerant age, the second command may seem daunting. But if I ignore your sin because the truth will

hurt your feelings or make me appear less "nice," I'm giving you less respect and dignity, not more.[25]

However, even the process of confrontation is marked by deep respect for others. First, Jesus says, you need to go. Don't ignore your brother's sin; don't stew in anger; don't gossip about it; just go and deal with it. If that doesn't work, take someone else with you (Mt 18:16). This process is direct and careful before it leads to the last resort: excommunication. It's a slow, almost tedious approach; there's no room for mob scenes or witch hunts. These hard but good conversations should be routine in the new community of Jesus. And we should expect to be on both ends of them—the one who does and the one who receives the correction. Our hearts are prone to wander, so these conversations are needed often.

When we act like child-beginners walking beside other child-beginners, our hearts are free to love. We don't indulge in self-righteous finger pointing. Even our truth-telling conversations are marked by gentleness and humility (see also Gal 6:1-2). We see ourselves in the great tradition of Horton: utterly astonished that Christ chose us, and then utterly committed to defend Jesus' little people.

THE UNNATURAL ACT OF FORGIVENESS
Matthew 18:21-35

There are few absolute guarantees in life, but here's one: someone will hurt you. Someone will rip you off, ditch you, disappoint you, misunderstand you or just fail to love you. This offender may be a stranger, but more likely it will be someone you love deeply. One more guarantee: the hurt will tear a hole in your heart. And the tear may last a long, long time.

When the hurt comes, when the heart tears in two, we all have to decide how to handle the issue of forgiveness. It's easy to talk about forgiveness when we're not feeling hurt, rejected or betrayed; it's a fascinating theological and psychological discussion. But if our heart has been torn, it's no longer a "discussion"; it's an agonizing choice: forgive or don't forgive. Many people choose not to forgive. Psychologist Robert Karen observes, "In talking to people about forgiveness I've been surprised at the resistance that some smart, sensitive, people feel to this subject."[26]

My friend Steve told me up front that he couldn't fathom the concept of forgiving and being forgiven. As we wolfed down McDonald's fish filet sandwiches, he blurted out, "Matt, I don't think God could ever forgive me. Okay, maybe he could forgive 70 percent of my sins, but not all of them." When I tried to explain that Jesus always cleans up the entire load of dirt, as in one hundred percent or nothing, Steve interrupted, "Yeah, fine, but you don't know the stuff I've done." Then he told the following story:

> Nineteen years ago this guy stole my wife away from me. They got married and moved to Florida while my life unraveled. After I was arrested for assaulting a police officer, this guy smirked through the entire hearing. When I was convicted he flipped me the finger. I've hated him for nineteen years. He's coming up here next week. I have a thirty-two-caliber pistol strapped around my ankle, and when I see him I will kill him. I've thought all about it. I'm sixty-three years old. I'll get a life sentence, but I'll also get free medical and dental and a warm bed and three meals a day. It's not a bad way to end my life.

Why forgive? Why bother? According to Philip Yancey, "Forgiveness is achingly difficult. . . . Forgiveness is an unnatural act. . . . The very taste of forgiveness seems somehow wrong."[27] What should followers of Jesus tell Steve? What should we tell ourselves, especially after our heart has been torn in two?

The Bible is clear: choose forgiveness. It's not easy; it will feel unnatural, but choose it anyway. Choose it because that's how God treated us. Forgive "just as in Christ God forgave you" (Eph 4:32). Of course, many of us know this and accept it—at least on an intellectual level—but Jesus wants us to embrace forgiveness with our heart, not just as a concept. So as usual he tells a story. It starts with a question from Peter, who wanted a nice, reasonable lesson on forgiveness: "How often should we forgive—seven times?" he asks. Seven instances of forgiveness for the same offender seems awfully generous. But Jesus shoots back, "No, Peter. Try seventy times seven."

Then Jesus launches into a story about a man who owes his boss ten thousand talents. Right away everyone understands that Jesus is telling a funny story with a serious punch line. In that day a talent was the largest unit of currency, and ten thousand was the largest number in the Greek language. So this guy in the story owes about 1.5 gazillion dollars. It's ridiculous but you get the point: the guy is in deep trouble with no hope of getting bailed out. When the day of reckoning comes, the situation takes a shocking turn: the boss cancels the 1.5 gazillion dollar debt. Unbelievable! Preposterous! According to Jesus, "The servant's master took pity on him, canceled the debt and let him go" (Mt 18:27).

Jesus isn't giving us a lesson on finances or debt collection; he's showing us a glimpse into his Father's heart. Just like the prodigal farmer who flings his seed in every direction (Mt 13:3, 24-25), God the Father generously cancels unbelievable debts. In Matthew 18:27 the Greek word for "take pity" is the same word used for Jesus' compassion in Matthew 9:36: "When he saw the crowds, he had compassion on them." Christians sometimes have intense debates about theories of the atonement. What really happened when Jesus died on the cross, and why was it all necessary? There are different valid perspectives, but here's my view: Forgiveness always involves absorbing a debt. For instance, when my neighbor's dog mauled our tabby cat, the vet bill was over five hundred dollars. Someone had to pay it. The veterinarian could have treated the cat for free, but then she would have absorbed the debt. My neighbor could have paid the entire bill, or we could have paid it, but someone had to absorb the cost.

It's the same with my sin and your sin and the sin of the entire planet: someone has to absorb the debt. So what was Jesus doing for us when he died on the cross? Well, lots of good things happened, but one thing is certain: he paid a debt that we could never have paid. Like the guy in Jesus' story, morally speaking we were 1.5 gazillion dollars in debt with no chance of getting bailed out. But in and through Jesus' love and mercy, God the Father took pity on us, canceled our debt and let us go.

In the first half of this story we see God's grace in motion. The gospel doesn't begin with orders or edicts or even good religious rules. God doesn't say, "Take my advice. Forgiveness is a good thing, so try hard to forgive others. Work at it until you master it and then let's talk about

improving our relationship." Instead the gospel begins with Jesus saying, "Look at my Father's heart. He is good and generous. He creates a
plan to absorb our debt of sinfulness. Let his love sink into your heart.
He steps into the dirty water of baptism with sinners, he eats with sinners, he heals sick sinners, he becomes a ransom for sinners, and then
the one and only Son of God dies for you and forgives you—not just
seventy percent but one hundred percent. He's better than you could
ever imagine, even while you still act like a sinner."

Once we gaze at God the Father's gracious, forgiving heart, it makes
many of our resentments look petty, or at least less monstrous. That's the
point of the second half of this story. Released from certain death, the
servant steps into the clean, sunlit air, takes a deep breath, says a prayer
of gratitude and starts strolling down the street. At last, he's free! Suddenly he spots a business acquaintance, a slovenly fellow who owes him
money. The acquaintance approaches him with open arms, but our hero
can't forget an unsavory memory: eight months ago they were both
standing in line and the guy needed four bucks for a tall caramel latte
with whipped cream. Our hero generously donated the money, but now
this jerk acts like it never happened. So rather than hug the former friend,
he grabs him by the collar, shaking and slapping the latte thief as he
screams, "Where's my four bucks, you rat? You sure enjoyed that latte; it
was smeared all over your lips! Well, I'll have you pay for this." The
startled latte debtor chokes out, "Be patient with me and I'll pay you
back." (These are the same words the first guy used to receive mercy
from his master.) But in Jesus' terse words, "He refused" (Mt 18:30).

Once the boss hears about this, he hits the roof: "In anger his master
handed him over to the jailers to be tortured, until he should pay back all
he owed. This is how my heavenly Father will treat each of you unless
you forgive your brother or sister from your heart" (Mt 18:34-35). Jesus
isn't just making a theological statement here; he's providing a profound
psychological assessment. The desire for revenge, bitterness, and grudge-
holding extracts an enormous toll on us. When we don't forgive we think
we've corralled the one who has hurt us; actually, we've just enslaved our
own souls, and bitterness is a harsh tormentor.

Notice that Jesus doesn't say too much about what forgiveness entails.

He doesn't say it means forgetting a painful event, or that warm and gooey feelings will follow the act of forgiveness, or that it makes two estranged people best buddies again. Robert Karen criticizes people, especially church people, who ask too much of the forgiver: "They believe that to forgive is to condone somehow the harmful things that people have done . . . that to forgive is to lack the guts to call a spade a spade and to condemn what deserves condemnation. . . . What tarnishes forgiveness for some people is a church moralism that ignores ordinary human feelings."[28]

Jesus didn't ignore ordinary human feelings; this Gospel begins and ends with a God who enters our godforsaken places. Jesus shows what our resentments look like from God's perspective. Yes, you were hurt, but by holding on to your bitterness, by allowing the resentments to fester like a colony of streptococcal bacteria, your life has become sick. Jesus is saying, "Please, for my sake, for your sake, for the sake of the world, let it go. Let your offender go just as I am willing to let you go."

That's what I tried to tell Steve, too. I paused for a long time before I finally stammered, "Well, I guess it doesn't matter if you go to jail because you're already in jail. The guy who stole your wife and smirked at your hearing isn't in jail. You are. You're a prisoner of your own hate, and you're slowly killing yourself."

A week later he called me and said, "You know, I get your point. I put the gun away. I don't want to spend the rest of my life in jail—and I want to get rid of this bitterness, too." Of course it wasn't my point; it was Jesus' point. Forgiveness, like every other aspect of following Jesus, involves a long journey. Hopefully, by retelling the good news about Jesus, our hearts will soften, and as spiritual beggars (Mt 5:3) we'll want to forgive others. We'll want to start the journey, stumbling forward with hearts both torn by hurts and set free by grace. Slowly, before we know it, with Christ alive within us, we'll find more freedom to forgive than we ever imagined.

SHOULD WE CALL THE WHOLE THING OFF?
Matthew 19:1-15

"Let's call the whole thing off." That's the marriage advice dished out by Sandra Tsing Loh in a recent edition of *The Atlantic* magazine. "Sadly, and to my horror," she writes, "I am divorcing. . . . I am a 47-year-old woman whose commitment to monogamy, at the very end, came unglued." The article is subtitled "The author is ending her marriage. Isn't it time you did the same?" Loh concludes her article by warning her readers to avoid marriage altogether:

> In any case, here's my final piece of advice: avoid marriage—or you too may suffer the emotional pain, the humiliation, and the logistical difficulty, not to mention the expense, of breaking up a long-term union at midlife for something as demonstrably fleeting as love.[29]

As I read the article, I got the impression that the author thought her stance would sound original and shocking, perhaps even scandalous—"I sense you picking up the first stone to hurl," she writes. Actually, the article doesn't break any new ground. It's an old story. Two people get married. One or both partners find the marriage dull, stifling or heartbreaking. One or both partners want out. The marriage ends. People who love them pick a side in what often becomes a mini civil war. The two ex-married people, along with their small civilization of loved ones, grieve the death of a dream and move on with their lives. But none of this is new; nobody wants to hurl stones.

According to Matthew 19, Jesus and his contemporaries dealt with the same issues. Just like us, these "ancient" people debated and dissected the landmines of marriage and the lure of divorce. According to Matthew, Jesus entered the debate in verse 3 when some Pharisees asked him a question about divorce: "Is it lawful for a man to divorce his wife for any and every reason?"

They wanted to know where Jesus stood on a touchy theological dispute within the ranks of Pharisaism. Basically, the dispute centered on how to interpret Deuteronomy 24:1, which mentions a man divorcing his wife if "he finds something indecent about her." What, exactly, is indecent wifely behavior? One group within Pharisaism, followers of the famous Rabbi Hillel, offered a broad definition of indecency, even including the notoriously indecent act of burning your hubby's supper. A second party, followers of Rabbi Shammai, advocated a stricter interpretation. Either way, husbands—even religious husbands—were shedding their wives at an alarming rate. As Craig Keener notes, in Jesus' day, "if marriage did not work, divorce was a relatively simple option. Many sages considered it a duty to divorce a 'bad' wife."[30]

Jesus doesn't enter the debate on the Pharisees' terms. Instead, he offers a fresh perspective on marriage and divorce. Rather than start with Deuteronomy 24, he backs up to Genesis 1 and 2. "Haven't you read," he replies, "that at the beginning the Creator 'made them male and female,' and said, 'For this reason a man will leave his father and mother and be united to his wife, and the two will become one flesh'? So they are no longer two, but one" (Mt 19:4-6).[31] Jesus addresses divorce by offering God's original vision for marriage, just like a doctor might approach disease by offering a vision for health. Yes, the doctor might say, the human body breaks down; yes, viruses and disorders attack us. But let me start with a picture of the human body's original wholeness and beauty.

Whether you agree with Jesus or not, at least he was consistent in his approach to life in an imperfect world. While honestly acknowledging human brokenness and even human evil, Jesus never grew cynical. Instead, whenever he saw torn and battered human beings, he responded with compassion (Mt 9:36). Even in the midst of hostility and violence, he maintained his confident hope in the "renewal of all things" (see Mt 19:28).

Many people grow disillusioned and even jaded about marriage because it so often fails, terminating in divorce or dangling by a thin thread of contempt. No wonder we're tempted to call the whole thing off. But in this passage in Matthew, Jesus treats marriage like he treats human beings: with incredible dignity, because in the beginning they were good. Although people are flawed and failure-prone, they are worth defending and redeeming even as they sway like bruised reeds (Mt 12:20). By pointing to Genesis in the midst of this divorce-happy culture, Jesus upholds the original beauty of God's dream for marriage: two people—one man and one woman, to be precise—standing before each other naked and not ashamed, clinging and growing together through life's wild uncertainties, giving and receiving forgiveness often, until they are parted by death.

Jesus knows that every marriage is based on that audacious dream, but he also knows that marriages fail. As a result, he agrees with the Pharisees on one thing: some marriages can, and on rare occasions should, end.[32] Both Jesus and the Pharisees have the tradition of Moses and the Old Testament on their side. But the Pharisees have been using this Mosaic concession as their golden opportunity to ditch their defective wives and find improved models.[33] Jesus views it more like an amputation: if a doctor must sever a patient's leg, the procedure will invariably produce a sense of irretrievable loss.[34]

So if marriage is such a glorious institution, why do so many of these unions end with an amputation? Jesus faces the question without a whiff of cynicism. Instead he identifies the real culprit behind broken marriages (and just about every other broken thing in the universe): the human heart. "Moses permitted you to divorce your wives," Jesus bluntly says, "because your hearts were hard. But it was not this way from the beginning" (Mt 19:8). Marriages fail for the same reason people fail, which is the same reason we desperately need God's grace: our hearts are sick, corroded with arterial damage, and we require the intervention of a skilled surgeon.

Jesus drives married couples back to the little way of discipleship. The two people in a marriage aren't just a couple: they're also two sinners, spiritual beggars hungering for righteousness, needing to display mercy as they have received mercy, needing to forgive as they have been forgiven. They are also called to focus first and foremost on themselves: mourning for their sin, observing the speck in their own eye, growing in their personal purity of heart.

This isn't easy. Both Matthew and Mark place Jesus' teaching on marriage at the border of his descent to the cross.[35] In other words, marriage is linked with suffering, especially the suffering of identifying our sin, acknowledging our hardness of heart, coming to grips with our botched attempts to love like Jesus. But as we shall see, the cross and resurrection are also linked together. Thus marriage is also an ascent into the glory of the resurrection. Marriage propels us to ask for and receive the power of the resurrection, the presence of Jesus. As a married couple, as two broken but forgiven and forgiving sinners, we humbly obey Jesus when he says, "Come to me" (Mt 11:28). As a married couple, we are sent into the world in mutual mission to bless others and proclaim the gospel.[36]

The dream is so audacious and the calling is so high that at some point every married person will ask, "If that's the case, maybe it's better not to marry" (see the disciples' response in Mt 19:10). But then how will we immerse ourselves in the death and resurrection of Jesus? How will we learn to love? Marriage isn't the only way to learn about love, but for many people it's certainly one of the primary schools for deep transformation. If you are married, in this passage Jesus is saying, "Stick with it and it will yield fruit beyond your wildest dreams."

However, Jesus doesn't just bless marriage and married couples; he also blesses single people called to a life of celibacy.[37] It doesn't matter how they enter celibacy—by birth or heredity, by a traumatic or unwanted life event, or by a free choice (the three options outlined by Jesus in verse in Mt 19:12)—all celibates share one thing in common: their lives are blessed by God. In this passage, Jesus offers a beautiful plan for both marriage and celibacy. Both states offer an invitation to join Jesus in the way of the cross and resurrection. Both states are a gift—not only for the individual follower of Christ but also for the church and the world.

So what does this passage imply for those who don't or can't "stick with it" in their marriages? What about the masses of divorced people, those who often define themselves by their biggest and most painful failure? What would Jesus say to them?

First, the divorced often have the gift of coming face to face with their spiritual poverty. They know they need a spiritual doctor. You don't have to browbeat them to heed Jesus' command to "come to me, all you who are weary and burdened." If Jesus is not for them, he is not for anyone.

Divorce can also provide the opportunity for an honest whole-life evaluation. On the one hand, it is a tragedy when people divorce and remain stuck in the hardheartedness of contempt (Mt 5:22-23), judgment (Mt 7:1-5) and bitterness (Mt 6:12-15). But it's truly beautiful to watch people grow closer to Jesus even while enduring the tragedy of divorce. In the mysterious providence of God the Father, in the resurrection power of Jesus, God intervenes and softens the hearts of divorced people, causing them to overflow with meekness, mercy, compassion and forgiveness. Their lives serve as a sign of the power in Jesus' little way.[38]

EVERYBODY NEEDS AN INTERVENTION
Matthew 19:16-31

Sometimes people need an intervention. After an addict descends into denial and self-absorption, his loved ones must step in and jolt him back to his senses. It's usually a last resort. People have tried to get his attention, but now his family and friends, joined by a counselor or pastor, need to get in his face with total truth in love. The message usually involves something like this: "We love you, but you are hurting yourself and others. Everyone around you knows that your life has become unmanageable, but you don't see it. We're giving you a gift: discomfort, even pain, enough pain so that you'll wake up, get help and turn your life around."

The scary thing about interventions is that they can fail. After listening calmly or tearfully to his circle of loved ones, the addict can refuse to change. He can continue to spiral downward in addiction until he loses everything—family, friends, self-respect and perhaps even his life.

In Matthew 19:16-31 Jesus offers a no-nonsense but loving intervention. A rich young man has a gaping wound of addiction in his heart, but he doesn't see it. So with brutal honesty Jesus identifies the wound and performs a swift one-person intervention. After listening carefully to Jesus, the man chooses to walk away. It's a sad story: the intervention—even directed by Jesus himself—fails.

At first glance the man doesn't appear to need an intervention. Most addicts are easy to spot (and therefore easy targets for our contempt): alcoholics wobble in the street; gamblers may lose ten thousand dollars in one night; sex or love addicts can juggle three separate affairs. However, something less obvious has hooked this man's heart: an addiction to greed.[39] Literally translated, Matthew 19:22 states that "he was having many things." The "having many things" implies a spirit of materialism: the insatiable craving for more—more stuff, more shopping sprees, more comfort, more products, more experiences.

Once again (see Mt 6:19-34), Jesus declares that our approach to possessions and money matters to him. When we grasp them too tightly, they become the false god Mammon. For Jesus this isn't an innocent side issue. I know many contemporary followers of Jesus who condemn others for their moral failures, particularly in the realm of sexuality, but they blithely ignore Jesus' teaching on economics and wealth. They are addicted to more and better things. Although they see the speck of sin in the eyes of others, they do not see the log of materialism in their own eye.

Like most of us, the rich young ruler doesn't see himself as a hopeless, fall-on-your-face drunk. Being a decent, take-charge person, he cozies up to Jesus and asks, "Teacher, what good thing must I do to get eternal life?" (Mt 19:16).[40] This man may be wanting to identify that one additional thing that would secure eternal life. After attaining money and success and even morality, he now wants to add salvation. Apparently he doesn't see a problem with his lifestyle, but then again maybe he hasn't completely covered his religious bases.

Unfortunately, he drastically underestimates both Jesus' vision for goodness and the depth of his own addiction. After the rich young ruler's initial query, Jesus shoots back, more or less, "Are you kidding? Do you have any idea about the long and steady path to true goodness?" This rich young man is acting like a brash young basketball player who wants to get stardom by performing one amazing, 360-degree, two-handed, bounce-off-the-backboard slam dunk. Somebody like LeBron James needs to intervene and tell him, "Don't ask for shortcuts, kid, because it's a lifelong effort, not just one shot."

Jesus provides the lifelong path to goodness with what on one level sounds like simple advice: "Keep the commandments" (Mt 19:17).[41] Jesus starts with commandments five through ten, or those that focus on human relationships.[42] The path into the kingdom of heaven goes through, not around, how we treat our fellow human beings. This man wanted to "do" eternal life like he would "do" a business transaction with God—cozy and private, just him and God. Instead, Jesus points him in a different direction: care for your neighbors.

Jesus has moved into the heart of the man's problem and his deep denial. First, he treasures the wrong thing (see Mt 6:21; 13:44-46). He does not value Jesus and the kingdom of heaven as life's greatest treasure. Second, this man doesn't keep the love commandments; he can't respond to his neighbor. His possessions possess, trap and bind his heart. Just like a raging drunk won't give up his beer or vodka, or a sex addict won't give up strip clubs or emotional affairs, or a workaholic keeps fleeing into her job, this guy won't give up his disordered love for money and possessions.

So Jesus performs an intervention. With as much love and truth as possible, Jesus tells the man to let go of his grasping attachment to more and better stuff. "If you want to be perfect," he says, "go, sell your possessions and give to the poor, and you will have treasure in heaven. Then come, follow me" (Mt 19:21). Sadly, unlike the first story of discipleship in which the fishermen drop their nets and follow Jesus, this tale ends with a refusal. Matthew soberly records, "When the young man heard this, he went away sad, because he had great wealth" (Mt 19:22).

After my friend Dana, a new follower of Jesus, read this passage for the first time, she told me, "You know, I feel really bad for the guy in that story. It's so sad. He had a great opportunity to follow Jesus and make a difference in the world, but he couldn't turn the corner on his life. But in a way, I feel like it wasn't his fault. I mean, don't you think Jesus asked him to do something impossible? How could that guy just drop everything and then follow Jesus?"

First of all, Jesus didn't make this drastic request of everyone he met. Zacchaeus, for instance, voluntarily offered to give up half of his possessions and make a fourfold restitution to anyone he had cheated. Pleased with this offer, Jesus never asked him for more (see Lk 19:8-10). As far as we know, Jesus never made Peter relinquish his house or his fishing business as a discipleship requirement. Clearly, Jesus didn't follow a formulaic script for his interventions and his call on people's lives.

But on the other hand, Dana was right: Jesus did ask this man to do something impossible. I've heard sermons that dilute the reference to a camel passing through the eye of a needle. "Not to worry," they say. "There's a logical explanation for all of this. In Jesus' day the hole in the wall outside of Jerusalem was called 'the eye of the needle.' In order to pass through the wall, a camel had to unburden itself and slide through the needle's eye." Unfortunately, this concept didn't develop until the Middle Ages. Jesus meant what he said: take a camel, the largest animal in Palestine, and thread it through a tiny needle's eye. If you can do that, you can save a rich person. That's why the disciples, utterly shocked, asked Jesus, "Then who can be saved?" Jesus' point: no one . . . unless God takes the initiative to save us.

Jesus was circling back to one of his core ideas: "Blessed are the poor in spirit" (Mt 5:3), or "Congratulations to those who embrace their powerlessness over sin." Rather than walk away, this man should have fallen on his knees and cried out, "Jesus, I'm successful at knowing about the commandments and how to work the system and get things done. But I'm still not free. Trapped in a cage of my greed, I'm only a beginner at real love. I can't fly toward you, Lord. I'm addicted, my life has become unmanageable and I'm powerless to change it."

Jesus understood our fundamental problem: we can't save or redeem ourselves. That's why this passage begins with Jesus' call to become a child. Children don't assume that they're self-sufficient. Children know that some things are impossible for them but not for their parents. And children aren't shy about asking for help. So ask, Jesus says. But this man doesn't ask; he refuses to be like a child or a leper or a demoniac. Instead, by walking away from Jesus' intervention, he rejects the ultimate offer of freedom and restoration—the restoration of his own soul and what Jesus called "the renewal of all things" (Mt 19:28).

If someone were to ask me why I am a Christian, I could honestly say, "Because I needed an intervention and Jesus offered to set me free." I still need an intervention. I'll need one every day until the day I die.

THE SHOCK OF GRACE
Matthew 20:1-16

My friend Ray, the recovering alcoholic who didn't like the Beatitudes (see pages 56-62), was utterly appalled by Jesus' parable in Matthew 20. After I finished preaching on this text, I received the typical litany of "nice sermon, pastor" until Ray used his massive body to block my exit from the church. Refusing to shake my hand, he bellowed, "Are you kidding me? That's *the* dumbest story I've ever heard! You can't run the world according to Jesus. You can't treat people that way. Good people should get rewarded; bad people—lazy latecomers and slackers—should get punished. This story turns everything wrong side up. It isn't just dumb, it's messed up and downright dangerous!"

I sure liked Ray's honesty. And he's right about one thing: this story is messed up and dangerous. Of course that was probably Jesus' point. On more than one occasion, Jesus' simple teachings about grace and forgiveness left people bewildered and even ticked off. According to Jesus, God's grace initially may feel hot and raw, like the aftermath of a sunburn, before it soothes and heals.

This parable begins innocently enough. A farmer has an urgent job to get done so he starts hiring day laborers. At sunrise he calls his first crew, a bunch of early risers who start working at the crack of dawn. Then at intervals throughout the day—the morning coffee break, the lunch break, afternoon tea time—the farmer returns to the job center to hire more workers. Finally, an hour before quitting time, he hires his last crew. When all the crews line up to get their paychecks, the boss surprises the latecomers with a fat check for a full day's work. Based on that hourly wage, the early birds who sweated all day in the hot sun assume they've just won the lotto. Instead, the boss surprises them with a check for the same amount as the one-hour crew. Naturally, the first crew gripes: "Hey, this isn't fair: we work all day in the hot sun and these guys sign on an hour before quitting time and yet we get treated the same?" The boss doesn't budge. Instead, he asks, "Did I really gyp you? You got what was fair and honest, didn't you? If I want to fling my money at those latecomers, that's my choice. But you have no right to be jealous because I'm generous."

Obviously, Jesus isn't giving lessons about employer-employee relations or fair labor practices (although the Bible has plenty to say about that elsewhere—for example, see Jas 5:1-6). Although Jesus never uses the word "grace" in this story, this parable gushes with it. And at least initially we probably should respond like Ray—bristling at the unwanted and unfair intrusion of God's grace.

That's the point Jesus makes before and after this parable: God's grace turns our lives upside down and inside out—although it actually gets turned right side up and outside in. Jesus makes this point by tucking the parable into two bookends. In Matthew 19:30 he introduces the story by saying, "But many who are first will be last, and many who are last will be first." He concludes by saying it again in Matthew 20:16— "So the last will be first, and the first will be last." In Jesus' day (and often in our day) there were two clearly defined groups: the "firsts" who sat at the table gobbling up course after course of spiritual blessings, and the "lasts" who sat under the table waiting for a few spiritual crumbs to fall their way. According to Jesus, God's grace threatens to upset these predictable seating arrangements: the "lasts" get raised to the best seat and the "firsts" might start missing the meals.

Primarily, this story serves as a warning to the "firsts," those who received the first invitation to the table of grace, those who had the first chance to obey and serve the living God. In Jesus' day, the Jewish people and in particular the religious leaders possessed these spiritual privileges. They were the "firsts." In our day, I could easily qualify as one of the "firsts." After years of knowing Christ, attending small groups and worship services, and living in a country with an abundance of spiritual growth resources, I've been sitting at the table devouring blessings for a long time.

Jesus constantly warns the "firsts" not to take their firstness for granted. In the Gospel of Matthew God despises spiritual smugness and delights in the spiritual poverty of a Jesus-liberated heart (Mt 5:3). This theme is deeply rooted in the Hebrew Scripture, where over and over again God warned his people to remember the privilege and duty of their firstness. They were chosen by God to be blessed and to bless the whole earth (see Gen 12:1-3; Is 49:6).

But God must have known of the fatal temptation his "firsts" would face: spiritual smugness and arrogance that belittles or excludes the "lasts." "Firsts" can start to resent the fact that those people also get God's grace—and not just scraps of grace, but the exact same heaping portions. In Jesus' story they basically complain, "We got in first, we've been here from the beginning, we heard the call before anyone else, we've been serving God for a long time, we never wallowed in the pigsty of sin like they did, and then God invites them to his table of mercy just like us. We deserve better treatment and they deserve worse."

This is Matthew's version of Jesus' prodigal son story. In Luke's version, the elder brother gripes, "All these years I've been slaving for you and never disobeyed your orders. . . . But when this son of yours who has squandered your property with prostitutes comes home, you kill the fatted calf" (Luke 15:29-30). In Matthew's parallel story, the "firsts" complain, "These who were hired last worked only one hour . . . and you have made them equal to us who have borne the burden of the work and the heat of the day" (Mt 20:12). In both stories, the "good people" with spiritual privileges and a prime seat at the table fail to see the Father's heart.

How did these "firsts" get off track? Jesus' story gives us a clue: on four occasions he tells us the farmer "went out" in search of workers (see Mt 20:1, 3, 5, 6). The fact that these "firsts" are in the Lord's vineyard at all depends on God's gracious call. The farmer "went out" seeking them, drawing them into his vineyard and giving them a job. Again, Jesus' Bible, the Old Testament, constantly proclaimed the sheer mercy of God's call and choosing (see Deut 7:6-9). The apostle Paul makes the same point in describing God's freedom to lavish his grace wherever he chooses: " 'I will have mercy on whom I have mercy.' . . . It does not, therefore, depend on human desire or effort, but on God's mercy" (Rom 9:15-16). In Jesus' story the farmer gives the same message in Matthew 20:15: "Don't I have the right to do what I want with my own money?" In other words, God says, "You got in, you became a first, only through an act of my freely given mercy and call on your life. The 'lasts' will get in exactly the same way. You couldn't stop me from blessing you and you can't stop me from blessing them. You do not control the flow of mercy; I do."

The story ends with the farmer's speech quelling the gripes of the "firsts." That's Jesus' point: Grace stuns and silences us. It's not what I deserved and it's not what those people deserved either.

This thought hit me as my friend George shared his journey to Christ. He was sitting in a dingy church basement confessing a sordid tale of sexual sin. After starting with pornography, he moved on to high-priced escort services. But then he hit bottom: his life unraveled, he lost his job, his family disowned him and his wife was leaving him. But now, like the prodigal son, George had finally "come to his senses" (see Lk 15:17). When he finished this tale of filth and mercy, George asked to share a poem he had just discovered. With hands shaking, he unraveled a scrap of paper and told us, "I've been carrying this all week and it's one of the most beautiful things I've ever read. You guys have probably never heard this before but it goes like this: 'Amazing grace, how sweet the sound, that saved a wretch like me; I once was lost but now am found, was blind but now I see.'"

As tears of joy and relief streamed down his face, I realized that I didn't understand God's grace. I've heard that old hymn a thousand times and it usually bores me. Grace can leave us angry, stunned, bewildered, delighted or grateful, but it will never make us bored. George, one of the "lasts," a latecomer to the vineyard, a desperately lost and hungry sinner, "discovered" God's grace and he wept for joy. On that day, George became my mentor in the ways of God's grace.

According to my friend Ray, Jesus' story about the farmer and the workers is "messed up and downright dangerous." I can imagine the objections from all the decent "firsts" who live good and moral lives, faithfully remaining in the Lord's vineyard: "You mean George and people like that just get into God's presence? They can just come without groveling and working off their debt? You mean God invites George and those people right into the house, seating them at the table with full benefits with people like us?"

There's an unwavering answer from Jesus to all these questions: yes, yes, yes. Of course George will have to make a long journey toward spiritual renewal, becoming like Christ and making amends to those he's betrayed. He will need to keep coming to Jesus, asking Jesus to transform his heart and his character. But, yes, at the moment of true repentance, George received an invitation to the lavish banquet of king Jesus.

If you don't like it, Jesus warns in this parable, watch out: as George becomes a first, you could become a last. Our graceless resentment can slowly move us away from the table of mercy. We can become "lasts"— as much of a last as George used to be. Based on God's free choice to

display mercy, the Georges of the world do indeed become "firsts." Yep,
it's all crazy and upside down, but remember what Jesus said in the Beatitudes: I'm turning the world right side up.

Be aware, Jesus said, be very aware.

JESUS AND THE CULTURE OF CELEBRITY
Matthew 20:17-34

Forbes magazine's 2011 list of the top one hundred famous people,
based on a composite score of wealth and fame, held a few surprises.
Lady Gaga worked her way back to the top of the list, while Oprah,
the previous year's number one, slipped to number two. The band U2
jumped to four while, thank goodness, Dr. Phil came in at a respectable number eighteen. As for athletes, golfer Tiger Woods (number
five) beat out basketball champion LeBron James (number ten), soccer
star David Beckham (number thirty-five) and tennis pro Roger Federer
(number twenty-five). The list did not include any nurses, case workers for refugees, stay-at-home moms or dads, pastors of small churches,
adults with Down syndrome or waitresses.

We sure love our celebrities.[43] By tracking them, grading them, adding new ones to the list and dispensing with old ones, we've created a
massive culture of celebrity.[44] For some reason, just knowing about
well-known people makes our lives feel a little more substantial. And
perhaps we all have celebrity envy. After all, being a celebrity—even a
low-level and local celebrity—has its perks: fame, power, control over
others, admiration. When you're a star, even a plain star in a tiny gal-
axy, people assume you're successful, smart, funny, holy, Christlike or
just plain amazing. Achieving celebrity status feeds our famished ego
like nothing else.

In Matthew 20:17-34, the disciples have a bad case of celebrity envy—
and it nearly kills their fragile community. The story begins with Jesus
reciting (for the third time) the details of his impending death. It's a terrifying list of cruel acts ("They will condemn him to death . . . to be
mocked and flogged and crucified," Mt 20:18-19), but the worst item on
the list is the word "betrayed" in verse 18 or "turn him over" in verse
19—it's the same Greek verb in both verses. Matthew will use this word

often to describe the process of Jesus' death.[45] It's his sober and shocking passion verb. Jesus, God with us, the Son of God, will be handed over for judgment not for his sins but for ours.

The disciples should have been appalled and devastated. Instead they start scrambling for the best seats in the house. Actually, it all begins with the mother of James and John, who approaches Jesus and requests a "small" favor: "Grant that one of these two sons of mine may sit at your right and the other at your left in your kingdom" (Mt 20:21).[46] In other words, she boldly asks Jesus to make her boys into instant celebrities. This trio's request not only displays bad timing and poor tact; it also exposes the tragic bent of the human heart. In the midst of Jesus' sad news, the disciples are still stuck on themselves, enslaved to their trinkets of celebrity power, control, admiration, applause and success. Lost in the celebrity story, they miss the grand Jesus-restoring-the-cosmos story.

For three years, or through twenty chapters in Matthew's Gospel, Jesus has been training his followers to take the little way of discipleship. "Follow me," he says, and the following leads down before it leads up, down from the transfiguration into the world's suffering and pain, down into the haunts of lepers and demoniacs, down into sharing meals with ordinary sinners, down into life in a painfully flawed community, down into spiritual poverty and persecution, down into unspectacular displays of mercy and forgiveness. Jesus has been leading them down into hidden and marginal places to serve little people. It's the anti-celebrity path. But apparently the disciples don't get it: they still think Jesus should lead them right up into glory, power and fame.

Jesus responds graciously by asking, "You don't know what you are asking. . . . Can you drink the cup I am going to drink?"[47] They answer simply, "We can" (Mt 20:22). It's the wrong answer. This entire Gospel has been training them to respond to Jesus' "Can you?" with one answer: "I can't, but with God all things are possible." On our own we will be like Peter, taking a few glorious steps on the water before plunging into powerlessness (Mt 14:29-31). But the gospel of God with us declares that we aren't alone. By his grace we can move mountains (Mt 21:21).

The Zebedee trio starts acting like a pathetic troupe of clowns, run-

204

THE GOSPEL OF MATTHEW

ning and tripping all over each other—except nobody's laughing. In Matthew 20:24 the other ten disciples are "indignant with the two brothers" (apparently nobody got upset with Mama Zebedee). Perhaps they're ticked that they didn't think of it first. In the culture of celebrity there's never enough room for multiple stars on the stage of life. So the disciples turn their community into a vicious episode of *Survivor*, vying to form alliances and stay on the island while they vote someone else off. They puff and preen with the immature cries of every celebrity wannabe: "Notice me," "I was first," and "I'm better than you." Sadly, this celebrity craze ruptures community. Jesus' small band of followers, instructed by the master in the little way of the kingdom, tears and bleeds with open wounds of resentment, arrogance and discontentment. The refreshing new community of salt and light now looks like every other community.

So Jesus intervenes and calls them together with a very simple message: there's a wrong way and a right way to live. First, the wrong way: "You know that the rulers of the Gentiles lord it over them, and their high officials exercise authority over them" (Mt 20:25). Throughout most of history, this wrong way has appeared utterly natural. In Jesus' day every time someone picked up a copper coin, he or she saw the head of the reigning emperor Augustus (and later Tiberius) with the inscription "He who deserves adoration." As obnoxious as that sounds, most of us wouldn't mind a little more adoration coming our way. What could be more appropriate and sensible?

On the other hand, Jesus' prescription for the right way to live feels shockingly abnormal. "Not so with you," he warns them. "Instead, whoever wants to become great among you must be your servant, and whoever wants to be first must be your slave" (Mt 20:26-27). The word for "servant," *diakonos*, refers to a common table waiter, or an ancient busboy. The word for "slave," *doulos*, refers to an ordinary slave.[48] Both words would have repulsed Jesus' hearers as much as they repulse us. Nobody voluntarily chooses the role of table waiter or slave.

Jesus jolts us out of our attachment to fame, power, success and human praise not just by giving us advice (as helpful as that is), but also by becoming our servant and slave. That's the gist of Matthew 20:28, perhaps the most powerful verse in this section: "Just as the Son of Man did not come to be served, but to serve, and to give his life as a ransom for many." This verse contains part of Jesus' "theory of the atonement." He came as our ransom. A ransom is offered on behalf of someone who is being held captive against their will. A ransom, either in the form of money or personal presence, takes the place of the captive. In this sense, the disciples weren't just captives of an oppressive Roman conqueror; they were also bound against their will by their attachment to fame, power and privilege.

From the very beginning of Matthew's story Jesus has stepped into our shoes, taking our place, becoming our ransom. From his birth in the stable to his status as the hunted refugee to his meals with sinners, Jesus has been descending into our suffering, walking with us, offering his personal presence in the midst of our sin and brokenness. By becoming our ransom through his sacrificial death, Jesus died the death we should have died.

In the next scene, Matthew 20:29-34, Jesus encounters two blind men and demonstrates how to live out of the limelight of celebrity status. Two ordinary blind men get healed. We often forget that this little story—and most of Jesus' life—occurred away from the centers of power and influence. The real celebrities of Jesus' day—political and religious—were far removed from Jesus and his little band. By healing the blind men, Jesus demonstrates one way to break the grip of bondage to fame and power: pay attention to little people. Go to marginal places and show extraordinary love for ordinary and even lowly people. Respect the disrespected. Offer generous portions of mercy to the mercy-starved.

As our ransom Jesus took our place, dying the death we should have died. As he heals the blind men, demonstrating humble servanthood, he lives the life we should have lived. No matter how the *Forbes* list changes from year to year, Jesus alone deserves praise, adoration and worship. In his life and death and resurrection he hasn't made it to the top of the list; he *is* the list. Thankfully, as the humble king, he invites us even in our poverty and shame to join him as guests and brothers and sisters on the stage of glory.

WHO PUT YOU IN CHARGE OF US?
Matthew 21:1-27

Throughout his career as the owner of the New York Yankees, George Steinbrenner epitomized a ruthless, domineering, egotistical approach to leadership. Nicknamed "the Boss," Steinbrenner canned fourteen general managers, fired twenty-five team managers (one got the axe four times) and routinely blasted his players, even calling one high-priced superstar a "fat toad." Everybody knew that Steinbrenner was in control. On one occasion, after team manager Joe Torre requested a visit to his pregnant wife, Steinbrenner let him go but warned, "After the baby is born, your a** is mine."

A recent *New York Times* article argued that we need and even want take-charge leaders like Steinbrenner. According to leadership psychologists, "Recent research on status and power suggests brashness, entitlement, and ego are essential components of any competent leader." And when you're in power, "[you] want to stay there. . . . You are expected to live your role as a dominant, decisive, absolute authority—and to internalize it."[49] In other words, we expect leaders to sniff and get high on the influence of power.

That's why Jesus proves to be such a conundrum. Throughout Matthew's Gospel, and now especially in this series of stories, Jesus at times acts like a "decisive, absolute authority." He's the Lord, knocking over tables, cursing innocent fig trees, refusing to answer direct questions. Then he subverts expectations with his sweet tenderness, riding on a lowly donkey, embracing people with disabilities, inviting tax collectors and prostitutes to join him. In this string of four scenes in Matthew 21:1-27, Jesus displays a strange combination of abject humility and divine lordship. Naturally, people don't know what to do with him. They keep demanding, "What kind of leader are you? You're a nobody and yet you act like the world's boss. Who put you in charge around here? Just who do you think you are?"

In the first story in this passage (Mt 21:1-11), Jesus rides into Jerusalem on a donkey. It's a strange fusion of authority and humility. On the one hand, the donkey was a beast of burden for the working poor. Unlike snorting war horses, donkeys epitomized ordinariness and even powerlessness.[50] But the Gospel writers also link this image to Jesus' power and authority. In 21:4 Matthew uses his familiar preface, "This took place to fulfill what was spoken through the prophet," before quoting part of Zechariah 9:9:

Say to Daughter Zion,
"See, your king comes to you,
gentle and riding on a donkey,
and on a colt, the foal of a donkey." (Mt 21:5)

Riding on a donkey implies that Jesus, the world's rightful king, is ushering in the peace and rule of God. But, surprisingly, Matthew omits a few crucial words from the ancient prophecy—"triumphant and victorious is he." Jesus is the world's leader, Matthew suggests, but watch carefully, because he will take our standard concepts of power and authority, line them up like fish on a table, gut them, repack them with new meaning and bring them back to life.

In the second scene (Mt 21:12-22) Matthew records, "Jesus entered the temple courts and drove out all who were buying and selling there. He overturned the tables of the money changers and the benches of those selling doves" (Mt 21:12). It's always tempting to reduce Jesus to one-dimensional qualities like "compassionate" or "accepting," but this vignette reminds us that Jesus wasn't just a nice guy, even a loving nice guy. He also displayed incredible strength and authority. The word for "drove out" in verse 12 is the same word Matthew used when Jesus drove out a demon. It's easy to drive out one person, but Jesus drove out an entire strip mall filled with happy and profitable vendors.

Then in 21:14 Matthew reports that "the blind and the lame came to him at the temple, and he healed them." On one level, this scene records Jesus' quick switch from outrage over injustice to gentleness toward outcasts. But it's also a statement about his messianic authority. When David assumed power as king, he excluded the blind and the lame from entering his palace (see 2 Sam 5:8). Now Jesus, the greater-than-David king, gathers the blind and lame back into the temple. Jesus fulfills even King David's story.

It's a shocking scene because Jesus, the self-educated carpenter from Nazareth, strolls into town and acts like he owns the place. Imagine a standard Western movie where a town gets overrun by thugs until a masked stranger arrives, slinging his guns, shooting up the bad guys, defending women and children, tending the wounded and letting the good guys out of jail. At some point one of the villains hisses, "Just who do you think you are? Apparently nobody told you this is our town." Our hero twirls his gun as he coolly replies, "Not anymore, partner. I'm in charge now." Then he removes his mask and says, "Remember me? I'm the sheriff, boys. I'm back in town and I'm setting things right." Throughout this passage Jesus speaks and acts like the town-saving sheriff.

In the third scene in this passage, Matthew 21:18-22, Jesus gets hungry, spots a fig tree and doesn't find fruit, so he curses the tree, which instantly withers and dies. Some very bright people, including the atheist philosopher and mathematician Bertrand Russell, have misunderstood this passage. Based on Jesus' treatment of the fig tree, Russell rates Jesus' character lower than that of Socrates and Buddha.[51] But that misses the point. Throughout the long section of Matthew 21–22, Jesus searches for and expects to find spiritual fruitfulness as demonstrated by obedience to God and mercy toward others. Jesus is like a gardener who plants, waters, weeds and naturally anticipates a harvest. The shocking (and even offensive) aspect of this story isn't the untimely death of a fig tree; it's that Jesus, the donkey-riding carpenter from Nazareth, acts like he's the gardener for the whole world. And when we don't produce appropriate fruit, he takes it personally.

After three incidents displaying Jesus' authority and humility, the religious bigwigs are fed up. So in Matthew 21:23 they send a posse to confront Jesus and ask, "By what authority are you doing these things? . . . And who gave you this authority?" The showdown has been coming for a long time. If we look at all of chapters 1-20, we realize they're probably saying something like, "You little pipsqueak! Who do you think you are? You come from nowhere. Your followers are nobodies. You eat meals with sinners. You break our carefully ordered Sabbath laws. You interpret our Scripture. Then you come to our temple and start acting like you're in charge. Okay, big shot, if you're really the boss around here, who gave you the authority?"

In a humorous and brilliant counter move, Jesus asks them a question: "John's baptism—where did it come from? Was it from heaven, or of human origin?" (Mt 21:25). Right away the religious leaders know they're in a quandary. Answer A, John is from heaven, will lead them into a jam; Answer B, John is from men, will lead them into a pickle. Jam or pickle? They choose neither, saying, "We don't know." Unimpressed, Jesus replies, "Neither will I tell you by what authority I am doing these things" (Mt 21:27). Even as he plummets into his own crucifixion, Jesus makes his point loud and clear: I'm in charge.

All four scenes in this passage radiate practical and theological truth and beauty. On a practical level, unlike George Steinbrenner and millions of other flawed leaders—bosses, rulers, presidents, dictators, pastors, fathers and mothers—Jesus demonstrated authentic, life-giving, nonwounding leadership. He displayed the perfect balance between tenderness and strength, authority and humility, gentleness and severity. Once again, Jesus lived the life we should have lived.

But this section also quietly unveils what theologians call the "dual natures of Christ," his full divinity and full humanity. At times he seems completely human. Like every other person he feels hunger pangs (Mt 21:18) and anger at injustice (Mt 21:12). On other occasions he operates with an air of Godlike authority. He acts like he owns the temple. He freely receives praise and adoration from the masses (Mt 21:16). He implies that he's David's Lord and master (Mt 22:41-46). The Gospels present a simple, clear theological formula: Jesus is one hundred percent God and one hundred percent human. If you dilute the formula even a fraction of a percentage point in one direction or the other, it's not the gospel.

So in response to the original question posed in this passage—"Just who do you think you are?"—Matthew tells us that Jesus is both human and God: a man who hungers and the God who gives food, a man who worships and the God who receives worship, a lowly slave and the God who liberates the oppressed, the hero of the story and the God who writes all of our stories.

AND THEN WHAT HAPPENED?
Matthew 21:28–22:14

In a new collection of short stories, the editors ask a series of questions: "What is the thing that keeps us reading? Where do we find the magic of stories? Why do we care about books and tales?" For them it comes down to a simple, four-word phrase: "And then what happened?" Those are the "four words that children ask, when you pause, telling them a story. The four words you hear at the end of a chapter. The four words, spoken or unspoken, that show you, as a storyteller, that people care."[52]

Jesus knows how much we crave stories; after all, he told plenty of them. Jesus' stories grab our attention and keep us asking, "And then what happened?" Most people gravitate toward Jesus' big-name stories, such as that of the prodigal son. They usually don't recall the tales in Matthew 21:28–22:14. But with marvelous brevity, beauty and simplicity, Jesus uses these stories to crack our eyes and ears open to the wonder of God's grace—and the danger of rejecting it. These three stories encompass more than our personal salvation or our personal relationship with Jesus. In Jesus' context they also focus on how God chooses a community of people who will reflect his character as they work to restore a broken world. And yet because God's kingdom is both big and little, global and personal, we can apply these stories on a personal level as well.

In the same way that Rembrandt drew rough pencil sketches for some of his paintings, Matthew 21:28-32 looks like it could be a raw sketch for Luke 15. Both stories focus on two sons—a bad son who repents and a good son who doesn't want to repent. In Matthew, when the father asks for help, the first son bluntly says, "'I will not,'" but then he changes his mind (see Mt 21:29). The other son tells his father he wants to help, but then he never goes out into the field. When Jesus asks his followers, "Which of the two did what his father wanted?" (Mt 21:31), everybody gets the right answer.

So far, so good—a simple story suitable for children: no surprises and nothing offensive. But then Jesus adds a shocking twist: "Truly I tell you, the tax collectors and the prostitutes are entering the kingdom of God ahead of you" (Mt 21:31). The tax collectors and prostitutes believed

John the Baptist's message, while the religious leaders ignored his invitation to repent (see Mt 21:32).

In other words, the father approached despicable spiritual outsiders with an invitation, and they said no. But then, just like the prodigal son, they came to their senses and returned to the father. Then God came to the spiritual insiders, and they gave lip service to his invitation. "Oh, yes sir," they shouted and saluted, but then they walked away. Once again, Jesus criticizes people who honor him with their lips but whose hearts are far from him (see Mt 15:8).

This story cuts two ways: first, it warns those who arrogantly assume they have the inside track, when in reality they aren't obeying the Father's will. It's hard for us to imagine the depth of Jesus' offensiveness in this little story. He took the most despicable groups of sinners anyone could imagine and then said they were more spiritually advanced than the religious elites. This kind of talk could get a would-be Messiah killed.

Second, it opens a door of grace and mercy for unlikely people far from God, people who have ruined their lives by saying no to God: the toothless meth addict and the white-collar porn addict; the busy overachievers and the developmentally disabled; the obese, the anorexic and the beauty queens; the smugly self-righteous and the spiritually poor. In a hundred places this Gospel proclaims, "Come to me, all you who are weary and heavy-laden. Come to me all you screwups and little-faiths, good and bad, wheat and tares, and I will give you rest."

The second story, Matthew 21:33-46, describes the crazy love of a farmer for his vineyard. In this story Jesus reaches back to an Old Testament image for God's care for his covenant people (see, for example, Is 5:1-4). In a sense, this story captures *the* story of the entire Bible. First, God initiates a love relationship with his people. Notice that all the active verbs in verses 33 and 34 ("planted," "put a wall," "dug," "built," "rented," "moved," "approached" and "sent") begin with the farmer. The biblical love story is from beginning to end held together by God's love and energy, not ours. With persistent, patient love, the landowner continues his relationship with the vineyard even when its occupants try to throw him out.

The scene of persistent love from God's side soon degenerates into persistent rebellion from the human side. When the farmer sent his servants to collect the fruit, they "seized his servants; they beat one, killed another, and stoned a third" (Mt 21:35). This describes the overwhelmingly irrational nature of our human rebellion. God loves the vineyard with passionate intensity, but his people are "hell-bent" on rejecting that love. Like a warped bow that curves away from the bullseye, the human heart bends away from God's presence—unless God intervenes.

But the farmer matches this irrational rebellion with a more powerful irrational love. At first he continues to send his servants, but the servants continue to be pulverized. Then, for some strange reason, he chooses to send his son. "They will respect my son," he says (Mt 21:37). Why would he ever reach that conclusion? Doesn't he know the track record of these people? The evidence is overwhelming: they don't want the farmer managing their lives. Has he forgotten what they've already done to his procession of servants? Is his memory that short? Is he really that naïve?[53]

No, he's not naïve; the farmer's love pulses with intentionality. He knows exactly what he's doing. Jesus is summarizing the plot line of the entire Older Testament—and the plot line of our lives as well. God loves his people; they routinely rebel against that love; God keeps pursuing them; then, finally, God does the unthinkable: in and through Jesus he becomes one of us. God steps into the messy, bloody, ongoing cycle of violence and hatred, becoming the next and the greatest victim-ransom: "They took him [the farmer's son] and threw him out of the vineyard and killed him" (Mt 21:39).

The farmer responds by removing his original cast of tenants and using workers who will actually share the vineyard's fruit (see Mt 21:41). As with the story of the two sons, Jesus concludes with a shocking and offensive twist: "Therefore I tell you that the kingdom of God will be taken away from you and given to a people who will produce its fruit" (Mt 21:43). Once again Jesus delivers a searing one-two punch:

- The smug, self-righteous, unfruitful insiders have failed to accept Jesus and reflect the Father's heart of mercy and thus share the vineyard's fruit.

- The outsiders, the spiritual beginners, the little children and the spiritual beggars, accept Jesus and reflect the Father's heart of mercy and thus share the vineyard's fruit.

The third story in this series, Matthew 22:1-14, repeats the same themes with different images. God, this time pictured as a wedding host, initiates a cosmic love story: "The kingdom of heaven is like a king who prepared a wedding banquet for his son" (Mt 22:2). But once again the invitees irrationally reject God's invitation to the feast. In Jesus' words, "They refused to come," or, literally, they "kept refusing to come." And once again God's ability to love his unresponsive people matches and exceeds their ability to reject that love. In Matthew 22:4 the host pleads with his guests to show up, even providing a detailed description of the wedding reception menu (perhaps it said something like, "Entrée number one includes a roast rib of oxen smothered with shitake mushrooms, while entrée number two includes filet of fatted calf covered with pomegranate chutney"). Initially the guests snub the host with a passive smirk—"They paid no attention and went off" (Mt 22:5)—before they resort to their familiar violent rejection (see Mt 22:6).

Finally, just as in the two previous stories, there are consequences to this blatant rejection of God's invitation. The host fires the original list of wedding guests and reissues his invitation to a new group of people, an unlikely assortment of riffraff: "anyone you find," "the bad as well as the good" (Mt 22:9-10). The wedding host just wants the banquet hall filled with guests.

But then this final story in the trilogy takes a strange twist as Jesus ends it on a sobering note. In Matthew 22:11 the king, or wedding host, spots a guest who clearly didn't get the dress code memo. He is not "wearing wedding clothes," and he doesn't have an excuse ("the man was speechless," Mt 21:12), so the king boots him out of the wedding dance.

It's not the ending most of us expect to hear, especially from our gentle Jesus. Personally, I'd prefer a happier ending: the wedding host tells the underdressed guest, "Oops. Hey, it happens to the best of us. Come in anyway, but next time, let's be a little more careful about how we dress for weddings." Instead Jesus dishes out a brutal warning: don't come to the party unprepared.

Throughout the ages Christians have offered different interpretations of what the wedding garment represents.[54] But we can see throughout Matthew (Mt 7:21, for example) that people want to follow Jesus and get the benefits of the kingdom on their terms. So, for instance, they refuse to admit their spiritual poverty. They're offended by getting lumped in with little children (Mt 11:25-30) or, horror of horrors, with tax collectors and prostitutes. Or they assume they can sign up with Jesus but not actually follow him (Mt 8:20) or listen to him (Mt 13:1-24). Or they can respond to Jesus without building their lives on his words (Mt 7:24-27).

Throughout this Gospel Jesus has made it clear that we don't follow him on our own terms. We don't come to him with our own choice of wedding garments. As we respond to his invitation of "Come to me" (Mt 11:28), he will change our heart first and then our behavior and relationships to others. In other words, we'll start wearing the right clothing for the wedding feast, removing the soiled clothes of racism, bitterness, self-righteousness, anger and rage, lust and marital unfaithfulness, dishonesty, materialism, anxiety, contempt toward vulnerable people and greed—to name just a few of our inappropriate garments. But in circling back to Jesus' doorway statement in Matthew 5:3, "Blessed are the poor in spirit," we'll also realize this isn't a heroic journey for spiritual superstars. It's a simple journey for little-faiths who constantly cry out for mercy.

JESUS' QUIET SUPERPOWER
Matthew 22:15-46

On a recent airplane ride I sat next to a bright young woman who offered her theory of religion. "It's sort of like Greek mythology," she informed me, "where people utilized mythic storytelling as a vehicle to explain frightening natural phenomenon. For instance, they conjured up stories about Zeus sending bolts of lightning as a way to understand weather patterns. Religion does the same thing. It's all totally irrational, using mythic symbols and stories in an attempt to explain the inexplicable. But due to our intellectual advancements, we don't need myths or religion anymore."

I replied, "Wow, that's an interesting theory. Unfortunately, and no offense, that's a very narrow, reductionist and culturally imperialistic viewpoint on a very broad and complex subject." Completely unfazed, she said, "Well, of course you see it that way. You're probably a religious person, so you have faith while people like me rely on reason."

My airplane seatmate was expressing a common opinion in our culture: reason and faith exist in separate realms; you can have only one or the other. As popular author Sam Harris contends, "Where we have reasons for what we believe, we have no need of faith; where we have no reasons, we have lost both our connection to the world and to one another. People who harbor strong convictions without evidence [i.e., religious people] belong at the margins of societies."[55] In other words, like fire and ice, faith and reason can't coexist in the same place (in Harris's view, reason eventually consumes the ice block of faith).

Jesus' life rebuts this assumption. Throughout Matthew's Gospel, Jesus has demonstrated his tender, compassionate heart, but now in a series of three "controversy stories," he displays his rational, brilliant mind. The result will leave Jesus' critics with a stark conclusion: Jesus is claiming to be the Messiah, the long-awaited Son of David (which Matthew promised all the way back in Jesus' genealogy in chapter 1). As the Son of David and the full and perfect human being, Jesus perfectly reveals reason and faith, love and logic. As a "superhero," Jesus has a vast array of superpowers—powers to heal disease, calm storms, defeat the demonic, love the unlovable. But one stands out in this passage: his sheer brilliance. In particular, the stories in Mathew 22:15-46 reveal three characteristics of Jesus' brilliance:

- the ability to think deeply about complex issues of politics, theology and philosophy

- the ability to think creatively, viewing subjects from fresh perspectives

- the ability to communicate clearly, using concise and simple language, speaking without verbal clutter (or, as we might say, the ability to cut to the chase)

The first story starts with the Pharisees making plans "to trap him in his words" (Mt 22:15) by forcing Jesus to make an inflammatory comment about a touchy political matter. Flattering him with the title of "Teacher," they ask, "Is it right to pay the imperial tax to Caesar or not?"

It's a dicey question. In that day your views on taxation could get you killed. Prior to Jesus' ministry a rebel named Judas had led an anti-taxation revolt, which the Romans crushed by pinning Judas and his cohorts to crosses.[56] If Jesus answers, "No, it is not lawful to pay taxes," he's a dangerous political rebel. If he answers, "Yes, it is lawful to pay taxes," he's clearly in cahoots with the unjust oppressors. It's a nicely laid trap, filled with a slab of bloody bait.

Instead of grabbing the bait, Jesus asks to see the coin used to pay taxes (Mt 22:19). As they remove it from their pockets and hand it over, Jesus has exposed their hypocrisy (since they are participating in the dreaded tax system) and provided a powerful object lesson. "Whose image is this?" Jesus asks. "Whose inscription?" When they say, "Caesar's," Jesus gives his verdict: "Give back to Caesar what is Caesar's, and to God what is God's" (see Mt 22:20-21). With this brilliant and incisive answer, Jesus refuses the bait and turns the tables on his critics, forcing a series of questions back on them: Are they the ones who are compromised? Have they really given full allegiance to God? Are they playing games, keeping Caesar happy while speaking of God?[57] After this incident, "they left him and went away" (Mt 22:22).

In the second controversy story, found in Matthew 22:23-33, it's the Sadducees who approach Jesus. Known for their hip, urbane appreciation of Greek culture, the Sadducees, like other rational intellectuals of that day, rejected any form of bodily afterlife. To them the concept of a resurrection was crude and uncool. So reaching back to an obscure and largely unused Old Testament text, they concocted a bizarre story about seven brothers who died one after the other, each marrying the same woman according to a brother's duties (see Deut 25:5). So, they ask Jesus, after all of these weddings and funerals, when the resurrection comes (snicker, snicker), "whose wife will she be of the seven, since all of them were married to her?" (Mt 22:28).[58]

Notice that in this scene Jesus isn't moved by compassion. Instead he employs his critical powers to their logic. "You are in error," he says, "because you do not know the Scriptures or the power of God" (Mt 22:29). According to Jesus, the Sadducees' problem is both spiritual (they don't fathom the power of God) and intellectual (they don't know the Scriptures). Jesus dismantles their supposition about the resurrection—namely, that the resurrection yields the same set of relationships we had in this life. In Jesus' mind, resurrection life is much more nuanced and creative than the Sadducees' (and their Greek counterparts') literal and cynical ideas about the afterlife. Instead, Jesus contends, "At the resurrection people will neither marry nor be given in marriage; they will be like the angels in heaven" (Mt 22:30).[59]

Jesus then leads them to a central Old Testament text (Ex 3:6) where God meets Moses at the burning bush and declares, "I am the God of Abraham, the God of Isaac, and the God of Jacob" (Mt 22:32). And he makes another logical point: if God is still in relationship with three dead guys (who had God's promise of resurrection life beyond the grave), then those dead guys must still exist.

Jesus is responding to the Sadducees by appealing to their brains, not just their hearts. And his conclusions about the resurrection result from the total immersion of his mind in the biblical texts. In Jesus' humanity we find reason fused with faith, a clear mind joined with a warm heart.

In the third and final controversy story, in Matthew 22:34-39, the Pharisees are back for a rematch. They present an "expert" who asks, "Teacher, which is the greatest commandment in the Law?" (Mt 22:36). It's a respectable question. Out of the maze of six hundred and thirteen Jewish laws, how would the religious pollsters rank them? Jesus doesn't even pause to think as he ticks off the top two: " 'Love the Lord your God with all your heart and with all your soul and with all your mind.' . . . 'Love your neighbor as yourself' " (Mt 22:37-39). Again, Jesus responds with a warm heart and a clear mind. Because he has thought so deeply about this question, he quickly summarizes the Old Testament by focusing on two commandments found in Deuteronomy 6:5 and Leviticus 19:18 respectively. According to Jesus, everything hangs on these two large hooks.

As an important side note, in Matthew (as well as in the Gospel of Mark) Jesus substitutes "mind" for the word "might" found in the original verse in Deuteronomy 6:5. In other words, Jesus himself seems to stress the role of the mind in loving God. We love God with our whole self, including our brain.

Jesus concludes the three controversy stories by switching roles from questioned to questioner. After receiving four questions, Jesus draws from Psalm 110 and asks four questions (see Mt 22:42-45):

• What do you think about the Christ?

• Whose son is he?

• How is it that David, speaking by the Holy Spirit, calls him "Lord"?

• If then David calls him "Lord," how can he (i.e., the Christ) be David's son?

Jesus' questions challenge the religious leaders' preconceived notions about the Messiah. It's a brilliant (and ultimately gentle) attempt to change their hearts by changing their thoughts. Jesus is merely trying to plant a seed and let it grow. He seems to be saying, "Why don't you try looking at the Messiah in a new light? Could he be David's son (human) and yet at the same time the divine Lord?" Will Jesus' questions hit home? Will these seeds blossom and bear fruit? Only time will tell.[60]

Notice the collective responses to Jesus' quiet but simple superpower:

• "When they heard this, they were amazed. So they left him and went away" (Mt 22:22).

• "When the crowds heard this, they were astonished at his teaching" (Mt 22:33).

• "No one could say a word in reply, and from that day on no one dared to ask him any more questions" (Mt 22:46).[61]

Fully God and fully human, Jesus lived the life we should have lived. What does it mean to be a fully alive human being? Certainly we will feel deeply, but as we follow Jesus, we will also strive to think deeply. This doesn't mean that every disciple must become an intellectual and a scholar. The greatest command is to love, not to think. But as Jesus himself said, we are called to love God with and through our minds. Therefore, as a fully alive follower of Jesus, like my Lord and master I will commit to use my mind, thinking deeply, reading widely, studying old texts, creatively making new connections and drawing conclusions so that I can grow in love for God and others.

CHRISTIANS BEHAVING BADLY
Matthew 23:1-39

My friend Walter calls me his favorite Christian; I call him my favorite atheist. Walter is dumbfounded by the level of hypocrisy found among religious people. During a casual conversation I asked him how he "converted" to atheism, and his answer surprised me:

> It started when I was sixteen years old waiting to enter a worship service. My whole family used to attend church every Sunday at a posh downtown church in Atlanta. One day as I was sitting on the steps watching the people stream in, a black family approached the church's front door. Before they could get in, a couple of ushers intercepted them and said, "Excuse me, but this is a whites only church. There's a church for colored people down the road." Surprised and humiliated, the family slipped back down the steps and onto the street. This was before the civil rights movement, but that scene revolted and enraged me. On that Sunday morning, sitting on those beautiful church steps, my faith shattered. Later on while attending college I discovered the philosophical framework for my atheism, but that was my initial "conversion."

I'm not sure if Walter knows how much he and Jesus have in common. Both Walter and Jesus are repulsed by Christians behaving badly. In Matthew 23, Jesus lambasts the religious leaders of his day who weren't reflecting the beauty of the coming kingdom. This chapter isn't pretty or nice. After taking a big wind-up, Jesus hurls a series of unrelenting, unsparing strikes against religious hypocrisy. We like to read this chapter and cheer for Jesus, as if we're fans sitting in the bleachers. We're on Jesus' team and he's creaming the evil Pharisees. Unfortunately, we miss the fact that while this passage takes aim at the first-century religious leaders, it also takes aim at our hearts, especially for those who are spiritual leaders. On nearly every page of this Gospel, Jesus critiques false religion and distorted spirituality—and the critique isn't just for his direct hearers; it's a critique of you and me.

One key word sets the tone for Jesus' assessment: "woe," as in "watch out" or "you're in big trouble" or "you'd better duck." The

woes keep piling on top of each other until the tally finally stops at
seven. It's a landslide victory for Jesus, but this isn't a game; he is
methodically dismantling the danger of hypocrisy.[62] It's a long, with-
ering critique, but Jesus emphasizes the following telltale signs of religious hypocrites:

1. Hypocrites don't walk the path. In Jesus' words, "They do not practice what they preach" (Mt 23:3). In particular, they do not follow
   Jesus' little way of discipleship. Instead they live in *theathenai*, or they
   make a theater of their lives. They want the best and brightest awards.
   They are narcissistic servants of God. Jesus' way, however, is for those
   going down, not up, for the poor in spirit, not for spiritual experts, for
   the unnoticed rather than the applauded. For the hypocrites of Jesus'
   day, good deeds weren't interesting or energizing unless they were
   noticed, praised and rewarded by other human beings.

2. Hypocrites keep others off the path. As Jesus puts it, "They tie up
   heavy, cumbersome loads and put them on other people's shoulders,
   but they themselves are not willing to lift a finger to move them. . . .
   You shut the door of the kingdom of heaven in people's faces. You
   yourselves do not enter, nor will you let those enter who are trying to"
   (see Mt 23:4, 13-14). For the Pharisees of Jesus' day this meant making rules that were virtually impossible for ordinary people living ordinary lives. Their motto seemed to be, "Do as I say, not as I do." As
   a result, they were barred from experiencing the mercy of the living
   God in their lives.

   In our day, we can continue to "tie up heavy loads and put them
   on men's shoulders" by insisting that people follow Jesus' difficult
   way without offering any assistance or sacrificing our comforts to
   help. For instance, we might take a strong stand for the sanctity of
   life (which we should), but then we ignore the single mom and her
   Down syndrome son. Or we stand for the unique beauty of hus-
   band-wife sexual love (which we should), but then we turn a blind
   eye to the loneliness of a young gay man who doesn't have a cozy
   nuclear family like we do. In other words, we basically send this
   message: "I'm not going to lower the standard for you; you must

struggle alone against difficult odds. But, my friend, you can sure count on me to warn you about the high cost of spiritual failure— from a distance, of course. God forbid that following Jesus should cause me and my family to suffer for your sake. God forbid that I should inconvenience myself so you don't have to be alone. That would be unfair!"

3. Hypocrites focus on externals. In woes four through six Jesus accuses the religious leaders of cleaning the outside of the cup while the inside seethes with filth. For Jesus, two things sully and rot the inside of our heart: greed (or economic injustice) and self-indulgence (or sexual immorality).[63] In our culture, we tend to separate these two stances. We must be either (a) for social justice or (b) for sexual purity. But in this series of woes Jesus weds social justice with sexual purity, just as the Old Testament prophets did. Cleaning the inside of our cup, becoming Christlike and holy, involves heeding the cry of the poor and avoiding pornography, feeding the hungry and living a chaste life until marriage, fighting for fair housing and championing the sanctity of life. Almost everyone in our culture separates these two categories; the community of salt and light must honor both kinds of cleanness in the beauty of Jesus.

4. Hypocrites major on the minors. Finally, the ancient hypocrites of Jesus' day passionately emphasized minor points of the spiritual life while ignoring or minimizing the major points. In Jesus' example, they've diligently tithed their mint, dill and cumin but then neglected "the more important matters of the law—justice, mercy and faithfulness" (Mt 23:23). As a result, they "strain out a gnat [the smallest unclean animal found in the Levitical dietary code] but swallow a camel [the largest unclean animal]" (Mt 23:24). In other words, they practice diligence in minor matters (notice that Jesus doesn't dispense with these minor matters) while being slack about major matters like loving one's neighbor, forgiving enemies, displaying mercy to sinful people and calling on Jesus in their need.

I'm not sure what I told my friend Walter, but I wish I would have said something like this: "Walter, this may surprise you, but you and Jesus actually have much in common. You both hate any form of hypocrisy, especially allegedly God-sanctioned hypocrisy.

"Those church ushers you described—and that entire system of church-based institutional racism—didn't please Jesus. They weren't acting in Jesus' name. At one point in his ministry, Jesus even got rip-roaring mad when supposedly godly people barred others from getting in the front doors of God's presence. On this issue, Walter, you and Jesus are definitely on the same side. For me, the solution to that church's hurtful racism would be to act more like Jesus, not less like Jesus."

In the end, this passage doesn't just focus on those nasty, uptight, hyperreligious Pharisees; instead it leads us to focus on the beauty and glory of Jesus himself. In Matthew 23:34, after this relentless series of red-hot woes, Jesus offers a surprising and poignant statement: "Therefore I am sending you prophets and sages and teachers." After reading that line we should think, *Wait a minute! I thought only God could send prophets and sages and teachers.* In a startling claim, Jesus is stating that he not only existed during the days of Jeremiah and Isaiah and Hosea, but he dispatched prophets.

In the end, Jesus breaks into a heartrending love song for his wayward people. Rather than scream, "Out of my sight," he passionately cries out, "How often I have longed to gather your children together, as a hen gathers her chicks under her wings" (Mt 23:37). Once again, Jesus' heart breaks like that of a jilted lover (see also Mt 11:20-30). Although this passage brims with woes and threats, it isn't just a tirade against evil. Each hypocrite addressed in Matthew 23 is a dearly beloved human being for whom Christ will die. Even in the midst of this unrelenting assault, Jesus fights for the hearts of the "elder brother" Pharisees (see also Lk 15:24-32).

That's why we have to be careful as we apply this passage. Rounding up and then blasting the "bad guys" produces a splendid adrenaline rush. I often hear people heap unrelenting scorn on "those Pharisees," which includes "church people" who don't run church the way I want it run—or just people who hurt my feelings. Our working assumption often sounds like this: "You are more pharisaical than I, so you deserve my seething contempt. Unlike you, I am free from judgmental attitudes (except toward judgmental people like you)."

In other words, as we rush to expose and stamp out the hypocrites in our midst, we become the new wave of phonies. In our war against violence, at times we merely shed more blood.

So based on Jesus' words I have to critique myself on a regular basis. As I condemn hypocrisy, do I hunger and thirst for righteousness? Jesus came to restore all things; is that my passionate desire for everyone—even the hypocrites? As I confront distorted spirituality, do I confront it with tears in my eyes and a lump in my throat? As I critique others, do I allow my heavenly Father to critique me for my unhelpful attitudes and words?

If I can answer yes to these questions, Jesus' Spirit lives in me even as I confront religious hypocrisy. If not, I should keep my mouth shut and ask God to search my heart, exposing the log in my eye.

A LONG, PAINFUL, MESSY BIRTH
Matthew 24:1-35

Over the course of my life, some very knowledgeable people (a mother and four sisters, then a wife, a daughter and numerous female friends) have told me that childbirth is long, messy and painful. And after watching my four children enter the world, I can only stand in awe at the women who walk through this process. Apparently human beings are one of the few mammals that experience intense pain during child delivery. Nevertheless, every day courageous women all over the globe endure the pain of childbirth because they know the end result: a living, breathing baby boy or girl.

According to Jesus, the process of giving birth—complete with all the contractions, anguished cries, sweat and blood—is an apt metaphor for the coming of the kingdom of God. After predicting all sorts of painful events—deceptions, wars, famines and earthquakes—Jesus says, "All these are the beginning of birth pains" (Mt 24:8). In other words, there's a new world coming. God with us will restore the brokenness, making all things as fresh as a newborn baby. But as history lurches forward, the pain of life will become intense and it will seem to never end. That's half of Jesus' message in Matthew 24:1-35: things will get worse. The contractions will intensify in duration and frequency.

But then Jesus promises that things will get better. When the kingdom of heaven comes in fullness we'll find joy and relief beyond our wildest dreams. That tiny mustard seed will bloom into an incredible nation-sheltering tree and world-nourishing loaf. So hold on, Jesus says—through the pain, through the contractions, through the long day and night of suffering—because there's a new world waiting to be born.

Matthew, Mark and Luke all agree that Jesus' long discourse in this section started with a shocking statement about the temple. For the people of that day, the temple was the most stunning, beautiful, sophisticated building that had ever existed. It also served as the center of religious life. So imagine the shock of Jesus' comment about the temple's imminent ruin: "Not one stone here will be left on another; every one will be thrown down" (Mt 24:2). For the average American that would be like someone predicting, "By the end of the month, every single symbol of national pride—the White House, the Washington Monument, the Jefferson Memorial and the Lincoln Memorial, to name just a few—along with every church building in the country, will be reduced to rubble." We would shake our heads and say, "You've got to be kidding! Not in my lifetime!" But in this passage Jesus predicts the temple's demise and much worse, because that's how childbirth progresses: it always gets worse before it gets better.

Not surprisingly, this sprawling passage has caused much confusion for Jesus' followers throughout the years. New Testament scholars are still debating the exact timetable for the "contractions" Jesus described.[64] Was he referring to immediate events or distant news? Did his predictions apply just to Jesus' disciples or should we sift through current events and look for clues of Jesus' coming in our day? The best answer is that Jesus wanted us to view these events through a double lens: a close-up lens (the immediate future of Jesus' day) and a long-distance lens (the end of history or perhaps future traumatic events throughout history).[65]

Regarding the close-up viewpoint, we know that soon after Jesus' life historians recorded major famines (A.D. 46), earthquakes (A.D. 61), "wars and rumors of wars" (A.D. 66-73) and, of course, false messiahs and false prophets. Within a generation after Jesus spoke the words in this chapter, the Roman armies marched into Jerusalem and, stone by glorious stone, dismantled the temple. As a forewarning to this unthinkable destruction, Jesus said, "So when you see standing in the holy place 'the abomination that causes desolation,' spoken of through the prophet Daniel—let the reader understand—then let those who are in Judea flee to the mountains" (Mt 24:15-16). In A.D. 70 the Roman army fulfilled this prediction: according to the early church historian Eusebius, Christians fled to Pella so they wouldn't get trapped in Jerusalem.[66]

But we know that these convulsive events didn't lead to the end of human history, so Jesus also wanted us to look through a long-distance lens. Every age, and every age of the church, has experienced world-shaking, faith-jarring tribulations. In the past year alone earthquakes have devastated parts of China and Chile while nearly annihilating Haiti and Japan. Today wars and armed conflicts rumble throughout Iraq, Afghanistan, Somalia, Sudan and Mexico. With the constant threat of terrorism, "rumors of war" hang like smog over formerly safe places like the United States. Famines, violence, the global sex trade, AIDS, possible pandemics and persecution—all of these could compose the modern day "birth pains" mentioned by Jesus. So although Jesus' discourse in this chapter fits the first generation of the church, it also fits every age, especially the church that has suffered, is suffering or will suffer. Every age has the potential to experience "great distress, unequaled from the beginning of the world until now—and never to be equaled again" (Mt 24:21).

The double-lens approach to this passage also helps explain the perpetual existence of those pesky, faith-rotting spiritual termites—false messiahs, false prophets and false teachers. "Watch out" (literally, "keep watching out"), Jesus warns, "that no one deceives you. For many will come in my name, claiming, 'I am the Messiah'" (Mt 24:4-5). According to Jesus, these false prophets will flash impressive spiritual resumes. They will perform "great signs and wonders" (Mt 24:24). With an air of authority, they will declare Jesus' exact whereabouts: "There he is, out in the desert. . . . Here he is, in the inner room." Unlike those boring ordinary disciples, these "messiahs," prophets and teachers will talk and act like spiritual experts. But Jesus tells us that we won't need their expertise and insider knowledge. When he returns, it will be as obvious as lightning stretching across the sky, a kettle of vultures circling a carcass (see Mt 24: 28) or a darkened sky filled with falling stars (see Mt 24:29).[67] When Jesus returns the nations will see him and start weeping.[68]

This chapter's crescendo of birth pains—false teachers with their phony spirituality, wars and rumors of wars, earthquakes and famines, persecution and hatred—will cause many to turn away from the faith and their love to grow cold (Mt 24:10, 12). When all hell breaks loose, when the world around us shatters, when darkness falls and everyone starts looting in the streets, it's tempting to plunge into the cold night and grab what we can. With sober and simple words, Jesus warns the church in every age, "See, I have told you ahead of time" (Mt 24:25).

In the midst of earth-shattering global news, it's tempting to revert to our default mode of frenetic activity—do more, look busy, try harder, sign up for bigger projects, stomp out more evil. Or perhaps it's more tempting to numb the pain, disengage from the world's plight and hang on until Jesus comes back. We vacillate between heroic activism and cowardly escapism. According to this passage, neither option would please Jesus. Instead, he asks for ordinary practices that help us stay present to him and to the world around us: watch out (Mt 24:4), keep your love warm (Mt 24:12), stand firm (Mt 24:13) and endure the labor pains. Even as the world seems to unravel under our feet, Jesus invites us to follow him, living one day at a time (Mt 6:34), trusting our Father for daily bread (Mt 6:8), practicing forgiveness (Mt 6:14-15), making peace with our neighbors (Mt 5:9), shining a light into dark corners (Mt 5:16), listening to Jesus (Mt 17:5) and being with the God who is with us (Mt 11:28). God's promise to be with us makes it possible to remain steadfast.

As we continue with him, Jesus offers an amazing promise: "This gospel of the kingdom will be preached in the whole world as a testimony to all nations" (Mt 24:14). It's the theme of this passage again: things will get worse, then things will get better. But how? After all, birth pains seem to dominate history and today's news. How or why would anything get better? And how could Jesus give this extraordinary promise to such an unlikely group of followers, the little faith band of spiritual paupers, those hated and hunted non-experts, the community that waits in anguish like a woman in childbirth? Somehow in the midst of their poverty and gentleness they proclaim the good news to the whole world.

Notice that Jesus does not say, "Yes, things will get worse, but keep your chin up and keep trying harder to preach the good news anyway." He says the gospel "will be preached in the whole world." The message of Jesus' transforming power will be preached not just in a few places by timid disciples; it will be shared with the whole world and to all the nations. Jesus knows it will happen—just as sinners will be forgiven, just as the mustard seed will become a huge tree, just as the blind will see, just as lepers will become whole, just as the crucified Messiah will rise again after three days.

In one sense, this passage prefigures the story of Jesus' death and resurrection. As Jesus was misunderstood, arrested, betrayed and killed only to rise again in splendor and new life, so the church, united with God with us, is also called to suffer and rise again. The second-century theologian Justin Martyr claimed, "But the greater the number of persecutions which are inflicted upon us, so much the greater the number of other [persons] who become devout believers through the name of Jesus."[69] It's a classic redemption story: we're not spared the hard things, but in the sovereign plan of God, the pain turns into something good and beautiful—just as labor pains lead to a new baby.

The transfiguration in Matthew 17 reminded us that despite the peasant garb Jesus is the king. Now Jesus speaks about himself: "All the peoples of the earth will . . . see the Son of Man coming on the clouds of heaven, with power and great glory" (Mt 24:30). At a specific point in the future, Jesus' identity will become unmistakable. His glory will be obvious to all of creation. Born in a stable, hunted as a refugee, plunged into the waters of baptism, the one who still humbles himself through his flawed church, Jesus will return not as a lowly beggar but as the glorious Lord to make all things new (Rev 21:5). And when that happens, it will have been worth the wait—and even the anguish of giving birth.

PLANTING GARDENS IN JUNKYARDS
Matthew 24:36–25:30

My friend Amy doesn't always appreciate institutional Christianity. In her mind a lot of organized religion doesn't help people; at times it either hurts them or is a colossal waste of time, churning up effort and money that could be spent on racial reconciliation, the tutoring of Somali immigrants or a microloan for a Bolivian sandal-maker.

So on Palm Sunday I took her to a little church in a drug-infested area of downtown Atlanta. We worshiped in a small room with sixty people, a mixed group of blacks and whites, and the pastor preached on Jesus' triumphal entry into Jerusalem on Palm Sunday. Then he invited the entire congregation to get out of our seats, leave the building, walk across an abandoned lot strewn with chunks of concrete, and march through the neighborhood, which was filled with burnt and boarded-up houses. It felt like we were walking through a war zone. In the midst of these sad signs of ugliness and despair, the pastor led us to a beautiful garden, a one-acre plot with new trees, raised flower beds, green grass and picnic tables. Then he told the story of how the church, compelled by their hope in Christ, had reclaimed this plot of land, purchasing it from an auto junkyard so they could create beauty in the midst of wreckage.

Sometimes when Christians think about Christ's second coming they want to engage only in "heavenly" or "otherworldly" activities. But Matthew 24:36–25:30 contains a "worldly" approach to hope that's as earthy as planting a garden in a junkyard. This doesn't mean we can dilute Jesus' message about his second coming. This passage starts with some very clear words about the end of the world as we know it. In dramatic fashion Jesus promises to come again and finish the restoration of all things, which produces a new, improved and perfected creation. The miracles he's done so far—healing lepers, curing the blind, calming storms—serve merely as trailer clips to the real show. But at the end of Matthew 24, Jesus warns that the suddenness of his coming will catch many people unprepared. In his words, "No one knows about that day or hour" (Mt 24:36 NIV 1984). For some people it will feel like unpleasant guests are crashing a wedding party, just like the floodwaters crashed the party scene in Noah's day (Mt 24:37-38). For others it will feel like a burglar is sneaking into their home (Mt 24:43-44). With these strong images, Jesus warns us to "keep watch" (Mt 24:42) and "be ready" (Mt 24:44).

Jesus also helps us sort out how to get ready for his coming. How do we stay alert so it doesn't catch us off guard, overwhelmed and ultimately lost? Surprisingly, at least perhaps to people like Amy, Jesus never told us to prepare for his return with a spiritually disengaged escapism, withdrawing from this world's pain and joys, hanging on by our fingernails until he extracts us from this evil place. Instead, by presenting three images of readiness—a household, a wedding and a pot of money—Jesus tells us to prepare for his return and for our eternal destiny by caring more and not less about our present life.

Jesus begins by telling us that staying alert for his return means caring for our household, "to give them their food at the proper time" (Mt 24:45). Feeding people at the right time involves simple, ordinary acts of love for people who need you. In our day, it's the equivalent of going to the grocery story, buying chicken breasts and rice, cooking the ingredients, setting the table, eating the meal together, cleaning the dishes and sweeping the kitchen floor. In other words, preparing for Jesus' return means completing the unspectacular physical duties required to run a household.

Certainly we should start with those who are nearest to us—our spouse, children, friends. This is our literal household. But according to Jesus' vision for the kingdom (see Mt 5:38-48), our household extends beyond this exclusive unit of nuclear family and a few likable friends. Throughout Matthew's Gospel we've watched Jesus expand the concept to include unlikely people—the marginalized and forgotten, unattractive people with oozing wounds, sinners who don't meet our standards of goodness and sometimes even our enemies. They are also destined for the care of our household.

For Jesus, our purpose isn't fulfilled when we get a job and a house; it's fulfilled as we care for our household—the people (and the places where those people live) who need our hands-on care. Thus preparing for Jesus' return moves us to ask searching questions: what is my household? Who is included under the roof of my household? I can't care for everyone on the planet, but how am I caring for the people in my life? Am I faithful to my household responsibilities? (Notice that once again Jesus requires faithfulness, not success; see Mt 24:45.) Or am I careless and negligent? In Matthew 24:49 Jesus uses the image of the servant in charge beating up his fellow servants. The implication is that we can wound others with our hurtful words or our lack of loving initiative.

How we live in response to these questions leads to either blessing by the master ("He will put him in charge of all of his possessions," Mt 24:47) or trouble from the master ("He will cut him to pieces and assign him a place with the hypocrites," Mt 24:51). Jesus uses these strong metaphors to make a clear point: households matter because people matter to God. So preparing for Jesus' return never leads to loveless escapism; instead it curves us back into the world with down-to-earth acts of love and service.

Back in Matthew 9:15, Jesus referred to himself as the world's bridegroom. In one sense the Bible is one long story about marriage: it starts with a wedding in Genesis 2 and it ends with a wedding in Revelation 21. God wants to marry his people (see, for example, Jeremiah 2 and the entire book of Hosea), so when Jesus implied, "Yes, I'm the bridegroom," it must have sent shockwaves of anger, confusion and perhaps excitement into the lives of the people who first encountered him.

Now in Matthew 25:1-13 he's doing it again. Jesus is implying that he's the world's bridegroom, the fulfiller of the great big wedding story between God and the human race. If this is true, if Jesus is who he claims to be and one day he'll return to finish the wedding he's started, there's only one proper response: celebrate! Party on like this is the world's greatest wedding. In other words, live with radical joy right now, in this life, not just later when Jesus returns.

Unfortunately, in this story, the bridegroom's apparent delay ("The bridegroom was a long time in coming," Mt 25:5) squeezes the joy out of the wedding party. The real problem isn't that the attendants fell asleep— both the foolish and the wise virgins did—but that the foolish virgins weren't prepared to celebrate with the groom. The rendezvous in Matthew 25:5 is a joyful prewedding receiving line in honor of the groom, just as we often make a joyful postwedding receiving line to hug, kiss and throw rice. In Jesus' day, the groom's friends and family were required to stay awake and alert for the groom. Not staying awake would have been an insult. Joyless, sluggish, lackluster partyers were not tolerated. According to Craig Keener, "Palestinian Jewish people regarded weddings as critical social events . . . and a breach of etiquette was therefore serious."[70]

Again, hope for Jesus' return gently arcs into our life in the present, causing us to live with joyful anticipation right now. When Amy and I attended the service in that tiny, inner-city church, we were overwhelmed by the depth of the congregation's joy. Surrounded by gangs, drug wars, charred houses and ugly slabs of concrete, they meet every Sunday and sing with gusto. In the middle of the service they greet each other with hugs and kisses, and even Amy and I received a hug from everyone in the room. These people know their bridegroom has come and he will come again. They're my new mentors in how to prepare for Jesus' return.

In Matthew 25:14 Jesus, the master of metaphors, switches to a new image: "Again, it will be like a man going on a journey, who called his servants and entrusted his wealth to them." The master gives his three servants different levels of wealth—five talents, three talents and one talent. In case you think the master gypped the one-talent guy, keep in mind that a talent was the greatest unit of money in Jesus' day. One denarius was a day's wage; one talent equaled ten thousand denarii or ten thousand days' worth of earnings—about $1.8 million.[71] So even the one-talent guy hit the jackpot.

In this parable Jesus returns to one of his primary themes: the utterly lavish, outlandish generosity of God. That's the heavenly Father Jesus knew—as no one else has ever known him ("No one knows the Father except the Son," Mt 11:27). The God Jesus knew (and the God he was, as God with us) sent his sunshine on the just and the unjust (Mt 5:45), flung good seed in his fields (Mt 13:1, 24), put new wine into old wineskins (Mt 9:17) and called flawed people to become bold and remarkable disciples (Mt 10:1-4). According to Jesus, God his Father is better, kinder and more generous than we could ever imagine.

So the question becomes: as we wait for this gracious God with us to come again, how will we spend the jackpot he allotted to us? We didn't earn it. We just got lucky—or, more accurately, we "received" it through sheer grace (see Mt 25:16, 18). And now, through even more sheer grace, God the Father gives us the freedom to manage, spend and increase it.

Notice the active, creative, initiative-taking verbs in this story: "The man who had received five bags of gold *went at once* and *put his money to work* and *gained* five bags more" (Mt 25:16).

In contrast the third servant, the one-talent guy, proceeds to slink away from any form of hopeful creativity. Instead, he justifies his passivity by blaming the master. He basically says, "I have to escape and hide and it's your fault. You're unfair and you might condemn me if I fail." But throughout this Gospel we've seen the disciples fail—big, frequent failures are on almost every page—and yet the mercy of Jesus abounds even more. So there is no excuse for this servant's cringing lack of courage. The fear of failure is no excuse. Preparing for Jesus' return implies taking risks and living creatively.

In all three stories hope for Jesus' return makes us more engaged in this life right here, right now. Like a boomerang, we fling hope into the future, looking for Jesus' return, waiting for the coming bridegroom, but then the boomerang circles back, gliding toward where we stand today until it finally bonks us on the forehead. In other words, yearning for the restoration of all things causes us to live better today—serving, celebrating and risking. At times it's as practical as planting a garden in a junkyard.

Amy was impressed. Over the next few weeks I overheard her excitedly tell this story at least four times. "I went to church with my friend Matt," she stated, "and you would not believe what this church has done." I think that's what Jesus had in mind when he told us we were salt and light. So, thank you, little church in downtown Atlanta. My friend Amy saw your good deeds and, in her own small way, she glorified our Father in heaven (Mt 5:16).

JESUS' VERSION OF THE BUTTERFLY EFFECT
Matthew 25:31-46

On an ordinary winter day in 1961, an MIT meteorologist named Edward Lorenz ran some routine experiments and found some unusual results. He discovered that tiny and seemingly insignificant changes in his data could produce huge differences in the final result. At first, Lorenz and other scientists in the field of chaos theory explained this by referring to "the sensitive dependence on initial data." Fortunately Lorenz also used a more poetic term—"the butterfly effect." In 1972, at the urging of a colleague, Lorenz presented a scientific paper titled "Predictability: Does the Flap of a Butterfly's Wings in Brazil Set off a Tornado in Texas?" According to Lorenz's theory, the butterfly won't directly cause a tornado, but it might start a chain reaction that leads to profound changes in worldwide weather patterns. In others words, even tiny, insignificant movements or actions can produce huge changes that affect millions of people.[72]

In Matthew 25:31-46 Jesus describes a similar "butterfly effect" for the spiritual life. At its core, this spiritual butterfly effect states that even tiny deeds of love done for little people have huge results. Or, if we break it down a little further, it could look like this:

> Small, seemingly insignificant acts of love, such as visiting someone or making a meal at a homeless shelter or offering hospitality . . .
>
> . . . done on behalf of apparently unimportant, powerless, invisible people, such as an immigrant, a fetus, a soldier with post-traumatic stress disorder or a drunk homeless man . . .[73]
>
> . . . produce huge results, such as providing warmth and comfort for the homeless man, which in some real sense gladdens the heart of Jesus.

This passage contains Jesus' last official teaching in Matthew's teaching-filled Gospel. He leaves behind this story as he goes to the cross. It's so like Jesus, especially the Gospel-according-to-Matthew Jesus. Throughout this account Jesus has revealed the Father's overflowing heart of mercy for "good people" and "bad people" (Mt 5:45). He has defended the mercy-deprived and stated his mission in terms of mercy-giving (Mt 9:9-11). Now in this final teaching segment he again focuses on mercy. In particular, he addresses his disciples, those who have received his mercy, and asks them to display the Father's heart and his heart of mercy to other human beings.

For Jesus mercy isn't just an abstract theory or an inaccessible ideal, like a dusty old book perched on a shelf. No, for Jesus mercy remains utterly accessible, practical and "doable." Notice the specific actions of

mercy listed in this passage (Jesus states them twice so we won't forget): feed the hungry, bring water to the thirsty, invite lonely people
into your house,[74] give clothing to the naked, visit the imprisoned and
spend time with sick people (Mt 25:35-36). Nothing on this list exceeds our grasp. Ordinary people can fulfill Jesus' high call to show
mercy. Rather than tell us, "Earn your Ph.D. in microeconomics so you
can eliminate world poverty in ten years," Jesus simply says, "I was
hungry and you fed me." The call to mercy compels us to do something
so simple: pay attention, show up, then do something practical to alle-
viate the misery of a fellow human being.

Here's the crux of this passage: mercy requires personal presence.
This simple truth flows from the reality that Immanuel is God with us
through Jesus (Mt 1:23). This doesn't mean mercy is simple to practice.
We'd rather do almost anything—write a check, give advice, manage a
program, give a one-time handout—than be present and walk beside
someone in pain. For instance, my friend Lydia is a beautiful young
woman who suffers from full-body spasms that, when they hit, feel like
a charlie horse in every muscle in her body. During a particularly horrific
series of spasms, she called me from the ER at three a.m. When I showed
up, she just wanted me to sit beside her until the medicine kicked in and
the spasms subsided. One set of friends had already "freaked out" and
headed back to the university dorm rooms. The doctors and nurses had
already pumped her full of painkillers and muscle-relaxers, so they didn't
need to be present. She just wanted someone who wouldn't flee from the
reality of her physical anguish. Helping Lydia meant showing up and
staying present in the midst of her pain.

On my visit to Mexico City, my friends Saul and Pilar gave me the
same message. Saul kept saying, "I love my friends from the United
States, but you always want to fix the poor by giving them a handout
or starting a massive program. The poor do *not* need another handout!
You cannot fix them. Yes, we can and must provide the poor with options and resources, but more than anything, they need you, and you
need them. We need to give one another our time, our heart and our
friendship. Then the poor will grow and change just like everyone
else: through personal presence, through the power of relationships

and person-to-person involvement."

Notice that in this passage Jesus provides extra motivation for our personal presence: when we show up for others, we also show up for him. When we're present to others, we also encounter the presence of Jesus. "I tell you the truth," Jesus says, "whatever you did for one of the least of these brothers and sisters of mine, you did for me" (Mt 25:40). In other words, when we walk with the "least," we are walking with Jesus. Whenever we feed a hungry child in the name of Jesus, somehow Jesus receives real nourishment. When we offer water to one thirsty person, we quench Jesus' thirst. When we visit the sick, we show up for Jesus. Even small acts of mercy done for the meanest, most thankless human beings have huge ramifications.

But according to Jesus' words in Matthew 25:41-46 there's also a reverse butterfly effect: consistently failing to display small acts of mercy (i.e., living a merciless lifestyle) has a profound negative impact on others, on us and on Jesus. Just as we can encounter Jesus in the presence of hurting people, so we can ignore him when we neglect hurting people. Goatlike individuals (see Mt 25:33) fail to show up and meet the needs of the hungry, the thirsty, the lonely, the naked, the imprisoned and the sick. In response to this glaring sin of omission, Jesus says, "Whatever you did not do for one of the least of these, you did not do for me" (Mt 25:45).

This should compel me to ask some difficult questions about my life: Who are the mercy-deprived in my world? Have I rushed past them and ignored their needs? Am I oblivious to the presence of Jesus in the love-starved people around me? Have I consistently failed to do something practical—feeding or clothing or visiting someone—as I strive for greater accomplishments and comforts?

This mercy-withholding lifestyle leads to a frightening conclusion— we've missed Jesus in this life and eventually we'll miss him forever. That's the brunt of Jesus' sober words in Matthew 25:41: "Depart from me, you who are cursed, into the eternal fire prepared for the devil and his angels." It's a scary threat. "Eternal fire" grabs your attention. Yes, it's a metaphor from Jesus, the master of metaphors, but it points to something awful and real: separation from God's presence.

For all of his beautiful words about mercy, Jesus does not hesitate to
warn us about separation from the source of mercy. "All the nations will
be gathered before him" prepares us for an urgent and awesome event.
The living God will "separate the people one from another as a shepherd
separates the sheep from the goats" (Mt 25:32). To this day Middle East-
ern farmers allow sheep and goats to graze together until they are sepa-
rated at night. In Jesus' vision of the world's end, humanity hurtles toward a great fork in the road, a cosmic separation into sheep and goats.
As we've seen before in Matthew's Gospel, Jesus, the master of mercy
and tenderness, also speaks with blunt urgency and brutal honesty. "On
your journey through life, you'll find a fork in the road," he warns us. "If
you take the wrong turn, it will hurl you off a cliff. So take my advice:
when you come to the fork, listen for my voice. Obey my voice, veer toward me, and you will be safe." Jesus urges, woos and even threatens us
to steer us away from the cliff of our own destruction and damnation.

Based on Jesus' call here, we might conclude that we're accepted by
God (or invited to come to the Father) based on our good deeds of mercy.
But that's not consistent with the rest of Matthew's teaching. First of all,
the believers who receive the Father's blessing of eternal joy gasp with
surprise when they hear Jesus' words of approval (see Mt 25:37-39). After offering thousands of cups of cold water, they hardly give it a
thought.[75] They'd never say, "Look at what I did for God. Now God
owes me mercy in return. Now I deserve a place in heaven." Second, Jesus already gave us the one doorway to enter and receive the kingdom
with all its blessings: "Blessed are the poor in spirit, for theirs is the kingdom of heaven" (Mt 5:3). "Poor in spirit" people don't buy their way into
God's grace; they merely receive it as a gift.

So from the flow of Matthew's entire story, we could summarize
mercy in this way: (1) We receive mercy from God the Father; (2) We
display mercy because of God the Father. In other words, as we engage
in acts of mercy, even tiny deeds of love for little people, the world
changes. The kingdom comes. Our light shines and our Father in heaven
receives glory. Jesus is saying clearly and emphatically what the rest of
the Bible also tells us: receiving grace leads to extending grace; tasting
mercy leads to offering mercy to others (see Tit 2:14; Eph 2:8-10).

But then to disconnect Jesus' good news from his mercy mandate, to receive God's love and then withhold it from others, to be forgiven and then to refuse to forgive others . . . well, it just doesn't make sense. It's ridiculous. It's cold and heartless. Fortunately, Jesus keeps inviting and wooing us into a life of receiving and giving mercy. But there's a threat too: if we keep withholding mercy for others, if we see Jesus in the eyes of our love-hungry neighbors and then ignore them, we have also ignored Jesus. And we might even be on the path to hell—no matter how well we think we know Jesus, and no matter how much we talk about him.

THE DEATH AND RESURRECTION OF JESUS

Matthew 26:1–28:20

From the very beginning of this Gospel story, Matthew wants us to know something amazing about Jesus: he is Immanuel, the God who is with us. (Of course, he is also Son of David, Son of Man, Messiah, Son of God and Lord of the Sabbath, among others.) But just how far will Jesus go to be God with us? That's one of the central questions behind this Gospel.

It's a powerful question. We've all had friends, spouses, family members who joined us for part of our journey but then, for one reason or another, said, "I can't go any farther." Perhaps our sin and darkness was too deep. Perhaps we were too needy or just too human. Perhaps they had their own issues. Throughout this Gospel Jesus has demonstrated true love, a love that shows up, a love that stays present. Now in these last two chapters that true love shows up and walks beside us in the depths of human brokenness, sin, darkness and evil.

In terms of human sinfulness—both on a personal level and on a systemic institutional level—this section covers the gamut. The powers of human and demonic evil come to an apex in Matthew 26 and 27. Some of it is utterly banal and almost boring; some of the sinfulness is shocking and cruel. It all forms an incredibly ugly picture of the human race.

But in spite of the sordid reality of human evil, Jesus' identity and mission as God with us doesn't change. He will continue to walk with us, even into the depths of our spiritual darkness and bondage, even to the depths of our willful rebellion against God.

Of course Jesus wasn't just being nice and loving when he walked into human evil and died on the cross. According to his own understanding, he was giving his life as a ransom for many (Mt 20:28). He was setting the captives—us—free from our self-imposed bondage. He was "drinking the cup," draining the dregs of God's rightful judgment against human evil and sinfulness (Mt 20:22). Matthew 26–27 details exactly what happened when Jesus became our ransom and drank the cup we should have drunk.

But the story doesn't end with Jesus' death. Matthew 28 brings triumph and mission to the story. The resurrection means that this tale doesn't have a sad, hopeless ending. The resurrection shows how God can take weak and foolish, even brutal and cruel things, and turn them into redemption stories. And the resurrection leads to the stirring conclusion of this book: Jesus calls his followers to make disciples and to bring the good news to all the nations of the earth.

SMASHING INTO LIFE AND LOVE
Matthew 26:1-35

When my daughter Bonnie Joy celebrated her first birthday we threw her a huge party. We donned silly hats, blew tiny paper horns, waved bright streamers, carried in a cake, lit candles and blew them out. We ended our birthday celebration by gathering around and singing "Happy Birthday" as Bonnie smashed her face into the cake. One of our friends, a tall and regal Tanzanian named Festus, was watching his first American birthday party. So at each new phase of the party he would clap his hands and excitedly ask me, "Oh, my, good for Bonnie, but why do you do that now? Why do you blow those loud horns? Why do you wear the silly hats? Why do you light the candles? Why did she smash her face into the cake?" And then I'd pause and ask myself, *Yeah, why do we do that?* Even a simple birthday party included symbols, ceremony and ritual.

Of course American parents aren't alone in this: every culture has ways of relating that involve words and actions and symbols. Symbols—both symbolic objects and symbolic actions—communicate beyond words. If you take a bunch of reality, compress it and compact it and squeeze it into one object or one movement, you've created a symbol.

Throughout the Bible, from Noah's rainbow to the detailed instructions for the Tabernacle, God used symbols to reveal himself to us. For instance, when he wanted to show us the ugliness of sin and the cost of forgiveness, he told his people to choose a live animal, kill it, sprinkle the blood on their clothing and then burn the animal's fat. This may sound crude, but no one ever left those services muttering, "What the heck was that about?" You experienced the drama of sin and redemption. You watched it, felt it, smelled it. It stuck to your clothes. Symbols have that kind of power.

God wants us to know him, and we can't know him with our minds alone. That was the error of modernity—namely, that we could grasp God with verbal analysis and pure reason apart from deeper-than-rational symbols, gestures and actions. We need both. That's why ordinary events—birthday parties, weddings, dinners, baseball games and even two friends meeting on the street—include words and symbols/actions/rituals.

One of the most important symbolic events in the Bible was the Passover. Every year faithful Jews would gather to remember and reenact the story of how they were enslaved in Egypt, oppressed by the mighty and cruel Pharaoh until God came down and set them free. To this day our Jewish friends still remember the Passover by eating, drinking, touching, lighting candles, telling stories, enacting special rituals.

Matthew 26:17 records, "On the first day of the Festival of Unleavened Bread [another name for the Passover], the disciples came to Jesus and asked, 'Where do you want us to make preparations for you to eat the Passover?'" Jewish fathers were responsible to make arrangements for the Passover, so Jesus provides a detailed plan for what will happen next. He explicitly instructs his disciples to find a "certain man" and tell him, "My appointed time is near. I am going to celebrate the Passover with my disciples at your house" (Mt 26:18). Throughout the passion story Jesus wants his disciples to know that his death isn't a tragedy. It's painful and sad but it's not a tragedy. Once again, Matthew weaves a story of God's sovereign plan right into our bloody history.

As they gather for the Passover, "reclining at the table with the Twelve" (a picture of joy and unity and love, Mt 26:20) Jesus turns to the disciples and says, "Truly I tell you, one of you will betray me" (Mt 26:21). A sudden chill fills the air. The disciples still don't understand Jesus and his mission or their own hearts. They howl in protest, but Jesus quietly picks up the Passover bread, gives thanks (the Greek word is *eucharisto*, from which we get our word "Eucharist") and breaks it as he hands it to his disciples, saying, "Take and eat; this is my body" (Mt 26:26). Then Matthew records, "He took a cup, and when he had given thanks, he gave it to them, saying, 'Drink from it, all of you'" (Mt 26:27).

Like my daughter's birthday party, Jesus' celebration was imbued with the wonder of words, symbols and actions. Notice the ordinary, earthy, physical nature of this sacrament.[1] They didn't analyze the bread; they took it in their hands, bit it, chewed it, tasted it and then swallowed it; then they gulped the wine—the rich, bittersweet liquid burning in their throats all the way to their guts. In our postmodern, experiential culture, followers of Jesus still have this ancient, ever-relevant experience of God's presence in Christ—the Eucharist.

What did Jesus mean when he declared, "This is my body"? Some people argue that it's a mathematical formula, as in "bread = Jesus' flesh and blood." Others contend that the whole thing is just a mental reminder, like putting a string around your finger so you don't forget to take out the recycling.

But Jesus probably meant neither. He was asking his disciples to experience his presence, to feed on him in their hearts. Those ancient Jews would have understood it that way. When they gathered for the Passover, they were re-experiencing all the power and drama and God presence of that first Passover night. When he described how Jesus is present in the bread and wine John Calvin explained, "Now if anyone asks me how this takes place, I shall not be ashamed to confess that it is a secret too lofty for either the mind to comprehend or my words to declare. . . . I rather experience it than understand it."[2]

Of course, words were also part of the experience. As he quietly took the cup Jesus said, "This is my blood of the covenant, which is poured out for many for the forgiveness of sins" (Mt 26:28). Those words would have stunned the original hearers. They knew all about the old covenant in which God had said, "I will be your God and you will be my people." It was a good covenant, but one side of the covenant—our side—perpetually botched the deal. But God kept promising a new covenant, not to replace the old one but to fulfill it. Now Jesus has declared the unthinkable: the new covenant is here, right now, in the person and presence of Jesus himself.

Notice the key words in Jesus' mini-sermon: "This is my blood . . . poured out for many." My blood . . . poured out . . . for you. With beautiful simplicity this passage highlights the depth of Jesus' love for his disciples—and for us. Let's place ourselves in this story: we are the ones who fall away. None of us are righteous, but we keep defending ourselves and trying to prove our innocence. We have betrayed our Lord, and yet here he is, not only sticking with us, not only eating with us, not only preparing the meal for us, but giving his own self to us. He gave his own blood, "which is poured out for many for the forgiveness of sins."

There's only one person in this passage who understands the reality of God's poured-out love for sin-sick people: it's the unknown woman in Matthew 26:6-13. She "came to [Jesus] with an alabaster jar of very expensive perfume, which she poured on his head as he was reclining at the table" (Mt 26:7). After calculating the street value of the perfume, the disciples criticize her actions (Mt 26:8-9). But Jesus understands her love-driven heart (Mt 26:10-13). As Jesus pours out his love and life for us ("This is my body. . . . This is my blood . . . poured out for you"), the only adequate response is to pour back our love.

This unknown woman, who seems to be living the Beatitudes, demonstrates the movements of God's love story with all of us: the Lover pours out his love; the beloved, at first ignoring but then receiving the love, pours it back to the Lover; the Lover receives this imperfect offering and then lavishes more perfect love on his beloved—and so it goes for all eternity.

This love story is symbolized by two famous cups discovered in the ancient, marshy bogs of Denmark. The first, known as the Gundestrup Cauldron, is dated to the first century B.C. It's adorned with pictures of violent gods and warriors. Several panels feature animal or human sacrifice. One panel shows a gigantic "cook god" preparing to drop squirming humans into a boiling pot. The second cup, which appeared after the gospel transformed Ireland, is called the Ardagh Chalice. Like the cauldron it was forged for worship, but it presents a radically different view of God. God no longer demands our sacrifice to appease him; instead he pours out his blood for us. Jesus, the Lamb of God and the living God, gave himself for us. Yes, God is love![3]

In order to remind us over and over again that he loves us, God doesn't just preach love to us; he also lets us experience the reality of his sacrificial love. Like a loving Father, God gets on his hands and knees and shows us his love—with words, with symbols, with rituals and with action. So, yes, by all means, hear the words, process the experience with your mind. Think good thoughts about this truth. But then respond to God's wooing invitation to eat, drink, taste, see and feel. Go ahead and smash your whole life into God's love.

SHATTERING THE MYTH OF INNOCENCE
Matthew 26:31–27:66 (Part 1)

The author and pastor Fleming Rutledge once asked her friend Sally, a perpetual church shopper, if she had tried St. ABC Church. "Oh, I could never go there," Sally gasped. "They have a big cross with Jesus hanging there like a criminal." Then Sally shared a story that reinforced her horror. "While I was shopping in an upscale mall, I purchased a lovely new blouse but the clerk forgot to remove the security tag. When I tried to leave the store, the alarms started blaring and the security guards practically pounced on me." She was mortified. "But do you know the worst thing about the experience?" she asked. "It was being treated like a common criminal. That's not who I am!"

Fleming Rutledge commented on her friend's experience: "The truth is that Sally does not know who she is. . . . She does not believe herself to be guilty of anything. Wronged, yes; misunderstood, yes; undervalued,

yes; imperfect, yes . . . but not sinful. Because she believes herself to be
one of the good people, because she could never commit a sin like shop-
lifting, she cannot see the connection between Jesus' death as a common
criminal and herself."[4]

Like Sally, I'd be horrified to have others treat me like a shoplifter.
On some level, we all know we're imperfect, but we're definitely not one
of the "bad people"—you know, people who actually steal sweaters,
abuse dogs, solicit prostitutes, steal employee pensions or mock the disabled. We have small, respectable sins, moral blemishes such as a little
gossip, a little resentment and lust, a little racism. Of course we don't
hate anyone; we just don't have time to make friends with anyone outside our social circle. So if someone drew a line in the sand and asked us
to side with the good or the bad people, we'd definitely be on the good
people side.

Our desire to become part of the morally upstanding crowd makes
Matthew 26:31–27:66 painful and disturbing. Earlier in this Gospel we
noted Jesus' high view of the dignity of human beings, even the little,
"insignificant" people devalued by our society, who were created to reflect God's light (Mt 5:16) and imitate God's merciful heart (Mt 5:45-
48). But in the long and ugly story told in this passage, every person will
unwittingly confirm another aspect of Jesus' evaluation of the human
race: we are more sinful than we would ever dare to admit.

With brutal honesty—but also with love and tenderness—Jesus calls
us all sick. That's the essence of his diagnosis in Matthew 26:41: "The
spirit is willing, but the flesh is weak." The Greek word translated as
"weak" (asthenes) also means "sick." So Matthew tells us that Jesus
"took up our infirmities [astheneias] and bore our diseases" (Mt 8:17). In
other words, even when we want to do what's right, our fallen nature
doesn't cooperate. In some ways we're like a stroke victim who wants to
walk, who knows she can and should walk, but who just can't get out of
her hospital bed. Of course Jesus also proclaims beautiful good news
about our condition: if we're sick and he's the doctor, then we can become whole again.

In one way or another, every person and group in this passage displays the symptoms of our human sickness. Sadly, throughout the

church's history, some Christians have used this passage to heap scorn and even hatred on Jewish people, as if they alone crucified Jesus. But that misses the point. First, Matthew is only critical of some Jews—a select group of the religious leaders. Secondly, the Romans also initiated and finished the crucifixion of Jesus. Finally, in this passage God's searchlight shines in every dark corner of the human heart, exposing the sickness in all of us—and most of this exposure starts with Jesus' followers.

In five simple words—"You will all fall away" (Mt 26:31)—Jesus announces the complete collapse of his band of disciples. Peter resents this sober warning. Like Sally and the rest of us, he clings to what we might call "the myth of innocence," the naïve belief that we're the exception to Jesus' dire diagnosis, that although the world is filled with bad people doing bad things, we're innocent (or at least semi-innocent) because we're one of the "good people." Puffed up on the myth of innocence, Peter vehemently disagrees with Jesus' prediction. "Even if all fall away on account of you, I never will," he blusters with bravado (Mt 26:33). When Jesus tries to deflate Peter's airy confidence, Peter repeats his myth: "Even if I have to die with you, I will never disown you" (26:35).

The irony—and the shallowness—of Peter's boast becomes obvious in the next scene. In the midst of Jesus' sadness and grief, he asks for one favor from Peter and two of his friends: "Stay here and keep watch with me" (Mt 26:38). It's a simple assignment. You don't even have to pray, Jesus says, just sit there and watch me pray. A little friendship and concern would be nice too, but at the very least don't nod off. Instead, on three occasions Jesus returns from his prayers and, to his surprise and dismay (Mt 26:45), finds a troupe of snoozing disciples. After fervently declaring his willingness to die for Jesus, Peter can't even keep his eyes open for sixty minutes straight.

By the end of the night, it gets even worse for Peter. In Matthew 26:51, as the mob comes to arrest Jesus, Peter pulls out his sword and slices off the ear of the high priest's servant.[5] It's important to note that Peter is undoubtedly trying to help his buddy Jesus. Unfortunately, on almost every occasion when Peter barges forward with his "helpfulness" (walking on the water in chapter 14, lecturing Jesus in chapter 16, offering to

construct booths in chapter 17), the result is a mini-disaster. Our sincere
helpfulness doesn't prove our innocence. Even helpful people fail Jesus.
At the end of chapter 26 (verses 69-75), Matthew records Peter's sig-
nature moral belly flop. On three occasions, as Jesus courageously faced
the powerful crowd, Peter faced some powerless servants and vehemently
denied Jesus. "The rock" cracked and crumbled. Three times he dozed;
three times he denied. No one rose higher than Peter; no one sank lower
than Peter. Jesus was right about human nature: we're sick and we need
a doctor (recall Mt 9:9-11).

Peter wasn't the only failure among Jesus' disciples. Judas failed Jesus
by his outright act of betrayal, kissing Jesus on the cheek so the mob
could identify and arrest him. Worse, when Judas recognized his guilt
("I have sinned, for I have betrayed innocent blood"), he capitulated to
despair and hanged himself (Mt 27:4-5). By the end of the night, "all the
disciples deserted [Jesus] and fled" (Mt 26:56).

We can also note the failure of the Jewish religious establishment.
First, they accuse Jesus on largely flimsy, trumped-up charges (Mt 26:57-
68). Then, when Judas feels crushing remorse for his betrayal, they turn
away in disgust. "What is that to us?" they reply. "That's your responsibility" (Mt 27:4). Judas begs for a second chance, but they are either un-
willing or unable to offer forgiveness. Unlike Jesus, they will break a
bruised reed and snuff out a smoldering wick (Mt 12:20). But they know
how to make quick plans to spend those thirty pieces of silver (Mt 27:6-
10).[6] Again, Jesus was right about our nature, even our religious nature:
left to ourselves, we create systems that "shut the door of the kingdom of
heaven in people's faces" and neglect "justice, mercy and faithfulness"
(Mt 23:13, 23).

In this story, political institutions as represented by Pilate don't fare any
better. Pilate's supposed to be in charge; he's supposed to dispense justice
while maintaining order and decency. Instead, insecure and uncertain, he
caves to peer pressure. He asks the angry mob how to handle Jesus, which
is like a bullfighter politely asking the bull for his thoughts on the fight. In
the end, Pilate proclaims his own myth of innocence as he melodramati-
cally and hypocritically washes his hands and announces, "I am innocent
of this man's blood. It is your responsibility!" (Mt 27:24).

Finally, "the crowd" or "all the people" (representing the rest of us) vent their rage, demanding Jesus' death. Only hours after another crowd heaped praises on Jesus, they scream, "Crucify him!" (Mt 27:22-23). We repeat this same story over and over again: the world is screwed up and someone has to pay—the blacks, the Jews, the Hutus or the Tutsis, the Serbs or the Croats, our parents or our spouse, the Republicans or the Democrats, church people or atheists. We're innocent so it must be someone else's fault, and that someone must serve as our scapegoat. It's a long, sad story,[7] but once again Jesus has the right diagnosis: we are sick and we need a doctor.

In the end, this passage looks a lot like Bob Dylan's early song "Who Killed Davey Moore?" In Dylan's story, a fighter named Davey Moore drops dead during an ugly boxing match. Through six painful verses everyone involved denies their guilt. Everyone maintains their innocence—the referee, the angry crowd, the boxer's manager, the gambling man, the sports writer and finally the other boxer. Every stanza ends with a refrain of innocence: "It wasn't me that made him fall / No, you can't blame me at all."

In the same way, throughout this passage in Matthew's story, everyone is responsible but no one takes responsibility. No one confesses the sickness in his own nature. No one refutes the myth of her innocence. No one stands with the "bad people."

Except Jesus.

As everyone else sings Dylan' refrain of "It wasn't me" (see the disciples' "Surely not I, Lord," Mt 26:22 NIV 1984), as everyone else lines up with the good people, Jesus, the only innocent person in this story, the only one who has walked into and through Satan's fog, the only one who refused to find a scapegoat, quietly hangs between two common criminals in order to become sin for us. The physician bears our sickness. The innocent one bears our guilt.

According to Matthew and the other voices in the New Testament, this isn't an accident or tragedy. In the midst of his darkest, most tormented night, Jesus quietly says, "It must happen in this way" (Mt 26:54, 56). Earlier in the story, Jesus twice mentioned drinking from a cup (Mt 20:22; 26:40), a reference to the Old Testament prophets who spoke darkly about the cup of the Lord's wrath (Is 51:17-23; Jer 25:15-29). God promised that one day he would force all the wicked, cruel, God-rebelling people and nations to drink the cup of his righteous wrath. God would open their mouths and fill their throats and bellies with a concoction of bitter wine, making them drunk and helpless. It was a powerful picture of three things: (1) giving the wicked a taste of their own medicine, (2) setting the innocent captives free and (3) cleansing and renewing the earth with a fresh start.

Through Jesus, Matthew provides two major updates to the "cup" imagery. First, based on the story of Jesus, it's much more difficult to identify, round up and punish the standard lineup of bad-guy scape-goats. We're all part of the world's mess. But someone still has to drink the cup. God can't and won't act like the chief priests or Pilate, piously hovering over evil and injustice, washing his hands and declaring, "This isn't my problem." No, God will pour out the deep, dark, bitter wine of his judgment on sin—not to destroy and hurt the world, but ultimately to cleanse and restore it.

Second, in an unimaginable plot twist, God the Father and God the Son agree on a thing most shocking: Jesus will drink our cup. By doing so he shatters our individual and collective myths of innocence, leaving us bankrupt and empty-handed before God's blazing holiness. But as we stand empty-handed, we also have the marvelous invitation to receive his lavish grace.

GOD WITH US, ASKING OUR QUESTIONS
Matthew 26:31-27:66 (Part 2)

My friend Andy recently told me a powerful story. Eighteen years ago Andy and his wife decided to adopt a foreign-born child, so after a long process, Andy finally ventured into a South American country to bring their new daughter back to Long Island. At the time this country was gripped by corruption, violence and political chaos. After Andy ar-rived, they (i.e., anyone who could profit from Andy's plight) kept up-ping the price for the adoption. When he finally threatened to take the matter to the U.S. consulate, a mysterious figure confronted Andy, warning him of vague but dreadful consequences. It was like a spy thriller, except it was Andy who was caught in the middle of some sinister, dangerous plot.

He refused to leave without his daughter. The odd thing was that Andy had never even met this girl. She was small and helpless. She hadn't won any awards or aced any tests. He didn't know that one day her smile would light up their living room, or that she'd love their cats and dogs, or that she'd play Mozart pieces on the family piano. For all practical purposes, she was just an orphan condemned to a life of grinding poverty in a far-flung developing country. But for some crazy reason, Andy stayed there, negotiating with corrupt officials, spending oodles of money, squandering time and even risking his life to find and win this little girl.

Now, eighteen years later, Andy was telling me about an intimate high school graduation party for Maria, his adopted daughter. At one point during the meal, Maria unexpectedly stood up and gave a beautiful speech thanking everyone who had helped her find a better life on Long Island. As Andy told me this story, he was trying to fight back the tears. I got the impression that he could have lived a hundred more years, or even a hundred lifetimes, and nothing would compare to hearing Maria's spontaneous thank-you. Of course it all started when Andy, against all odds, walked into a hellish nightmare in an attempt to be with her.

When Andy finished this story it struck me that my non-Christian friend had discovered the heart of the Christian story: Love is better than anything. And the heart of love means presence, the desire and ability to be with someone else. I've read contemporary evolutionary biologists who explain Andy's "crazy love" (or altruism) by referring to the impersonal mechanism of natural selection. I find that explanation not only cold but intellectually untenable. Instead, I prefer a simpler and more satisfying explanation: we were made by love and for love. Throughout this Gospel Jesus has repeatedly presented his vision for reality: at the center of the cosmos there is a personal God, a heavenly community of Father-Son-Spirit who dwell in loving relationship, who also love us and who were willing to spend and risk everything to be present with us.

Many Christian thinkers have tried to analyze and explain Christ's death using their "theories of the atonement," but these explanations sound as cold and impersonal as Darwin's theory of natural selection. We (pastors, theologians, writers) often draw a stark but clear picture of our plight: God is on one side of a huge chasm and we're on the other and, quite frankly, God is always disappointed and usually disgusted with the abysmal failure of the human race. This picture isn't entirely wrong, but by itself, it certainly doesn't resonate with Matthew's story of Jesus, which is the story of Immanuel, God with us.

We could also call this the story of God's greatest gift—himself. Jesus called it the gift of his body (see Mt 26:26; Lk 22:19), that is, the gift of his personal and real presence to us. God did not say, "I send you my best wishes" or "I give you good advice, laws and commandments." In the person of Jesus, God says, "I give myself to you." And, wonder of wonders, Immanuel also says, "I want you to be with me." With profound yearning for our presence, on two occasions prior to his death Jesus made a simple request: stay with me (see Mt 26:38, 40). Does this mean that God is incomplete and insecure without us? No, it simply means that God (as demonstrated in Jesus, God with us) thrives on relationship just as we do. God the Father acts like Andy—searching for us, willing to stay until he finds us, sacrificing almost anything to take us home with him.

In this long and dark section of Matthew, God's passionate desire to be with us splashes with vivid colors in Matthew 27:46. Hanging from the cross, Jesus cries out a Bible verse (Ps 22:1) in Aramaic: " '*Eli, Eli, lema sabachthani?*' (which means 'My God, my God, why have you forsaken me?')" (Mt 27:46). Due to the emotional impact of that cry, Matthew and Mark leave it in Jesus' first language of Aramaic, while Luke and John omit it.

This raw, honest, simple question "reveals better than any sentence in the Gospel who Jesus is and what he does."[8] At the cross the promise of God with us from Matthew 1:23 finds its full expression in Jesus' anguished cry.

In Matthew's account, Jesus does not die in glorious triumph; he does not die soaring above human pain and suffering. Instead, he dies with a question on his lips: Why have you forsaken me? Why did you ditch me?

Ponder for a moment all of the things Jesus could have said (or that Matthew could have recorded) right before he died.[9] Instead he punctuates the air not with a statement but a question—and not just any question, but perhaps *the* question found on the lips of most fellow sufferers. Jesus not only walks among us; he not only becomes a hunted and homeless refugee with us; he not only plunges into the water of baptism with us; he not only eats with sinners like us; he not only bears our sickness and guilt; he also asks our most painful, perplexing questions. By living and asking our questions, Jesus can't be any more "with us."

Many well-meaning people often give the following advice: "Yes, I'm sure you've suffered, but it doesn't help you or honor God to ask 'why' questions." Unfortunately, at times the "why" questions don't disappear: Why did my mom get cancer? Why did our dad leave us? Why did they massacre that village? Why did my uncle molest me and my sisters? Why did that earthquake flatten Haiti of all places? Why did my doggie get hit by a car? Why torture, corruption, addictions, divorce, racism, injustice?

Life's "why" questions cut like shards of glass flung into our heart. Over time they settle in and find their place, but they rarely dissolve. After working with chronically ill people, I've also found that giving advice—even sincere, intellectually coherent, biblically based advice— usually doesn't help either. Most people crave our presence before they crave our answers (although, later on, advice may also help heal the wounds of suffering). So, astonishingly, Jesus not only provides answers to life; he also asks our questions, even our most anguished, doubt-riddled questions.

In Matthew 27:46, the Greek word for "cried" (*anaboao*, the only use in the New Testament) implies a "powerful emotion . . . [and] an agonized expression of a real sense of alienation."[10] In other words, Jesus felt ditched, abandoned, discarded. According to a traditional phrase for Jesus' question, it was a "cry of dereliction." In this haunting question, our anguish became his anguish.

Despite his anguish, Jesus didn't descend into despair.[11] In the midst of haunting questions and gut-wrenching feelings of abandonment, Jesus did not renege on his promise to drink the cup. He couldn't feel, see or hear his heavenly Father, but he still appealed to "my God." Like David, Jesus trusted and obeyed the Father who, based on all the evidence, appeared to have abandoned him. Once again, Jesus lived the life we should have lived.

This wasn't the first time Jesus walked with us into the storm of our sorrow. Back in Matthew 26, as he tried to pray at Gethsemane, Matthew records that Jesus was "sorrowful and troubled" (Mt 26:37).[12] The Greek word for "troubled," *a-demos*, literally means "not at home," confused, bewildered, stunned, at a loss. How could God feel not at home, bewildered, at a loss? Aren't these feelings sinful? Perhaps they can be for people, but then again we can also feel not at home through no fault of our own. Some all-too-human events—sudden death, war, divorce, unemployment, natural disaster, cancer, mental illness—make us feel not at home. As he prays in the garden, Jesus identifies with and walks into our sorrow and trouble.

As Jesus descends into the darkness of the cross, he offers his presence, his "with-us-ness" for our "not-at-homeness." At one point (Mt 27:29-30) the Roman soldiers mock and spit on Jesus. You can't get much lower than spitting on someone. A few moments later (Mt 27:33-34), someone offers Jesus wine mixed with bitter gall. As usual in Matthew, Jesus completes the journey of Old Testament believers, particularly the "poor one" of the Psalms, who wrote, "I looked for sympathy, but there was none, for comforters, but I found none. They put gall in my food and gave me vinegar for my thirst" (Ps 69:20-21). Standing with a long line of fellow sufferers, Jesus joins the mocked, the scorned, the overlooked, the taunted, the rejected and the degraded. At each stage of this story, Matthew wants us to know that love drove Jesus to be with us, bearing not only our sin and guilt but also our questions, heartaches, betrayals and dislocation.[13]

Of course Matthew also wants us to note that this fully human Jesus is also fully God. That's the wonder and the irony laced throughout this passage. For example, as the soldiers mock Jesus, spitting on him in contempt, dressing him up and declaring his phony kingship, bowing and scraping before this pathetic authority figure, Matthew wants us to remember that underneath the bruised and swollen face, the crown of thorns and the tattered robe, Jesus really is the world's one and true ruler. At his birth, Matthew announced the royal blood coursing through Jesus' veins. At the transfiguration, Jesus declared his hidden but incomparable glory.

That's what makes the gospel story unique and beautiful (and, in another sense, shocking). Like my friend Andy, in and through Jesus God has chosen the path of personal and sacrificial involvement with us. This statement doesn't make sense without the phrase "in and through Jesus" because only the Gospels proclaim that God knows our suffering and pain from personal experience.

For most of us, the real sting of suffering isn't just the physical pain or disruption; it's the isolation and abandonment. It's the feeling that we are utterly alone. As John Stott wrote, "Pain is endurable, but the seeming indifference of God is not. Sometimes we picture him lounging, perhaps dozing, in some celestial deck-chair, while the hungry millions starve to death."[14] In their song "Blame It on the Tetons," the indie band Modest Mouse sings about this: every person's a burning building, and there's no one around to extinguish the flames. Or we're all like someone drowning in the ocean, with no one to help us get some air.

But Matthew's story of Jesus' death dismantles this view of God as it proclaims, "You are not alone! There is someone to put the fire out; there is someone to show us how to get better air. God isn't dozing on some celestial deck-chair. Instead, our God has wounds; our God has even felt our desolation and asked our most painful questions."

After Andy shared his amazing story with me, I wanted to cry with him. I wanted to grab my agnostic friend and thank him for telling me about Maria and teaching me more about Jesus. For years I've tried to find a way to show Andy who God really is, that God the Father is better than he could ever imagine. After listening to Andy's story, I want to tell Andy—and the whole world—that there's another story of daring, risky, spend-it-all, sacrificial love. But it's the best love story ever told. And it's for Andy and Maria, and me and you, and every person on this planet.

GOD FOR US, SETTING THE CAPTIVES FREE
Matthew 26:31–27:66 (Part 3)

Most of my smart, sophisticated friends don't believe in sin. Or if they do, they don't think it's a major problem. For instance, my friend Emily grew up in a "sinless" family. It wasn't that her family members had achieved moral perfection; they just couldn't comprehend the concept of sin. As Emily recalls, "When I heard the word 'sin' I got angry. I used to say, 'What does that word even mean? Why would anyone hold to such an archaic, musty, oppressive concept?' And then some of my religious friends had the audacity to say that we were enslaved to sin or by sin or whatever. Ugh, what a dreary and depressing thought!"

A few months ago Emily, who now has three children of her own, told me that it's no longer hard to accept the concept of her own sinfulness. "At times I act so wonderful and kind," she says, "and then I'll fly off the handle, or I'll realize how much of my life revolves around me and getting my way. My flaws suddenly appear obvious and repulsive. It's not just that I do bad stuff. It's deeper than that: I feel trapped by my own junk. Sure, I need forgiveness, but I also need liberation. I don't need a little patching up here and there; I need a major renovation of my life from the inside out. I guess, after all these years, I realize those religious friends were right. I am a slave to sin."

It's still hard for many of my friends to swallow the whole enslaved-to-sin-need-a-Savior saga. But Matthew 27 demonstrates that the problem of sin lurks at a deeper level than we may have imagined. When Jesus said he would "give his life as a ransom for many" (Mt 20:28), we should imagine something along the lines of a thrilling rescue from a hijacking or kidnapping scenario. Unfortunately, most people misunderstand the nature of our plight. According to the Bible, sin involves much more than doing bad things or failing to do good things; sin implies living like a slave.

Throughout this Gospel, Jesus has described the enslaving power of a host of human captors: selfishness (like Herod, Mt 2:3-18), religious pride (Mt 3:7-10), anger and contempt (Mt 5:21-22), sexual lust (Mt 5:27-28), untruthfulness (Mt 5:33-37), revenge (Mt 5:38-42), social exclusion (Mt 5:43-48), people pleasing and self-promotion (Mt 6:1-18), anxiety and materialism (Mt 6:25-34), a judgmental spirit (Mt 7:1-5), shame (Mt 8:1-4), fear (Mt 8:23-27), guilt (Mt 9:1-8), arrogance (Mt 11:20-21), bitterness (Mt 18:23-35), addictions (Mt 19:16-24) and self-righteous hypocrisy (Mt 23:15-28). Of course, the Bible also implies that we aren't just victims because on one level we've freely chosen our own enslavement.

Yet when Jesus died on the cross, the sheer force of his daring rescue operation broke our bondage to our slavery. Now, if you saw Jesus dying on the cross, it wouldn't have looked like an overwhelming rescue mission. On the contrary, in every respect it would have looked like a botched undertaking. For example, in the process of mocking Jesus, at one point the religious leaders sneered, "Let God rescue him now if he wants him" (Mt 27:43). As far as taunts go, this one hit home. Accused and condemned, bruised and battered, stripped naked, drenched in sweat and blood, pinned to an instrument of torture, jeered at more often than the local thug Barabbas, discarded outside the city like a dead dog—honestly, who would want this man? He had sunk lower than the crooks on his right and his left. How could God want him? And how could this man, who claimed to be God in the flesh, act as our liberator?

But that is precisely the crux of this story. Jumping forward to the end of chapter 27, after all hell broke loose on the earth and Jesus "gave up his spirit" (Mt 27:50), Matthew begins to record the momentous events of Jesus' daring rescue mission. Matthew piles on seven passive verbs— "was torn," "was shaken," "were split," "were opened," "were raised," "were manifested," "were frightened"—to suggest that God the Father was at work, even when everything looked utterly dark and hopeless. Matthew doesn't wait for Easter to say that as Jesus died for us, God the Father was liberating the captives (us), raising the dead (us), reconciling sinners (us) to the Father and renewing the face of the earth (bigger than us). In other words, for Matthew the resurrection and crucifixion aren't two discrete, separate events. As "the hour" (see Mt 26:45) of darkness and betrayal descended on the earth, as the forces of evil converged to pummel Jesus with demonic hatred, as Jesus died with a question on his lips, God was working powerfully to set the captives free.

To add to this perspective, Matthew concludes his long passion story with the following detail: "So they went and made the tomb secure by putting a seal on the stone and posting the guard" (Mt 27:66). Matthew simply describes the scene, but based on the flurry of God's activity in verses 51-54, he was probably chuckling, "You've got to be kidding. They put a pathetic little seal on Jesus' tomb? That's like trying to wrap up a sleeping lion with a couple of twisty ties. Jesus will burst the seal just like he tore the veil from top to bottom, shook the earth, broke open the tombs and raised the dead. He came to set the captives free and your little seal won't stop that."

But what difference does all of this make in the ordinary life of an ordinary follower of Jesus? Perhaps three case studies will demonstrate how Christ's cross sets us free. The liberating power of the cross frees us from the captivity of shame, the captivity of ethnic exclusivity and the captivity of self-centeredness.

First of all, consider the hostage taker of shame. Most contemporary psychologists would say that a sense of guilt means I did something bad and now must repay the debt. In contrast, shame means I failed to live up to expectations—mine, my family's, my culture's—and this exposure of my failure makes me feel isolated and excluded from community. Of course, in some communities I don't just feel excluded; I am excluded.

So, for instance, take the following scenarios: a well-respected wife, mother and church member secretly struggles with an addiction to alcohol. A university student tries to meet the expectations of his immigrant parents but can't tell them he's failing biochemistry and really wants to become an inner-city youth pastor, not a research scientist. A much-loved pastor keeps looking at pornography on his home computer. A young woman can't share with anyone—especially her parents or her fiancé—that five years ago she aborted a baby. A struggling, ethnic-minority family can't ask for help because they've already lost their jobs and are on the verge of losing their home.

These people live in the grip of shame; shame has taken them hostage. Again, shame doesn't just mean that they feel guilty for their misdeeds; it means that they have failed to achieve communal standards. If others uncover the truth about their lives, they may feel like outcasts or become outcasts. So shame—that uneasy sense that we don't measure up and that our real self will cause others to reject us—propels us to work harder, achieve more, hide our dark secrets and look better. This load of shame drives us away from true intimacy and deep community.[15] Shame makes frauds, imposters and strangers out of all of us.

Matthew 27 tells us that Jesus not only bore our guilt; he also walked into, identified with and bore our shame. Craig Keener notes the shame of a typical crucifixion: "One being executed on the cross could not swat flies from one's wounds, not withhold one's bodily wastes from coming out while hanging naked for hours and sometimes days."[16] As we read the details of this chapter—the cruelty, rejection, mockery, humiliation and even the spitting—it's hard to imagine anyone sinking lower than Jesus into the abyss of human shamefulness. He blazed a path for us, providing an utterly safe place to bring our shame: the cross. Jesus, the Son of God, the only human being who had no reason to feel ashamed, became the shamed one for us.

As a result, the people who live under the cross and look to Jesus for his mercy can choose to leave their captivity to shame. I can bring to Jesus the most shameful things about my life—my addictions, failures and twisted secrets. Not only that, the church can become the place where we begin to heal from our shame and our secrets. As Richard Foster says so beautifully, "By living under the cross we can hear the worst possible things about the best possible people without so much as batting an eye. If we live in that reality, we will convey that spirit to others. They know it is safe to come to us."[17] In other words, as the cross sets us free from our shame, the new community of Jesus helps others break their own bondage to shame.

Matthew's passion story also shows us how the cross frees us from another form of captivity: our bondage to ethnic exclusivity. In the Gospel accounts there's a quick reference—almost a side comment—to an unnamed Roman solider who declares, "Surely he was the Son of God" (Mt 27:54; see also Mk 15:39; Lk 23:47). This isn't the first time the very Jewish Matthew refers to the inclusion of the Gentile outsiders. His story began with the ethnic outsiders in Jesus' family tree and then quickly moved to the inclusion of the foreign and even pagan Magi at Jesus' birth. Now at the moment of Jesus' death, another foreigner confesses Jesus' lordship. Like the centurion in Matthew 8 and the Canaanite woman in Matthew 15, these outsiders represent the millions and billions of people from every tribe, nation and tongue who will one day follow Christ.

The early church certainly understood this aspect of the bondage-breaking power of the cross. The apostle Paul taught that the cross equally liberates us from our individual separation from God and our ethnic and cultural separation from each other. "For he himself is our peace," Paul claims, "who has made the two groups [Jews and Gentiles] one and has destroyed the . . . hostility . . . to reconcile both of them to God through the cross, by which he put to death their hostility" (Eph 2:14, 16). Athanasius observed that it "is only on the cross that a man dies with arms outstretched," which he claimed symbolized Jesus' open-hearted and open-armed embrace of Jews and Gentiles.[18] The early theologian Hilary also noted that Jesus' death occurred "at the center of the earth, that it might be equally free to all nations," while later Anselm wrote that the shape of the cross signified "the church spread through the four quarters of the earth."[19]

However we say it—at the foot of the cross, through the power of the blood of Jesus, as we come to the cross—our life changes. Specifically, Jesus frees us from our bondage to all forms of ethnic exclusivity—racism, imperialism, elitism, even our "crossless" ethnic isolation from one another in the body of Christ. Centered in the cross of Jesus, the church becomes the beautiful new community committed to the hard, costly, time-consuming but liberating work of ethnic unity and growth.

Finally, the cross liberates us from our bondage to every form of selfishness. People who wryly say, "Yeah, must be nice trusting Jesus. You can do whatever you want and still find forgiveness" do not understand the power of the cross. Experiencing the power of the cross liberates us from our bondage to self-centeredness.

That was Maria's story from the last chapter. When Maria truly understood Andy's love for her, when she realized the costly love he had displayed for her, it changed her life. Specifically, at her family's graduation party, her eyes filled with tears as she humbly and joyfully said, "I was destined for a life of abject poverty. I knew my life could have been cruel and short, but you gave me the gift of new life." At that point, acting selfishly was the furthest thing from her mind.

There's only one appropriate response to the cross. Jesus has often already told us the response. Just in case we missed it, he'll tell us again in the last three verses in this Gospel. The one response to the cross is concise and clear: obey. Do what Jesus told us to do. Follow him. Take his words seriously, listening carefully, and then put them into practice.

ONE LITTLE WORD CHANGES THE WORLD
Matthew 28:1-15

In the history of failed prison breaks, this must rank as one of the worst. An inmate at the notorious San Quentin prison decided he'd had enough. So after longing for a better life and dreaming of freedom, he concocted a daring plan to break out. He'd hide in a dirty laundry bin, and an unsuspecting truck driver would grab the bin and its unseen guest—a convict stuffed under wet towels and dirty guard uniforms. The laundry company would drive him right through the prison gates into freedom. There was only one problem with this brilliant plan: the laundry trucks never left the property; they merely shuttled between the prison buildings. After a comfy but stinky ride around the familiar grounds, he went back to his cell and continued his sentence.[20]

In some ways, this failed prison break serves as a parable for our fallen human condition apart from Christ. The human spirit contains an irrepressible longing for a better life. Our best storytellers—spiritual and political leaders, musicians, filmmakers and writers—keep us dreaming about a world filled with justice, hope and freedom. But in many ways we're like the inmate who keeps riding around the prison yard. Yes, we are going somewhere; the truck and the laundry bin are moving around the buildings. But we never actually leave the grounds. We're all stuck in the same system. So even when prison life seems bearable and even safe and comfortable, deep down we know this isn't our home. We were made for freedom. Occasionally something tantalizes us from beyond the prison walls—a picture of the ocean, the shouts of children playing soccer, a flock of geese soaring overhead—and causes a longing for freedom to swell within us . . . until we realize we'll never get out of here alive.

But what if someone broke out of the prison? What if rather than just ride around and around in the laundry truck, someone actually escaped? And what if he not only escaped, but also returned to the prison—not as an inmate but as our liberator? I imagine he would say something like, "I beat the system and broke out. There really is a place where the sea roars and the children play and the geese soar. You don't have to be stuck here forever. But there is only one way: you have to trust me; you have to follow me. Take my hand and let's go."

To me, that's a small picture of the events reported in this chapter about Jesus' resurrection. In Matthew 1, we read that God in the person of Jesus became God with us. He entered our limited, walled-in existence. He became a prisoner with us. But then in the rest of the Gospel of Matthew, he spoke about life outside prison walls—a kingdom coming, a realm of salvation with God, a place of love and forgiveness and true freedom. He didn't just talk about it; with power he demonstrated this kingdom by healing the sick, casting out demons, raising the dead, loving the outcast, forging community. In the process, rather than squelch our desire, Jesus inflamed it. At last, we thought, here's someone who can lead us to a better place.

Then it all imploded. Just like the rest of us, Jesus died—and not just any death, a horrible, cruel, humiliating death. For two long chapters (Matthew 26–27) the crucifixion seemed to say, "Everything is broken. No one escapes. Every dream fades or gets trampled by reality. When Jesus said he could restore all things, we really believed him. But now, just like every other would-be Messiah, Jesus has crashed and burned in his plan to fix the world. He claimed to be God with us, but he's just another symbol for God's absence."

But then in Matthew 28 the entire mood of this Gospel story changes.[21] With complete authority Jesus arises from his brutal death and tells his disciples, "Do not be afraid. Go and tell my brothers to go to Galilee; there they will see me. . . . All authority in heaven and on earth has been given to me. . . . And surely I am with you always, to the very end of the age" (Mt 28:10-20). It's the confident assertion of the one—the only one!—who walked into and out of and back into the broken system of this world. It's as if Jesus is saying, "Don't be afraid. There is new life beyond these prison walls of sin, evil and death. All things can be restored. All broken lives can be healed. All sad tales can become untrue. I know the way out. I've blazed a trail to freedom. But you have to trust me; you have to follow me."

According to the Gospel of Matthew (and the entire New Testament), this joyful announcement isn't based on a vague belief in the triumph of impersonal forces or human effort to free us from the system we're all stuck in. After all, for Jesus the entire process of salvation begins by acknowledging our spiritual poverty, which Christ has awakened us to (Mt 5:3). In this passage our hope in Christ hinges on three simple words: "He has risen" (Mt 28:6). In the original Greek, that's only one word—*egerthe!* With one little word God turns the tables on evil, sin, death, injustice and tragedy. With one little word God changes a tool for torture into an instrument of hope. With one little word God does what we could never do with our many words and frenetic activity. With one little word Jesus escapes into freedom so he can lead us into freedom.

Jesus' resurrection isn't just an interesting theory or a theological concept. Its power makes it possible to enter a new world, a world of redemption and freedom beyond our wildest imagination. Surprisingly (or not surprisingly, according to the Gospel of Matthew), this new world started with two Mary's, one of them being Mary Magdalene. The Gospel writer Luke refers to her as "Mary (called Magdalene) from whom seven demons had come out" (Lk 8:2). It's not a nice picture of spiritual wholeness. In the language of twelve-step programs, her life had become "unmanageable." For Mary Magdalene, the crucifixion should have solidified her prison walls—the end of her chance for a fresh start in life, the end of a God-with-us life, the end of her dream for a better world. Instead, in light of the resurrection, Jesus ushers her into a new world of possibilities. She's the first person mentioned in Matthew 28. She's the one who receives the first announcement of the resurrection (Mt 28:5). She's the one who's told to find the male disciples of Jesus. The entire mission of the church will flow from Mary Magdalene's life-changing encounter with Jesus' resurrection.

The resurrection meant that this wasn't the end for Mary. For Mary, the woman most famous for her broken past, it meant the beginning of a brand new world. But why her? Why begin the new world with Mary

Magdalene? Based on the rest of this Gospel there's only one answer: God wants to prove that he relates to us by grace and not by our moral achievement. The power of the resurrection means that broken lives can be restored—even for someone like Mary Magdalene. Actually, in one sense, if we don't see ourselves in Mary Magdalene, if we don't see ourselves as one of those "sick people" who need a doctor, we can't follow Jesus to freedom. The power of the resurrection comes first and foremost to unlikely people, people who hunger and thirst for righteousness, people who know they need radical transformation, and because of their need they simply ask Jesus to save them.

The crucifixion should have been the end for the disciples too. Despite their macho bravado, despite their well-intentioned plans for success, when it came time for them to stand with Jesus in his darkest hour, they plunged into another round of colossal failure. Now Jesus was gone. Their dreams of redemption were gone. The hope of God with us was gone. The hope of forgiveness was gone. As they watched Jesus die, they also realized that the hope for life beyond death was gone. Like everyone else, the disciples would die in their sins. In every way imaginable, they had hit a dead end.

But now, in light of the resurrection, suddenly it's not the end for them either. After the resurrection Jesus seeks them out. He is still God with us. In Matthew 28:10 Jesus repeats the words of the angel from verse 7: "Go and tell my brothers to go to Galilee; there they will see me." Thus Jesus fulfills the promise he made before the crucifixion (see Mt 26:31-32), namely that he would meet them again. At the end of this chapter Jesus repeats the promise of his ongoing presence: "I am with you always, to the very end of the age" (Mt 28:20). The resurrection completes the central hope of this Gospel: God is for us and God with us.

There is a darker side to Matthew 28 as well. In verses 11-15 we see a countermovement away from resurrection reality. They "devised a plan" (see Mt 28:12) to counteract the good news of the resurrection. This attitude rings true with the rest of Matthew's Gospel. Faith in Christ isn't automatic. Some will resist it. In their minds, this repugnant, repulsive story must be squelched or at least resisted and ignored. This isn't the first time we've seen the dark underbelly of unfaith. But again Matthew wants us to note how often the human race—especially the "righteous" and the powerful—resist God's offer to walk with us. We don't want God to get that close. We don't want to let the coming kingdom change us. In the end, like all the powerful and privileged people in verses 11-15, our lives can end in a tragic rejection of Jesus and his little way of salvation and transformation.

Obviously, that's not what happened to Mary Magdalene and the disciples. They trusted Jesus and entered a brand new world. Because of the resurrection, for those who trust Jesus there is no "end" anymore. Nothing can prevent Jesus from being God with us—not our failure and sin, not human evil and violence, not the cup of God's wrath (his righteous judgment on human evil), not even the stranglehold of death itself. Through the crucifixion and resurrection, God the Father took every tragic, dead-end, broken thing and wove it into Jesus' victory. Now, through Jesus' resurrection, the disciples are ushered into the same story.

There are no dead ends for us, either. As he did for Jesus, God the Father takes the things destined to destroy us or at the very least cause us to hit a hopeless dead end—our failure, pain, suffering, even death itself—and weaves it all into our redemption story.

Recently a friend of mine was reflecting on his divorce. In some ways, the divorce stemmed from his moral failures. He had disappointed and hurt his wife. On the other hand, he had also tried to own and heal his contribution to the marital breakdown. In the end, nothing worked and the marriage shattered beyond repair. In the midst of the wreckage, my friend said, "You know, I didn't want this divorce. Actually, it's the worst thing that's ever happened to me. I feel devastated, but I'm not bitter. How could I be? After all, God has used this very worst thing to help me see my sin, make me more merciful toward others, cause me to trust him like never before, and open my eyes to the pain of this broken world. So I guess God took my very worst thing and made it into a very best thing for me and others. It doesn't change my views on the beauty of God's plan for marriage; it just changes my faith in God's ability to redeem the bad things in our lives." In the midst of my friend's painful apparent dead end, the risen Christ was not only with him; Christ was also transforming him. My friend described perfectly the power of the resurrection at work.

It's easy for us to minimize the profound social implications of the resurrection. Imagine people like Mary Magdalene and those first disciples grasping the message of the resurrection. In terms of their social status, they were near the bottom of the heap. Morally, they had failed to maintain a clean track record. Spiritually, they had often displayed their unremarkable little faith. But now, in light of the resurrection, a new world had opened for them. In and through the resurrection, these socially disregarded people found dignity and significance. Jesus bestowed honor and self-worth on them. The risen Jesus Christ breathed life-enriching promises into their souls: "Do not be afraid. Go and make disciples. I am with you always, even to the end of the age."

They were no longer defined by their past, their problems or their social standing. Even death couldn't define them. Ultimately, they were defined by only one thing: Jesus Christ had been raised. The first and only man to break free from our walled-in prison had come for them. Now there was only one thing that mattered: his promise "I am with you."

LIVING BETWEEN THE BOOKENDS—GOD WITH US
Matthew 28:16-20

After the glorious good news of the resurrection, we'd expect the disciples to finally get it. We'd like to see Matthew wrap up this Gospel with the hope that these little-faiths will arise; at last they'll become the mighty big-faiths, the irrepressible, unstoppable spiritual elites. Instead, Matthew 28:17 quietly mentions, "They worshiped him; but some doubted." It's so anticlimactic. Why even mention it? Why not cover it up? And yet it sounds just like the view of Jesus and the disciples we've seen for the last twenty-eight chapters of this Gospel. Following Jesus still puts us on the little way for ordinary sinners who trust an extraordinary Savior. It's still the way for spiritual strugglers who are, amazingly enough, called by Jesus himself to live as the salt of the earth and the light of the world.

Amazingly, in the midst of their doubt and struggle, Jesus doesn't condemn or reject the disciples. He doesn't shame them and say, "Away from me, you pathetic doubters." Doubt does not disqualify them from his way. Jesus will take doubting worshipers and continue to work with them on the path of discipleship. Once again, in Jesus there is hope for us, the disciples' fellow strugglers. In a way, this verse serves to end Matthew's Gospel the way he began: with the good news of a God who walks beside and transforms sinful people.[22]

But in the midst of Jesus' humble identification with sinners, this Gospel never loses its focus on the glory of Jesus, the God who is with us. We saw the glory of God with us in Matthew 17, when Jesus was transfigured and "his face shone like the sun" (Mt 17:2). Now in Matthew 28:18 this glorious and risen Jesus says, "All authority in heaven and on earth has been given to me." In our pluralistic culture, that statement is tough to swallow. If Jesus would have tempered it, toned it down—as in, "Some authority has been given to me"—it would have been much more palatable. But he claimed all authority had been given to him. It's a daring and audacious claim. If it's false, Jesus has a huge credibility problem. Of course, if it's true, then it's right and proper to fall down and worship him.

And if it's true, if Jesus does possess all authority over heaven and earth, then the next verse makes perfect sense. If Jesus is God with us who has all authority, and if Christ died for my sins and rose from the dead, then that good news compels me to spend the rest of my life fulfilling his words: "Therefore go and make disciples of all nations, baptizing them in the name of the Father and of the Son and of the Holy Spirit" (Mt 28:19).

Ultimately, Jesus' name (Immanuel, God with us), his crucifixion, his resurrection and his authority all point in the same direction: we have been called into mission for Jesus and with Jesus. Once we grasp who he is and what he's done, we can't stay the same. Our lives and our community as Jesus' people will never be the same. Because of Easter we are sent people. Once we grasp our "sentness," it will permanently alter our life.

Imagine, for example, that you're lounging on your back porch, sipping lemonade with your friends as you cook a batch of burgers and brats. The sun is setting on a lazy summer evening and you've kicked your feet up on a lawn chair. Ah, does life get any better than this? But

then suddenly from on the other side of the house you hear tires screech-
ing, glass breaking and metal smashing, then a long, ugly silence. Finally, after thirty seconds you hear at least a few people moaning. What
do you do? Initially, your cozy little party is over—or at least temporarily
suspended. You've been called into action. You and your friends throw
aside your drinks and leave the barbecue as you race to the street on the
other side of the house. Upon arrival you find a horrific scene of twisted
metal, rising steam, trickling blood and people in pain.

Naturally, you're overwhelmed by the sight of trauma and wreckage. But fortunately you and your friends aren't the first ones on the
scene. A mysterious stranger has already arrived and is starting to tend
to the victims. When he sees you and your friends, he looks into your
eyes and quietly says, "I am a doctor. I have taken charge here. Quick,
come over here and place this cloth on this man's wound. And you: go
over by the truck and hold that woman's hand. And you two: stay with
this child who is frightened and alone. All of you stay put until I tell
you what to do next."

You and your friends have been summoned. Someone with authority
and competence has called you into action. From now on he will define
your mission. Your job is to stay close to him, listen to his words and
obey his orders as you tend the wounded. You realize something exciting
is taking place within you: you are not bored! You will never be bored
again. And although you feel overwhelmed and inadequate, as long as
you listen to the doctor in charge, you can rest confidently in the fact that
you just have to do your part to bring healing to the wreck.

This Gospel began with the reassurance that God is with us, but
now it closes with the challenge that Jesus is also God with others.
God is with and for everyone on earth. Matthew 28:19 contains the
scope of our mission—"all nations."[23] It isn't just for our families or
our neighborhoods or our community or even our nation. No, "Make
disciples of all nations," Jesus said. Why didn't he make this a little
more modest? He could not because his love, his message of God with
us, isn't just for people like us: it's for everyone—outsiders, sinners,
even our enemies. So Jesus opens our eyes to his vision for all nations.
We've seen this before: ever so calmly and confidently, Jesus called us

the salt of the earth and the light of the world.

But as Jesus has emphasized before (see Mt 7:21-23), although the mission is daunting, we can't start defining it by big programs, colossal success, frenetic busyness or sensational results. Notice what Jesus tells us to do in Matthew 28:19. The emphasis of the verse is on the phrase "make disciples" (in Greek it's only one word). Making disciples always connects a person intimately to Jesus, and there aren't any shortcuts or formulas for forging intimate relationships. Making disciples also implies taking a student through the slow and personal process of learning a trade. As Jesus sends us into mission, he's calling us to do the slow and unspectacular work of walking beside people as they learn to hear and obey him. This kind of work isn't glamorous or dynamic. Likewise, the phrase "teaching them" (Mt 28:20) also implies a slow process. You seldom teach something when you're in a hurry, and if you do, you often do more harm than good. Teaching involves numerous hands-on, face-to-face encounters. The process involves "slow, corporate, and earthy ways of circling the same object, saying the same thing: disciple people—take your time with them, work carefully with them, bring them along gently."[24]

In the last verse Jesus returns to his central theme: God is with us. Actually, there are two clear bookends to this Gospel:

- "They will call him Immanuel (which means, 'God with us')" (Mt 1:23).

- "And surely I am with you always, to the very end of the age" (Mt 28:20).

Matthew's Gospel begins and ends not with a command or a threat or a philosophical pronouncement; it begins and ends with a promise: God is with us. According to the last verse, Jesus is God with us "to the very end of the age." I think most people get that part, and it's truly beautiful to know that Jesus will be with us to the end of the age—the end of this life and even for all eternity. But we tend to miss the fact that before this phrase Jesus says, "I am with you always." That little word "always" packs a punch because it literally means "the whole of every day."[25] The promise of Jesus' presence isn't just for the future. It isn't just for my old age or when I die and go to be with him forever. Jesus is present with me the whole of this day. That's powerful because I don't know if I can follow Jesus for the rest of my life—the rest of my life hasn't happened yet. But based on his presence in my life I have the strength to follow him this day. And then he'll be with me tomorrow so I can obey him that day . . . and the next day . . . and the next day. But I can only live for him today, because his presence is with me this day—the whole of this day. No wonder we're told to pray, "Give us today our daily bread" (Mt 6:11) and reminded, "Each day has enough trouble of its own" (Mt 6:34).

So "God with us" (Mt 1:23) and "I am with you always" (the whole of this day, Mt 28:20) form the two bookends of the Gospel of Matthew. Those promises also provide the bookends for my life in and with Jesus. Our lives—with all their twists and turns, failures and sorrows, joys and longings, degradations and triumphs, betrayals and loves—fit between those two bookends. Our entire mission—serving Jesus by preaching the gospel and healing the sick, doing the slow work of making disciples, building bridges across cultures until all nations hear the good news— also fit between those two bookends: God with us.

AFTERWORD

Despite having top billing in the New Testament canon, Matthew's Gospel often gets bypassed for one of the others. It doesn't have as much feel-good "love" language as John's writing, nor the currently popular emphasis on justice seen in Luke's. The length of Matthew's writing drives some people to the relative brevity of Mark instead, and others find Matthew's Jewishness difficult to navigate from a culture and time far removed.

Admittedly, Matthew is a lengthy and challenging book to study, but our apostolic writer is not without compassion on his readers. From time to time he does leave cookies on a lower shelf (if only to draw us to climb higher for greater rewards). For example, as Matt Woodley has stated in this book, Matthew bookends his Gospel with a single message that cannot be missed: In chapter 1, as Joseph is informed of Jesus' advent by the angel, Matthew identifies the child as Immanuel, "which means, God with us" (1:23); in the final verse of his book, Matthew is mindful to repeat this message, as Jesus, speaking to his followers before ascending to the Father, says, "Behold, I am with you always, to the end of the age" (28:20).

There, standing like mighty pylons from which he suspends his gospel bridge, is the heart of Matthew's message to the world: God is with us.

It may sound like a rudimentary idea, but God's presence with his people cannot be quickly passed over on the way to deeper theologies. It is a truth that must be deeply internalized and experienced in communion with him, because it is only when we come to a profound trust in his love and care for us—a truth verified by the incarnation, life, death and resurrection of Jesus Christ—that our vision of the world is transformed. Rather than seeing the cosmos as a threatening place that provokes fear, anger and violence, with the knowledge that our God is with us we can actually come to "fear no evil" because our Good Shepherd is by our side. From this posture of utter safety, like Jesus, we can subvert the world and display a kingdom not of this earth—a kingdom of peace, joy and healing.

With his pastoral touch, Matt Woodley reveals that the "God with us" message of Matthew is desperately needed today, and not just in the world but also within the church. As Christianity continues to face challenges, particularly in the Western world, we often respond with renewed calls to mission. We assume that our deficit is one of motivation or perhaps resources, and so enormous effort is put forth casting a vision for participation in works that will establish (or re-establish) the church.

But Matthew's Gospel reminds us that Jesus did not come merely to launch a mission. He came to reconcile us, along with all things, to his Father. And therefore a life with God must precede and encompass a life for God. Missional activism has its place, but it must always be submitted to a call for perpetual communion with our God—a communion gloriously revealed in Christ's coming, explained in Christ's teaching, inaugurated in Christ's death and sealed in Christ's resurrection. Without this foundation our efforts, while well intentioned, will be in vain.

This elementary message of Matthew's Gospel is among the more accessible treasures, but I do hope this commentary has helped you reach for the higher shelves as well. There the apostle invites us to savor truths about God's kingdom, feed on mysteries about the cosmos, and be sustained with the spiritual food to go and make disciples. But let us not forget amid our learning and teaching and serving; he is with us always, to the end of the age.

Skye Jethani

NOTES

Foreword

[1]Richard Burgin, "Isaac Bashevis Singer's Universe," *The New York Times Magazine*, December 3, 1978, p. 40

Introduction

[1]The Greek word for "renewal" in Matthew 19:28 is the descriptive word *palingenesia* or "the new genesis" (*palin* = again; *genesia* = genesis). It is a huge, happy and hopeful word. Philo used it for the renewal of the earth after the floodwaters subsided. The ancient Jews used it to signify the end of the world as we know it and the beginning of a new chapter in history. It's probably best to hear the beautiful voice of God use this word as he echoes through the prophet Isaiah (who greatly influenced Jesus in the Gospel of Matthew): "Behold, I will create new heavens and a new earth. The former things will not be remembered, nor will they come to mind" (Is 65:17).

[2]For the phrase "little way" I'm deeply indebted to St.Thérèse of Lisieux, a nineteenth-century French Carmelite nun who based her faith in Jesus on a very Matthewlike approach to the spiritual life.

[3]Matthew uses ten "formula citations," or quotations from the Old Testament that begin with something like, "All this happened to fulfill what was spoken by the Lord through the prophet." However, as Nolland notes, these formula quotes are "only the tip of the iceberg" when regarding Matthew's use of the Old Testament: "[Matthew] quotes the OT at least twice as much as any other Gospel writer. Here is a work saturated with the OT. . . . Though some of Matthew's text forms come to him straight from the Gospel tradition, the overall impression is of a man who freshly scrutinizes, at least on many occasions, the OT texts to which he appeals, and is able to do so in Greek, Hebrew (not always the Hebrew preserved in the MT) and occasionally in Aramaic. When it suits him to do so, he produces translations that reflect influences along more than one track of tradition." See John Nolland, *The Gospel of Matthew,* New International Greek Testament Commentary (Grand Rapids: Eerdmans, 2005), pp. 29, 33. See also pages 33-36 for Nolland's overview and conclusions about how Matthew used his Old Testament sources to tell the story of Jesus.

[4]For a detailed exploration of Jesus as teacher, prophet, Messiah, king, Son of God, Son of Man and judge-Lord-mediator, see Craig Keener, *A Commentary on the Gospel of Matthew* (Grand Rapids: Eerdmans, 1999), pp. 53-71.

[5]Ibid., p. 40. Although compare this with D. A. Carson's conclusion: "There are solid reasons in support of the early church's unanimous ascription of this book to the apos-

tle Matthew, and on close inspection the objections [against Matthew's authorship] do not appear substantial. Though Matthew's authorship remains the most defensible position, very little in this commentary depends on it." D. A. Carson, *Matthew, Mark and Luke* (Grand Rapids: Zondervan, 1984), p. 21.

[6]Personally, I agree with Carson's conclusion: "While surprisingly little in the Gospel points to a conclusive date, perhaps the sixties are the most likely decade for its composition." Carson, *Matthew, Mark and Luke,* p. 21.

[7]Keener best summarizes the purpose and audience for this Gospel: "Matthew probably functions as a discipling manual, a 'handbook' of Jesus' basic life and teaching, relevant to a Jewish-Christian community engaged in Gentile mission and deadlocked in scriptural polemic with their local synagogue communities." Keener, *Commentary,* p. 51.

[8]Although I agree with Carson when he writes, "No outline should be taken too seriously. The Gospels use vignettes—organized ones, doubtless, but vignettes nonetheless." Carson, *Matthew, Mark and Luke,* p. 51

Chapter 1: The Identity and Mission of Jesus

[1]In the words of N. T. Wright, "Matthew presupposes a telling of the Jewish story according to which Israel has failed, has ended in exile and needs a new exodus; and he undertakes to show that this new exodus was accomplished in the life, death and resurrection of Jesus." N. T. Wright, *The New Testament and the People of God* (Minneapolis: Augsburg Fortress, 1992), p. 390.

[2]J. R. R. Tolkien. *The Hobbit* (New York: Houghton Mifflin, 1997), p. 3.

[3]Jeremy Hsu, "The Secrets of Storytelling," *Scientific American Mind* 19, no. 4 (2008): 46.

[4]According to Carson, "The expression is found only twice in the LXX: in Genesis 2:4 it refers to the creation account (Gen 2:4-25) and in Genesis 5:1 to the ensuing genealogy." D. A. Carson, *Matthew, Mark and Luke* (Grand Rapids: Zondervan, 1984), p. 61.

[5]Some scholars don't take this phrase as far as I do. Nolland comments, "While a Genesis allusion is probable, its intention is likely to be less profound (use of a 'biblical' style?; offering another important account of origins?)." However, a few pages earlier, Nolland hints that Matthew may have been thinking along the lines of a new Genesis—or a new retelling of the OT. He writes, "In the genealogy with which Matthew begins his Gospel he echoes Genesis materials at the beginning and then draws on Ru. 4:18-22 supplemented by 1 Ch. 3:10-19. By evoking important aspects of the story of Israel's history the genealogy functions as a compressed retelling of the OT story." John Nolland, *The Gospel of Matthew,* New International Greek Testament Commentary (Grand Rapids: Eerdmans, 2005), pp. 71, 34.

[6]Carson comments, "Study has shown that genealogies in the Ancient Near East could serve widely diverse functions: economic, tribal, political, domestic (to show family or geographic relationships), and others." D. A. Carson, *Matthew, Mark and Luke* (Grand Rapids: Zondervan, 1984), p. 62.

[7]Adapted from Tom Wright, *Matthew for Everyone, Part One* (Louisville, Ky.: Westminster John Knox, 2004), p. 2. (Note: Elsewhere "Tom Wright" is cited as "N. T. Wright".)

[8]Carson notes, "'Son of David' is an important designation in Matthew. Not only does

David become a turning point in the genealogy (1:6, 17), but the title recurs throughout the Gospel (9:27; 12:23; 15:22; 20:30-31; 21:9, 15; 22:42, 45), God swore covenant love to David (Psalm 89:29) and promised that one of his immediate descendants would establish the kingdom—even more, that David's kingdom and throne would endure forever (2 Samuel 7:12-16). . . . [Thus] Matthew's chief aims in including the genealogy are hinted at in the first verse—viz., to show that Jesus Messiah is truly in the kingly line of David, heir to the messianic promises, the one who brings divine blessings to all nations." Carson, *Matthew, Mark and Luke,* pp. 62-63.

[9]Many scholars, including Carson and Nolland, argue for the symbolic significance of the fourteen by three in reference to the name of David. In the ancient world, letters carried numeric values. So, for instance, the name David, which in Hebrew had three letters (*dwd*), added up to fourteen ("d" or 4 + "w" or 6 + "d" or 4 = 14). Hence, David's three letters add up to fourteen or three lists of fourteen names in Matthew 1. However, Keener argues for a nonnumeric interpretation of the three by fourteen: "Perhaps fourteen was simply Matthew's average estimate of the generations from one period in Israel's history to the next. Matthew preferred a round number for each set of generations, perhaps for ease of memorization." Regarding the exact number in each of the three sets of "fourteen" (the last list only has thirteen names), Keener observes, "However one counts, not all Matthew's lists come to precisely 14; but Jewish interpreters did not expect numerical exactitude . . . and ancients could vary between inclusive and exclusive counting. Fourteen was a reasonable number of generations." Craig Keener, *A Commentary on the Gospel of Matthew* (Grand Rapids: Eerdmans, 1999), p. 74.

[10]I'm indebted to Dale Bruner for these two prominent themes from Matthew 1:1-17. See Dale Bruner, *The Christbook* (Waco, Tex.: Word, 1987), pp. 1-22.

[11]According to Nolland, Matthew's genealogy "locates [Jesus] firmly within, but at the climax of, the history of God's dealings with his people. In brief compass Matthew evokes the glories and tragedies of that story which the purposes of God foretold. . . . Matthew's story embraces the whole history of God's dealings with his people from the calling of Abraham to the end of the age." Nolland, *Gospel of Matthew,* pp. 70-71.

[12]Bruner comments, "This first genealogy in the New Testament has the surprising office of teaching us that the line that led from Abraham to Jesus, the Son of David, was intersected again and again by gentile blood. . . . Matthew wants the church to know that from the start . . . God's work has been interracial, and that God is no narrow nationalist or racist." Bruner, *Christbook,* p. 6.

[13]I heard this in a talk called "Theology of the Body 1" given by the brilliant Catholic theologian Christopher West at a conference of the same name in Lancaster, Penn., September 2009, put on by the Theology of the Body Institute.

[14]This is a paraphrase of a statement attributed to Martin Luther, who said, "Oh, Christ is the kind of person who is not ashamed of sinners—in fact, He even puts them in his family tree. . . . Now if the Lord does that here, so we ought to despise no one . . . but put ourselves right in the middle of the fight for sinners and help them." Martin Luther, "Sermon on the Day of Mary's Birth," quoted in Bruner, *Christbook,* p. 8.

[15]Paul Auster, *I Thought My Father Was God* (New York: Holt, 2001), p. xvi.

[16]Quoted in Christopher West, *The Love That Satisfies* (West Chester, Penn.: Ascension, 2007), p. 106.

[17]N. T. Wright comments on the virgin birth, "Matthew and Luke don't ask us to take the story all by itself. They ask us to see it in the light of the entire history of Israel—in which God was always present and at work, often in surprising ways—and, more particularly, of the subsequent story of Jesus himself. Does the rest of the story, and the impact of Jesus on the world and countless individuals within it ever since, make it more or less likely that he was indeed conceived by a special act of the holy spirit? That is a question that everyone must answer for themselves." Wright, *Matthew for Everyone, Part One,* p. 7. For a full discussion of the virgin birth in Matthew 1:18, see Carson: "That Mary was 'found' to be with child does not suggest . . . concealment ('found out') but only that her pregnancy became obvious. . . . There is no hint of pagan deity-human coupling in crassly physical terms. Instead, the power of the Lord, who was expected to be active in the Messianic Age, miraculously brought about the conception." Carson, *Matthew, Mark and Luke,* pp. 71-74.

[18]For a full discussion of this verse, especially in relation to Matthew's use of Isaiah 7:14, see ibid., pp. 77-80. Carson notes that Matthew here echoes the Gospel of John 1:14, 18.

[19]In the words of C. S. Lewis, "Think of a pearl diver, first reducing himself to nakedness, then glancing up in mid-air, then gone with a splash, vanished, rushing down through green and warm water into the black and cold water, down through increasing pressure into the death-like region of ooze and slime and old decay; then up again, back to color and light, his lungs almost bursting, till suddenly he breaks surface again, holding in his hand the dripping, precious thing that he went down to recover. He and it are both covered now that they have come up into the light." C. S. Lewis, *Miracles* (New York: Harper Collins, 1974), p. 179.

[20]This comment was made by a pagan philosopher named Porphyry in his ancient work *Against the Christians.* It is quoted in Thomas Molnar, *The Pagan Temptation* (Grand Rapids: Eerdmans, 1987), p. 27.

[21]Kenneth Cragg, *Jesus and the Muslim* (Oxford: Oneworld, 1999), p. 278.

[22]"Righteousness" is an important word for Matthew, who acknowledges that the word has different meanings (note the contrast between the righteousness required from Jesus that must "exceed" the righteousness of the religious leaders in Mt 5:20). R. T. France aptly summarizes Matthew's view of righteousness: "[It] is not just 'being good,' still less legal correctness, but rather a synonym for the Christian life, viewed as a relationship with God focused in obedience." R. T. France, *Matthew* (Grand Rapids: Eerdmans, 1985), p. 94.

[23]Philip Yancey, *The Jesus I Never Knew* (Grand Rapids: Zondervan, 1995), p. 29.

[24]For Psyche, a character in C. S. Lewis's *Till We Have Faces,* "the sweetest thing in my life has been the longing . . . to find the place where all the beauty came from." See C. S. Lewis, *Till We Have Faces* (New York: Harvest, 1956), p. 75.

[25]Walker Percy, *The Moviegoer* (New York: Ivy, 1960), p. 9.

[26]As Leon Morris notes, "Matthew is apparently saying that in some way the star kept

going ahead of them until it came to the place where the baby was and that it then stood (still)." Leon Morris, *The Gospel According to St. Matthew* (Grand Rapids: Eerdmans, 1992), p. 40.

[27]See Bruner, *Christbook*, pp. 43-50. Also see Keener's observation: "Without condoning astrology, Matthew's narrative challenges his audience's prejudice against outsiders to their faith (cf. also 8:5-13; 15:21-28); even the most pagan of pagans may respond to Jesus if given the opportunity. For one special event in history, the God who rules the heavens chose to reveal himself where pagans were looking." Keener, *Commentary*, p. 100.

[28]Keener observes, "These were the religious leaders, but they failed to act on their most critical biblical knowledge. Although these authorities did not desire to kill Jesus as Herod did, their successors a generation later did seek his death (Mt 26:57, 59). . . . Matthew also intended his vehemence against the religious establishment of his day as a warning to his fellow disciples. Matthew is emphatic that the sin of taking Jesus for granted, like the sin of wishing him dead, is a sin that can especially characterize those who claim to be God's servants." Keener, *Commentary*, pp. 103-4.

[29]As Keener notes, "News of a star signaling a new ruler in his realm would thus undoubtedly trouble a ruler as paranoid as Herod. . . . That the Magi seek one 'born King of the Jews' may further underline the challenge to Herod, who was widely known to have achieved rule by warfare and politics, not birth. If Herod had actually permitted some to hail him as deity . . . or otherwise revealed messianic aspirations, one can understand just what sort of threat the Magi's announcement represented to him." Ibid., p. 102.

[30]The exact quote from C. S. Lewis is, "We are not merely imperfect creatures who must be improved; we are . . . rebels who must lay down our arms." C. S. Lewis, *The Problem of Pain* (HarperCollins, 2001), p. 88.

[31]Anne Lamott, *Traveling Mercies* (New York: Pantheon, 1999), pp. 49-50.

[32]Since this exact phrase doesn't seem to occur in the Old Testament, scholars debate what Matthew meant by "So was fulfilled what was said through the prophet, 'He will be called a Nazarene'" (Mt 2:23). The two most common options are either Isaiah 11:1, which points to a "branch" (the Hebrew is *netser*) from the root of Jesse, or Judges 13:5, which mentions Samson's Nazirite vow. However, Matthew probably wasn't referring to a specific verse but to "a summary of a theme of prophetic expectation." In other words, "Matthew saw in the obscurity of Nazareth the fulfillment of Old Testament indications of a humble and rejected Messiah; for Jesus to be known by the derogatory epithet *Nazoraios* was not incompatible with the expected royal dignity of the Messiah, and thus fulfilled such passages as Psalm 22; Isaiah 53; Zechariah 11:4-14." France, *Matthew*, pp. 88-89.

[33]Carson comments, "Here [in Nazareth] Jesus grew up, not as 'Jesus the Bethlehemite,' with its Davidic overtones, but as 'Jesus the Nazarene,' with all the opprobrium of the sneer. When Christians were referred to in Acts as the "Nazarene sect" (24:5), the expression was meant to hurt. First-century Christian readers of Matthew, who had tasted their share of scorn, would have quickly caught Matthew's point. He is not saying that a particular OT prophet foretold that the Messiah would live in Nazareth; he is saying

that the OT prophets foretold that Messiah would be despised." Carson, *Matthew, Mark and Luke*, p. 97.

[34]Commenting on Matthew 2:15 ("And so was fulfilled what was said through the prophet, 'Out of Egypt I have called my son'"), Keener says, "Matthew expects all his readers to understand the primacy of Scripture and the centrality of Christ's mission in Scripture; but he expects his more sophisticated readers to catch his allusion to Israel's history as well. Contemporary commentators thus generally recognize that by citing Hosea 11:1, Matthew evokes the new exodus in Jesus, who embodies Israel's purpose and mission. Matthew emphasizes Jesus' solidarity with Israel elsewhere as well (cf. 1:1; 4:2). . . . Matthew emphasizes another point as well: God declares Jesus' Sonship in his return from Egypt, that is, outside the Promised Land. Jesus is not for Judea alone, but for all peoples." Keener, *Commentary*, p. 109.

[35]Matthew includes ten "formula quotations," or Old Testament "fulfillment texts." Half of Matthew's texts come from Isaiah, two come from Zechariah, and one each come from Jeremiah, Hosea and the Psalms. By using these ten texts, Matthew wants us to know that the Bible contains only one story: creation-election-exodus-law-promise-Jesus-kingdom-cross-resurrection-recreation. It all hangs together as one story, not two.

[36]Keener notes, "Rachel weeps for her children, but God comforts her, promising the restoration of his people (Jer 31:15-17), because Israel is 'my dear son, the child in whom I delight' (Jer 31:20; cf, again Mt 2:15). This time of new salvation would be the time of a new covenant (Jer 31:31-34). The painful events of Jesus' persecuted childhood are the anvil on which God would forge the fulfillment of his promises to his people, just as the cross would usher in the new covenant (Mt 26:28)." Keener, *Commentary*, pp. 111-12.

[37]Jean Vanier, *Becoming Human* (Toronto: House of Anansi, 2003), p. 45.

[38]Kathleen Norris, *Amazing Grace* (New York: Riverhead, 1998), p. 2.

[39]Richard Foster and James Bryan Smith, *Devotional Classics* (San Francisco: HarperCollins, 1990), p. 311.

[40]Bruner, *Christbook*, pp. 70-71, 77.

[41]Christopher J. H. Wright says, "To human eyes, Jesus was the son of an unimportant carpenter in insignificant Nazareth. In God's sight, however, he was 'My beloved Son in whom I delight.' That was his real identity. . . . The awareness of God being his Father and himself as God's son is probably the deepest foundation of Jesus' selfhood. . . . Jesus experienced a relationship with God, of such personal intimacy and dependence, that only the language of Father and Son could describe it." Christopher J. H. Wright, *Knowing Jesus Through the Old Testament* (Downers Grove, Ill.: InterVarsity Press, 1992), p. 105.

[42]As Bruner comments, "By surrounding Jesus' baptism with so many of the crucial Old Testament associations—Servant of the Lord, Son of God, Son of David, Spirit-bearer, Christ, etc.—Matthew is trying to say that in Jesus God has given us all his promises. In Paul's accolade, 'all the promises of God find their Yes in him,' they are fulfilled in Jesus (2 Cor 1:20). In Jesus we have everything we need: an open heaven, the presence

of the Spirit of God, and the closely identifying life of the Son of God himself. To solemnize this central truth, the whole Trinity is visible or audible here at the baptism: the Father in the Voice, the Spirit in the Dove, and the Son in the water." Bruner, *Christbook,* p. 88.

[43]Rick Bragg, "Florida Town Finds Satan an Offense Unto It," *New York Times,* March 14, 2002, p. 26.

[44]In his trilogy on the history of the demonic, Jeffrey Burton Russell summarizes his personal views: "[Satan is] a real force actively present in the cosmos urging to evil. This evil force has a purposive center that actively hates good, the cosmos, and every individual in the cosmos. . . . It has terrible and immense effects, but it is ultimately futile; every individual can defeat it . . . by drawing on the loving power of God. For Christians, then, the person of the Devil may be a metaphor, but it is a metaphor for something that is real, that really brings horror to the world every day and threatens to lay the entire earth waste." Quoted in Bruner, *Christbook,* p. 102.

[45]Carson comments, "Satan was not inviting Jesus to doubt his Sonship but to reflect on its meaning. Sonship of the living God, he suggested, surely means that Jesus has the power and right to satisfy his own needs." Carson, *Matthew, Mark and Luke,* p. 112.

[46]This wouldn't be the last time Jesus would face this same temptation. As he hung on the cross, people passing by said, "If you are the Son of God, come down from the cross" (27:40). In effect they were repeating Satan's primal and best temptation: "You aren't the Son of God; you don't have a special relationship with the Father; you are not loved. Instead, you are utterly alone in the coldness of the universe. So look out for yourself; save yourself; get your needs met your own way."

[47]"For that reason, because so much was at stake—no less than the salvation of the world—the devil's onslaught on Jesus' Sonship tried so desperately to deflect him from obedience to his Father's will. Aware that Jesus, through his obedience, would win the world for God, the Devil offered him the world in advance if he would sell out to him. But Jesus resisted and set himself deliberately on the path of loyal obedience to the Father, in full awareness that it would lead to suffering and death. There was no other way." Wright, *Knowing Jesus Through the Old Testament,* p. 132.

[48]As Carson notes, "Both Jesus' and Israel's hunger taught a lesson (Deut. 8:3); both spent time in the desert preparatory to their respective tasks. . . . The main point is that both 'sons' were tested by God's design, the one after being redeemed from Egypt and the other after his baptism, to prove their obedience in preparation for their appointed word. The one 'son' [Israel] failed but pointed to the Son who would never fail. In this sense the temptations legitimized Jesus as God's true son." Carson, *Matthew, Mark and Luke,* p. 112.

[49]In Morris's words, "The temptations proceed from the fact that he is the Son of God, and that accordingly he must live as the Son of God. The temptation narratives picture Jesus asking what that means. Is he to be a wonder-worker, using his powers to meet his own needs (and possibly those of others, too)? Is he to do spectacular but pointless miracles? Is he to establish a mighty empire ruling over the whole world? Matthew tells us that right at the beginning of his ministry Jesus looked at each of these and rejected

them all as the temptations of the devil." Morris, *Gospel According to Matthew*, p. 70.
[50]Bruner comments, "Jesus especially believed God's word. In all three temptations, Jesus got his victory by using the source accessible to the rest of us in Holy Scripture. . . .
Jesus used the same old source we have: Hebrew Scripture." Bruner, *Christbook*, p.
114.

Chapter 2: The Public Ministry of Jesus

[1]Leon Morris comments that the first part of Matthew 4:17 ("From that time on Jesus
began to preach") describes "either the beginning of a continuous action or marks a
fresh start or phase of the narrative." Leon Morris, *The Gospel According to Matthew*
(Grand Rapids: Eerdmans, 1992), p. 83.

[2]According to N. T. Wright, "The prophet Isaiah, in line with several Psalms and several
other passages, had spoken of God's coming kingdom as a time when (a) God's promises and purposes would be fulfilled, (b) Israel would be rescued from pagan oppression, (c) evil (particularly the evil of oppressive empires) would be judged, and (d) God
would usher in a new reign of justice. . . . The world was to be turned the right way up
at last. To speak of God's kingdom arriving in the present was to summon up that entire
narrative and to declare that it was reaching its climax. God's future was breaking into
the present. Heaven was arriving on earth." N. T. Wright, *Simply Christian* (San Francisco: HarperOne, 2010), p. 100.

[3]The other Gospel writers use the phrase "kingdom of God." In deference to his Jewish
readership, Matthew uses "kingdom of heaven." "Heaven" was a way to avoid being
disrespectful to the name of God.

[4]Notice Matthew 4:12, which mentions that Jesus made Galilee the "base camp" for his
ministry efforts. Bruner comments on the oddity of Jesus' strategic location: "Galilee is
a strange place for a Messiah to work. There is no early rabbinic reference to the Messiah's appearing or working in Galilee. Galilee was not just geographically far from Jerusalem; it was considered spiritually and politically far too. Galilee was the most pagan
of the Jewish provinces. . . . Galileans were considered by Judeans to sit rather loosely
to the law and to be less biblically pure than those in or near Jerusalem. Finally, Galilee
was notorious for being the nest of revolution and the haunt of Zealot revolutionary
movements. . . . Therefore when Jesus retreated into Galilee, he did more than head
north, he seemed to go wrong. . . . [But in Galilee] Jesus worked where Judaism touched
paganism, where the Nation intersected the nations, where light met darkness. Jesus
lived among the marginal people, on the frontier. This choice of venue . . . demonstrates
God's amazing initiative toward those who have never ever been considered" Dale
Bruner, *The Christbook* (Waco, Tex.: Word, 1987), p. 118.

[5]Henri Nouwen, "Moving from Solitude to Community," *Leadership* (April 1, 1995),
ChristianityTodayLibrary.com <www.ctlibrary.com/le/1995/spring/5l280.html>.

[6]Associated Press, "A dozen nations added to child, forced labor list," December 15,
2010, Yahoo! News <news.yahoo.com/s/ap/20101215/ap_on_bi_ge/us_child_labor>.

[7]The Greek word for "follow" is a present tense imperative, which means something like,
"Follow me and keep following me for the rest or your life." As Matthew's Gospel un-

folds we'll watch Jesus woo, challenge and confront people with a clear and personal invitation: will you follow and keep following me?

[8]Matthew 5:3-10 are called the "Beatitudes," derived from the Latin *beatus*, which means "supremely happy" or a "state of bliss."

[9]In contrast to Matthew, Luke records Jesus saying, "Blessed are you who are poor, for yours is the kingdom of God" (Lk 6:20). Gordon Fee and Douglas Stuart comment on this difference: "In Matthew the poor are the 'poor in spirit'; in Luke they are 'you poor' in contrast to 'you that are rich' (Lk 6:24). On such points most people tend to have only half a canon. Traditional evangelicals tend to read only 'the poor in spirit'; social activists tend to read only 'you poor.' We insist that both are canonical. In a truly profound sense the real poor are those who recognize themselves as impoverished before God. But the God of the Bible, who became incarnate in the Jesus of Nazareth, is a God who pleads the cause of the oppressed and disenfranchised." Gordon D. Fee and Douglas Stuart, *How to Read the Bible for All Its Worth* (Grand Rapids: Zondervan, 2003), p. 125.

[10]Nolland remarks, "The language of poverty is first and foremost the language of neediness. . . . The poor in spirit will be those who sense the burden of their present [impoverished] state . . . who patiently bear that state, but they long for God to act on their behalf and decisively claim them again as his people. To people like this belong the kingdom of heaven which has now drawn near." John Nolland, *The Gospel of Matthew*, New International Greek Testament Commentary (Grand Rapids: Eerdmans, 2005), pp. 200-201.

[11]Bruner, *Christbook*, p. 137. Bruner continues by stating, "The moment we begin to look back and down on those who have not come as far or high in consciousness or sensitivity or spirit as we, in that moment we have become rich in spirit and so fall out of the blessing of the first Beatitude."

[12]For a fascinating discussion of this translation, see Erasmo Leiva-Merikakis, *Fire of Mercy, Heart of the Word* (San Francisco: Ignatius, 1996), pp. 183-85.

[13]For more on "righteousness," see Morris, *Gospel According to Matthew,* p. 99.

[14]Henri Nouwen, *Life of the Beloved* (New York: Crossroad, 1999), p. 30.

[15]According to Morris, this state of spiritual poverty "is the exact opposite of Pharisaic pride in one's own virtue which Jesus so often confronted." Morris, *Gospel According to Matthew,* p. 95.

[16]Mark Kurlansky, *Salt: A World History* (New York: Walker, 2002), p. 6.

[17]Ibid., pp. 3-13.

[18]Morris notes, "*You* is emphatic and restrictive: Jesus is not talking about people in general but specifically about his followers. He says, *you are*: he is making a statement, not giving a promise." Morris, *Gospel According to Matthew,* p. 104.

[19]According to Morris, "This section comes fittingly after the beatitudes: it is the little people, those with no merit of their own to plead but who have been accepted by God in all their lowliness who are the salt and light." Ibid., p. 104.

[20]Kurlansky, *Salt,* p. 11.

[21]According to my biochemist friend Bob, modern-day salt is a very stable chemical com-

pound. Technically, it can't become "unsalty." But salt in Jesus' day was very impure (i.e., mixed with dirt or mud) and therefore had a tendency to lose its saltiness.

[22]Kay Redfield Jamison, *Nothing Was the Same* (New York: Knopf, 2009), pp. 43-44.

[23]Denis Haack, "Winsome Series: Part 1 What Does Winsome Look Like?" Ransom Fellowship <www.ransomfellowship.org/articledetail.asp?AID=34&B=DenisHaack&TID=7>.

[24]James R. Brockman, *Romero: A Life* (Maryknoll, N.Y.: Orbis, 2004), pp. 71, 242-45.

[25]According to France, the Greek word *plerosai* implies that "Jesus is bringing that to which the Old Testament looked forward; his teaching will transcend the Old Testament revelation, but, far from abolishing it, is itself its intended culmination." France also argues that the word may have carried connotations of the Jewish hope that the Messiah would provide the final exposition of the law, "sometimes amounting virtually to the promulgation of a new law." R. T. France, *Matthew* (Grand Rapids: Eerdmans, 1985), p. 114.

[26]Leiva-Merikakis, *Fire of Mercy, Heart of the Word,* p. 212.

[27]Christopher Wright notes, "Jesus, in tune with the whole ethos of the Torah, was enraged by the way the legal experts of his day had turned the law from its prime purpose of being a blessing and a benefit into being a burden for ordinary people. We must note carefully that Jesus did not condemn or reject the law itself. Nor did he condemn the scribes or Pharisees for their love and passion for the law. In fact he said that insofar as they taught what Moses taught, they were to be obeyed, but not imitated (Mt 23:2-3). What his penetrating observations exposed, however, was the way that detailed passion had robbed law of its whole point." Christopher J. H. Wright, *Knowing Jesus Through the Old Testament* (Downers Grove, Ill.: InterVarsity Press, 1995), p. 207.

[28]And again: "Jesus was bringing into full clarity the inherent values and priorities of the Torah. His own teaching certainly built on and surpassed the law itself. But it was facing in the same direction. . . . To a people who had lost sight of the forest for the trees, he brought back a sense of what really mattered first in God's sight. But he showed, by his quotation of Hebrew scriptures themselves, that he was not imposing on the Torah an inappropriate selectivity. Rather, the Torah itself, carefully read and understood, declares its own scale of values and sense of priorities. As we noted earlier, Jesus brought back to light the simplicity and clarity of the Torah from the layers of well-meant regulations that had been intended to protect it but had in effect buried it." Ibid., p. 219.

[29]Bruner, *Christbook,* p. 200.

[30]Actually, in all three of these Old Testament case studies—"Do not murder. . . . Do not commit adultery. . . . Do not break your oath"—Jesus displays a deep concern for human rights, for the dignity of each person made in the image of God. Anger, name-calling, contempt, sexual lust, infidelity, promise-breaking—all of these practices create broken relationships and wounded hearts. In contrast, working for reconciliation, treating others with respect, remaining faithful in our state of marriage or celibacy, standing by our words—these practices bestow dignity on others.

[31]Bertrand Russell, *History of Western Philosophy* (Taylor & Francis e-library, 2005), p. 529.

[32]N. T. Wright comments that striking someone on the right cheek isn't just an act of violence but an insult. "It implies that you're an inferior, a slave, a child (in that world, and sometimes even today) a woman. What's the answer? Hitting back only keeps the evil in circulation. Offering the other cheek implies: hit me again, if you like, but now as an equal, not an inferior." Tom Wright, *Matthew for Everyone, Part One* (Louisville, Ky.: Westminster John Knox, 2004), p. 52.

[33]Ibid.

[34]Emmanuel Katongole and Chris Rice, *Reconciling All Things* (Downers Grove, Ill.: InterVarsity Press, 2009), pp. 22-23, 37.

[35]This story has made the rounds in various books and Internet sites, but the original version was a short story written by the Yiddish writer Isaac Leib Peretz (1852-1915).

[36]Initially, this passage seems to contradict Jesus' statement in Matthew 5:16, in which Jesus says, "Let your light shine before men so they may see your good works." But in Matthew 5:16 the goal and motive of letting others see our good works is so that they may glorify our Father in heaven. In this passage, the motivation for letting others see our good deeds is so that they may glorify (or at least notice and affirm) not God but us.

[37]Commenting on the legitimate hunger for praise, C. S. Lewis wrote, "Pleasure in being praised is not pride. The child who is patted on the back for doing a lesson well, the woman whose beauty is praised by her lover, the saved soul to whom Christ says, 'Well done,' are pleased and ought to be. For here the pleasure lies not in what you are but in the fact that you have pleased someone you wanted (and rightly wanted) to please." See C. S. Lewis, *Mere Christianity* (New York: Macmillan, 1977), p. 112.

[38]The word "hypocrite" occurs seventeen times in the New Testament, but thirteen of those appear in Matthew (three times in Luke and once in Mark). "The word was used mostly for actors in a play, from which it is an easy step to those who speak words for effect and without regard to what is true." Morris, *Gospel According to Matthew*, p. 137.

[39]The verb occurs five times in Matthew and means to receive a sum in full and to give a receipt.

[40]Francis de Sales, *Introduction to the Devout Life* (Garden City, N.Y.: Image, 1972), p. 215.

[41]As Leiva-Merikakis notes, "Familiarity and awe, in tight conjunction, are the mark of Christian prayer." Leiva-Merikakis, *Fire of Mercy, Heart of the Word*, p. 256.

[42]The privilege of calling God "our Father" doesn't make any sense without Jesus' invitation and authority. Jesus is the one who taught us to call God "our Father." As Carson notes, "The overwhelming tendency in Jewish circles was to multiply titles . . . to God. Against such a background, Jesus' habit of addressing God as his own Father and teaching his disciples to do the same could only appear familiar and presumptuous to opponents, personal and gracious to his followers. . . . Jesus' use of *Abba* was adopted by early Christians; and there is no evidence of anyone before Jesus using this term to address God." D. A. Carson, *Matthew, Mark and Luke* (Grand Rapids: Zondervan, 1984), p. 169.

[43]Leiva-Merikakis mentions a Carthusian monk who, when preaching on the Lord's Prayer, couldn't stop repeating the first two words—"Our Father"—over and over again. The sheer miracle and joy of calling God Father had captured his heart with wonder and gratitude, and he could hardly move on to the rest of his sermon. Leiva-Merikakis, *Fire of Mercy*, p. 255.

[44]Bruner, *Christbook*, pp. 242-43.

[45]Keener, *Commentary on the Gospel of Matthew*, p. 216.

[46]Morris, *Gospel According to Matthew*, p. 145.

[47]Carson comments, "To pray 'your kingdom come' is therefore simultaneously to ask that God's saving, royal rule be extended now as people bow in submission to him and already taste the eschatological blessing of salvation and to cry for the consummation of the kingdom. . . . The third request is that God's will may ultimately be done on earth *in the same way* as it is not accomplished in heaven. . . . It is therefore impossible to pray this prayer in sincerity without humbly committing oneself to such a course." Carson, *Matthew, Mark and Luke*, pp. 170-71.

[48]In the words of the fourth-century pastor John Chrysostom, this request helps us not "wear ourselves out with the care of the following day." Cited in ibid., p. 146.

[49]Jon Mooallen, "The Self-Storage Self," *New York Times Magazine,* November 6, 2009, p. 26.

[50]Rodney Clapp, "The Devil Takes Visa," *Christianity Today,* October 17, 1996, p. 26.

[51]Jesus' reference to a "cubit" probably meant length of time and not height (which would have involved considerable growth). Anxiety doesn't add to the quantity or the quality of your life. Actually, Jesus knew what we know so well today: for most people, stress and anxiety produce health problems that usually shorten the span of our lives.

[52]Bruner comments, "If Jesus intended to create in us a suspicion of the beautiful, or even contempt for the aesthetic, he would hardly have used Solomon's court as a favorable comparison. The God and Father of our Lord Jesus Christ, this Word teaches us, is not only the Creator of basic things; this God is the Creator of beautiful things too. . . . The little flowers that grow wild on the hillsides, Jesus points out, effortlessly exhibit a radiance of beauty that the most powerful human beings 'fixed up' to the greatest possible extent—'Solomon in all his glory' (verse 29)—cannot begin to match." Bruner, *Christbook,* p. 268.

[53]Mark Buchanan, "Trapped in the Cult of the Next Thing," *Christianity Today,* September 6, 1999, p. 65.

[54]Nolland, *Gospel of Matthew,* p. 313.

[55]Mark Ashton tells an amusing true story about our inability to live without moral absolutes. Robert Wengert, a philosophy professor at the University of Illinois, would ask his students if they believed that truth was relative. Most students would raise their hands in approval. Then Wengert would tell them that short students would get A's and tall students would fail the course. When his students protested that his grading system was unfair, and that he could not grade the class on that standard, Wengert reminded them that moral absolutes don't exist, so they couldn't use words like "should" or "ought." Wengert's point is well taken: we can't live with moral relativism. But according to Je-

sus, making judgments is not the same thing as a spirit of judgmentalism. See Mark Ashton, *Absolute Truth?* (Downers Grove, Ill.: InterVarsity Press, 1996), pp. 9-10.

[56]Nolland, *Gospel of Matthew*, pp. 317-18.

[57]Carson comments, "Disciples exhorted to love their enemies (5:43-47) and not to judge (7:1) might fail to consider the subtleties of the argument and become undiscerning simpletons. This verse [Mt 7:6] guards against such a possibility. . . . What is sacred in Matthew is the gospel of the kingdom; so the aphorism forbids proclaiming the gospel to certain persons designated as dogs and pigs. Instead of trampling the gospel under foot, everything must be sold in pursuit of it (13:45-46). Verse 6 is not a directive against evangelizing the Gentiles. . . . 'Dogs' and 'pigs' cannot refer to all Gentiles, but as Calvin rightly perceived, only to persons of any race who have given clear evidences of rejecting the gospel with vicious scorn and hardened contempt." Carson, *Matthew, Mark and Luke,* p. 185.

[58]Quoted in Eric Metaxas, *Bonhoeffer* (Nashville: Thomas Nelson, 2010), p. 293.

[59]Leiva-Merikakis, *Fire of Mercy, Heart of the Word,* p. 291.

[60]Walker Percy, *Lost in the Cosmos* (New York: Farrar, Straus & Giroux, 1983), p. 1.

[61]This is from step three in the traditional twelve steps of Alcoholics Anonymous.

[62]Bruner, *Christbook,* p. 287.

[63]Some scholars will emphasize Matthew's rhythm of teaching and doing, particularly as it relates to his clearly marked, formulaic conclusions to Jesus' major teaching sections. On five occasions (Mt 7:28; 11:1; 13:53; 19:1; 26:1) he closes out one section and begins the next section by stating, "When Jesus had finished saying these things."

[64]Carson, *Matthew, Mark and Luke,* p. 193.

[65]With our assumptions about medicine, we often fail to see what the biblical authors saw about the holistic nature of health and sickness. A contemporary New Testament scholar argues for a holistic approach to health and medicine: "Jesus' healings and exorcisms are an indication that the kingdom of God is dawning. Their object is not only the alleviation of suffering but also bringing persons to participate in the reign of God. . . . Modern Western ideas of sickness and health are based on a disease model, which views sick people as diseased individuals with physical ailments that must be treated through medical intervention. The healing they need has little to do with salvation. By contrast, first century cultures believed that someone's sickness and health were connected not only with the physical state of that individual but also with that person's relationships, and even with the order or disorder of the cosmos. . . . Jesus' healings represent this holistic view. Jesus restores the sick to society as well as to health. His healings enable a leper, a demoniac and a woman who has been bleeding for twelve years to return to the community. . . . Through these acts of [salvation], Jesus is creating the healed and healing community predicted by the prophets." Brenda B. Colijn, *Images of Salvation in the New Testament* (Downers Grove, Ill.: IVP Academic, 2010), pp. 126-27.

[66]Dr. Bruce Perry, *The Boy Who Was Raised as a Dog* (New York: Basic, 2006), p. 153.

[67]I'm not implying that demonic evil is merely a symbol for human evil. This entire Gospel makes clear that Jesus believed in and battled against real and personal demons, evil spirits who are bent on the destruction of human beings made in the image of God.

[68]Leiva-Merikakis, *Fire of Mercy, Heart of the Word*, p. 379.

[69]Carson notes, "By touching an unclean leper, Jesus would become ceremonially defiled himself (cf. Lev 13-14). But at Jesus' touch nothing remains defiled. Far from becoming unclean, Jesus makes the unclean clean. Both Jesus' words and touch (8:15; 9:20-21, 29; 14:36) are effective, possibly implying that authority is vested in his message as well as in his person." D. A. Carson, *The Expositor's Bible Commentary* (Grand Rapids: Zondervan, 1984), 8:198.

[70]Bruner, *Christbook*, p. 325.

[71]Morris notes, "[Son of Man] is used over 80 times in the New Testament and, with the exception of Luke 24:7 and John 12:34 (both quoting Jesus) and Acts 7:56, it is always on the lips of Jesus. It was his favorite way of referring to himself. Matthew uses it six or seven times to refer to Jesus' earthly mission . . . 10 times for his rejection and suffering . . . and 14 times for his future glory. Such a threefold division is to be discerned in the use of the term outside the Gospel as well. . . . There is lowliness about it because the unthinking could see in it no more than the meaning 'a man.' But there is also greatness, for it is not unlikely that it is derived from the reference to the heavenly being described as 'one like the son of man' in Daniel 7:13-14. This points to someone especially close to God and thus has messianic significance. . . [Jesus used the term] firstly because it was a rare term and one without nationalistic associations. . . . Secondly, because it had overtones of divinity. . . . Thirdly, because of its societary implications. The Son of Man implies the redeemed people of God. Fourthly, because it had undertones of humanity. He took upon Him our weakness." Morris, *Gospel According to Matthew*, pp. 201-2. See also the long excursus on this title found in Carson, *Matthew, Mark and Luke*, pp. 209-13.

[72]It's fascinating that some of the first people to lead the relief work after Haiti's devastating earthquake of 2010 were from New Orleans. Out of their authority of personal experience, they were able to walk beside fellow-sufferers. See Bill Slasser, "New Orleans Reaches Out to Help Haiti," *The Christian Science Monitor*, February 14, 2010.

[73]As Bruner observes, "Matthew inserts these discipleship stories into his nexus of miracles to teach that faith in Jesus must always be united with obedience. Christians are not just patients, they are disciples. . . . For while the church exists indeed to comfort and to grace, she also exists no less centrally, and in Matthew's Gospel probably even more centrally, to challenge and to disciple. The commands are Jesus' main gift to the church according to Matthew's vision (Mt 28:20). . . . Jesus grips people not only to heal them; he grips them also to disciple them. . . . Jesus' love is not only tender, it is tough, and so into the healings Matthew inserts discipleship stories to keep the record straight and the gospel balanced." Bruner, *Christbook*, p. 313.

[74]Tim Keller, *Ministries of Mercy* (Phillipsburg, N.J.: P & R, 2007), p. 60.

[75]Josef Pieper, *Josef Pieper: An Anthology* (San Francisco: Ignatius, 1989), p. 28.

[76]J. R. R. Tolkien, *The Fellowship of the Ring* (London: Collins, 2001), p. 83.

[77]David Benoif, *City of Thieves* (New York: Viking, 2008), p. 98.

[78]Athanasius, *On the Incarnation* (Crestwood, N.Y.: St. Vladimir's Seminary Press, 1989), pp. 32, 34.

[79]See George Eldon Ladd, *A Theology of the New Testament* (Grand Rapids: Eerdmans, 1993), pp. 65-67.

[80]Leiva-Merikakis, *Fire of Mercy, Heart of the Word*, p. 536.

[81]Bruner, *Christbook*, p. 378.

[82]Jo Piazza, "Audiences Experience 'Avatar' Blues," January 11, 2010, CNN <edition .cnn.com/2010/SHOWBIZ/Movies/01/11/avatar.movie.blues/index.html>.

[83]Peter Singer, "The Sanctity of Life," *Foreign Policy Magazine*, August 30, 2005, p. 40.

[84]Tolkien, *Fellowship of the Ring*, p. 67.

[85]Douglas LeBlanc, "We Clean the Wounds of Those Who Hate Us," *The Living Church News Updates*, March 8, 2011, p. 1.

Chapter 3: The Varying Response to Jesus

[1]Laurie Goodstein, "Believers Invest in the Gospel of Getting Rich," *The New York Times*, August 16, 2009 <www.nytimes.com/2009/08/16/us/16gospel.html>.

[2]Ronald Rolheiser, *The Holy Longing* (New York: Doubleday, 1999), pp. 166-67.

[3]Dale Bruner, *The Christbook* (Waco, Tex.: Word, 1987), p. 417.

[4]N. T. Wright summarizes this passage by stating, "This is fighting talk. . . . When Jesus finally arrives in Jerusalem, these same things [in this passage] . . . are what get him arrested, tried and killed. Matthew wants us to see the shadow of the cross already falling over the story." Tom Wright, *Matthew for Everyone, Part One* (Louisville, Ky.: Westminster John Knox, 2004), p. 141.

[5]William Barclay, *The Gospel of Matthew, Volume 2* (Philadelphia: Westminster, 1975), pp. 25-26.

[6]As Morris remarks, "[Jesus] is saying that he, being who and what he is, can declare what are the rules for observing the Sabbath. . . . He, the Lord of the Sabbath, shows what the observing of the Sabbath really means; he determines how the principle of Sabbath observance is to be worked out. He makes the point that Sabbath observance means mercy. He has himself shown mercy to his disciples, and Matthew goes on immediately to the way he will show mercy to the man with the shriveled hand. Sabbath observance led to a full and rich life." Leon Morris, *The Gospel According to Matthew* (Grand Rapids: Eerdmans, 1992), pp. 304-5.

[7]The quotation comes from Isaiah 42. According to Keener, "In this passage Matthew reads Jesus as Isaiah's 'servant of Yahweh.' . . . God's servant Israel failed in its mission (Isa 42:18-19), so God chose one person within Israel to restore the rest of his people (Isa 49:5-7); this one would bear the punishment (cf. Isa 40:2) rightly due his people (Isa 52:13-53:12). As in 12:1-14, Matthew here provides a hermeneutical key for his entire Gospel. . . . Translating freely from the Hebrew, Matthew conforms the language of Isaiah 42 to God's praise of his Son in Matthew 3:17 ('my beloved . . . in whom I am well pleased'). As Matthew pointed out repeatedly in his Gospel (Mt 1:1; 2:15, 18; 3:15; 4:1-2), Jesus' mission is not merely a new event; it's an event rooted in the history of his people. From this text Matthew reminds his readers that Jesus was not a political or warrior messiah for the present time; he humbled himself as a suffering servant until the time he would lead 'justice to victory' (Mt 12:20)." Craig Keener, *A Commentary on the*

Gospel of Matthew (Grand Rapids: Eerdmans, 1999), pp. 360-61.

[8]Bruner notes, "The resurrection of the crucified Jesus will be God's one great sensation . . . delivered once and for all and for all time—take it or leave it, Matthew reports. . . . After Jesus' holy week, God is not in show business." Bruner, *Christbook*, p. 467.

[9]Nolland comments, "The possibility of forgiveness for people is fundamental to what Jesus came to do. . . . Matthew sets up the large frame of what Jesus is about as a 'forgiveness project' through the framing role of the key forgiveness texts in 1:21; 26:28. Both in relation to the origin of Jesus (1:18, 20) and in relation to his execution of his role (3:11, 16; 12:18), the presence of the Spirit is key. Presumably what makes the blasphemy of attributing to Beelzebub the work of the Spirit in Jesus unforgiveable is that it excludes people from participating in what God is doing in Jesus, and thus from the 'forgiveness project.' No doubt such blasphemy remains unforgiveable as long as it is sustained. It too may be repented of." John Nolland, *The Gospel of Matthew*, New International Greek Testament Commentary (Grand Rapids: Eerdmans, 2005), pp. 504-5.

[10]Maggie Jackson, "A Nation Distracted," *Utne Reader* (March-April 2010), p. 51.

[11]I use the word *prodigal* in its original sense—lavish, wildly extravagant.

[12]According to Carson, "The parable of the sower shows that though the kingdom will now make its way amid hard hearts, competing pressures, and even failure, it will produce an abundant crop." D. A. Carson, *Matthew, Mark and Luke* (Grand Rapids: Zondervan, 1984), p. 315.

[13]Morris, *Gospel According to Matthew*, p. 339. Morris also adds, "But in the New Testament [the word 'mystery'] usually carries the further thought that that which people can never work out for themselves God has now made known to them. . . . Nobody could know such truths unless they were revealed to them."

[14]Wright, *Matthew for Everyone, Part 1*, p. 162.

[15]Did Jesus cause or allow this condition of spiritual colorblindness? Bruner notes the difference between Mark's and Matthew's Gospels on this point: "When Mark said that Jesus taught in parables in order to (*hina*) harden, he was saying that hardening was Jesus' purpose in teaching! But when Matthew says that Jesus taught in parables because (*hoti*) the people were already hardened, he is saying that hardened people are the reason Jesus taught in parables." Dale Bruner, *Churchbook* (Grand Rapids: Eerdmans, 2004), p. 12.

[16]J. R. R. Tolkien, *The Hobbit* (New York: Houghton Mifflin, 1997), p. 194.

[17]In one of his last written works, Pedro Arrupe, the former superior general of the Jesuits, allegedly said, "Nothing is more practical than finding God, that is, than falling in love in a quite absolute, final way. What you are in love with, what seizes your imagination, will affect everything. It will decide what will get you out of bed in the morning, what you will do with your evenings, how you will spend your weekends, what you read, who you know, what breaks your heart, and what amazes you with joy and gratitude. Fall in love, stay in love and it will decide everything." Pedro Arrupe, *Pedro Arrupe: Essential Writings* (Maryknoll, N.Y.: Orbis, 2004), book jacket. I would add: Receive God's love; fall in love with the God who loves you, and then you'll always listen to the voice of Jesus.

[18]Many of us are uncomfortable with this language of spiritual darkness and demonology. We're very comfortable with the language of medicine ("she has bronchitis") or mental illness ("he has a narcissistic personality disorder") or therapy ("she was wounded by her rigid family system") or even politics ("we have to watch those liberals or conservatives"). Those are appropriate ways to describe reality, but according to Jesus' clear teaching there's another way as well: the language of spiritual warfare (see Eph 6:12). God's goal is always to weave a redemption story out of our lives and all of creation, but the enemy intends to weave a tragic, anti-human, anti-creation story. While he is a defeated enemy, he's still active and destructive. Bruner comments, "In the final analysis, the church teaches the existence of the devil because the biblical writers (who are normative for us) taught such an existence and instructed us that Jesus reckoned with such an existence, too. And 'a disciple is not above his Lord.'" Bruner, *Christbook*, pp. 101-2. See also Keener, *Commentary Matthew*, pp. 283-86.

[19]In Matthew 13:43, Jesus identifies two tarelike people: the scandals (those who cause others to trip and stumble on their journey toward Christ) and, literally, "those who are doing lawlessness" (those who think they can follow Jesus but don't have to obey what he says). Once again, although we are saved by faith (admitting our spiritual poverty), we are called to walk in love, good deeds and obedience to the ways of Jesus.

[20]Bruner, *Churchbook*, p. 31.

[21]Unfortunately, the NIV translates it as "a large amount of dough" instead of the literal Greek of three *satas*, or approximately one-half bushel or twenty-two liters.

[22]Morris A. Grubbs, ed., *Conversations with Wendell Berry* (Jackson: University of Mississippi Press, 2007), p. 42.

[23]Tolkien, *The Hobbit,* p. 126.

[24]Based on the incident in Mt 14:13-21, the feeding of the 5,000, we watch Jesus treat both people and food (and the act of people eating food) with utmost tenderness and respect. In Matthew's Gospel, references to food (eating, bread, banquets) appear in nearly fifty verses. Satan tempts Jesus with food (Mt 4:4). Jesus tells us to trust our Father for daily bread (Mt 6:11). Jesus compares salvation to a beautiful banquet (Mt 8:11 and 22:1-11). And prior to his death Jesus tells us to remember his presence through one simple act: Jesus takes bread, breaks it, and says, "This is my body given for you" (Mt 26:26).

Nearly two thousand years later we're still talking about the dynamics of food, people and the act of eating. For instance, I used to love wolfing down Hot Pockets, until I read Michael Pollan's book *In Defense of Food*. According to Pollan's definitions, a Hot Pocket isn't "real food" (just grab your magnifying glass and chemistry textbook and read the ingredients). Pollan is right (and biblical) on one major point: food matters. How we eat, what we eat, why we eat, how we get and prepare what we eat—it all matters. Gluttony matters. Malnourishment matters. According to the Bible, food matters because people matter. And people matter because God said so.

So this story in Matthew 14 isn't a unique incident in Jesus' ministry. It opens a window and displays a vital aspect of Jesus' mission. Desperate and weary people have been without food. They are hungry. They need help. The disciples offer their standard quick solution: They tell Jesus (notice they give Jesus a command), "Send them away." Jesus offers a better solution: "No, you offer them something to eat." Food and hungry people matter because they matter to Jesus, God with us. And we as disciples matter because we are the body of Christ on earth.

Personally, I agree with Dale Bruner that in this story "we hear echoes of the Lord's Supper" (Bruner, *Churchbook*, p. 70). At the very least, we can all agree that Jesus, in his amazing love, took the bread, broke it and then fed hungry people. This is the only miracle that appears in all four Gospels. Obviously the early church thought this was a crucial story; pictures of loaves and fish appear often in early Christian art. On one level, Jesus' miraculous feeding offers personal comfort to Jesus' followers. Our heavenly Father wants to provide for us. He doesn't want us to worry about our daily bread. It's also a challenging picture of our mission as a church. Faithful discipleship hinges, at least in part, on how we care for hungry people (Mt 24:38-45; 25:31-46). Once again, Jesus reminds us that we are "the church for the world," not "the church for the disciples' comfort."

[25]R. O. Blechman, *Dear James: Letters to a Young Illustrator* (New York: Simon & Schuster, 2009), pp. 30-34.

[26]Carson observes, "Although the Greek *ego eimi* can have the no more force than that, any Christian after the Resurrection and Ascension would also detect echoes of 'I am,' the decisive self-disclosure of God (Ex 3:14; Is 43:10; 51:12). Once again we find Jesus revealing himself in a veiled way that will prove especially rich to Christians after the resurrection." Carson, *Matthew, Mark and Luke,* p. 334.

[27]These words have been attributed to the Swiss psychologist Dr. Paul Tournier.

[28]Barbara Kingsolver, *The Poisonwood Bible* (New York: HarperCollins, 1999).

[29]For an extensive discussion of this passage see Bruner, *Churchbook*, pp. 84-91.

[30]Meir Soloveichik, "Locusts, Giraffes, and the Meaning of Kashrut," *Azure* 5766 (Winter 2006): 62-79.

[31]According to Bruner, "Tidy, catechetical Matthew [contra Mark in 7:22] then puts the infractions in their exact Ten Commandments order—Sixth, Seventh, Eighth, and Ninth Commandments: 'murders, marriage, breakings, sexual immoralities' (sexual infractions twice, as in the Sermon on the Mount, 5:27-30, 31-32, perhaps to stress their importance), 'stealings, false witnessings, slanders.' 'Slanders' (*blasphemiai*) may have been put last not only because they are the sin against the Ninth Commandment but also to point up one final time the key point of the passage: it is slanderous speech from the heart, not ritually unwashed hands, that ruins people's relations with God and others." Bruner, *Churchbook,* p. 96.

[32]Dr. Seuss, *Sneetches and Other Stories* (New York: Random House, 1961).

[33]Craig Keener, *Commentary Matthew,* p. 414.

[34]In the words of C. S. Lewis, "You discover gradually, in almost indefinable ways, that it exists and that you are outside it; and then later, perhaps, that you are inside it. It is not easy, even at a given moment, to say who is inside and who is outside. Some people are obviously in and some are obviously out, but there are always several on the border-line. People think they are in it after they have in fact been pushed out of it, or before they

have been allowed in: this provides great amusement for those who are really inside. It has no fixed name. From outside, if you have despaired of getting into it, you call it 'That gang' or 'They' or 'so-and-so and has set' or 'the Caucus' or 'the Inner Ring.' I believe that in all men's lives at certain periods, and in many men's lives at all periods between infancy and extreme old age, one of the most dominant elements is the desire to be inside the local Ring and the terror of being left outside." C. S. Lewis, *The Weight of Glory* (SanFrancisco: HarperCollins, 1980), p. 145.

[35]Regarding the "Son of David" title, Morris comments, "[It's an] expression Matthew has 8 times in reference to Jesus. . . . It speaks of a descendent of the great King David and came to be used of the Messiah, viewing him as a great warrior like David, one who would establish a mighty kingdom. It is curious to find the title being used by a Canaanite woman for whom an Israelite ruler would presumably have no attraction." Morris, *Gospel According to Matthew,* p. 402.

[36]Francis Collins, *The Language of God* (New York: Free Press, 2006), p. 259.

[37]Of course there's one glaring exception to this: the pagan, troubled, foreign woman with the family problems in Matthew 15:21-28.

[38]C. S. Lewis, *Surprised by Joy* (Boston: Harcourt, 1955), p. 227.

[39]Collins, *Language of God,* p. 229.

Chapter 4: The Growing Conflict with Jesus

[1]Charles M. Blow, "Spirit Quest" *The New York Times*, February 20, 2010 <www.ny times.com/2010/02/20/opinion/20blow.html?ref=opinion>.

[2]Robert C. Fuller, *Spiritual but Not Religious* (Oxford: Oxford University Press, 2001), p. 4.

[3]According to Keener, this area was "famous for its grotto where people worshipped the Greek god Pan; its earlier name Paneas persisted even in its modern Arabic name Baneas and public pagan rites reportedly continued there until a later Christian demonstrated that Jesus was more powerful. . . . Following Mark, Matthew emphasizes that God moves where he wills, fitting the theme of Jesus' universal mission in his Gospel." Craig Keener, *A Commentary on the Gospel of Matthew* (Grand Rapids: Eerdmans, 1999), p. 424.

[4]Dale Bruner, *Churchbook* (Grand Rapids: Eerdmans, 2004), p. 122.

[5]Keener notes, "'The gates of Hades' is a familiar Semitic expression for the threshold of the realm of death (cf. 11:23; Rev. 1:18). Pagans also employed the image of the 'gates of Hades' for the realm of death; they often spoke of the house or realm of Hades as the realm of the dead, as in Jewish texts. The words used here suggest that death itself assaults Christ's church, but death itself cannot crush God's people. The church will endure until Christ's return, and no opposition, even the widespread martyrdom of Christians or the oppression of the antichrist, can prevent the ultimate triumph of God's purposes in history. The promise precedes Christ's summons to martyrdom (16:24-25)." Keener, *Commentary*, pp. 428-29.

[6]The Greek word for church, *ekklesia*, appears twice in Matthew (here and in Mt 18:17). As Carson comments, "Matthew insists that Jesus predicted the continuation of his small group of disciples in a distinct community, a holy and messianic people, a 'church.'"

D. A. Carson, *Matthew, Mark and Luke* (Grand Rapids: Zondervan, 1984), p. 31.

[7]As Rolheiser says, "The church is always God hung between two thieves. Thus, no one should be surprised or shocked at how badly the church has betrayed the gospel and how much it continues to do so today. It has never done well. Conversely, however, nobody should deny the good the church has done either. It has carried grace, produced saints, morally challenged the planet, and made, however imperfectly, a house for God to dwell on earth." Ronald Rolheiser, *The Holy Longing* (New York: Doubleday, 1999), p. 128.

[8]Ibid., p. 140.

[9]See Thomas C. Oden, ed., *The Parables of Kierkegaard* (Princeton, N.J.: Princeton University Press, 1978), pp. 40-45. I have taken some liberties with Kierkegaard's original parable, but I love his conclusion: "For this is the unfathomable nature of love, that it desires equality with the beloved, not in jest merely, but in earnest and truth."

[10]In the words of Pope Benedict, "The mountain is the place of pure ascent. . . . It is the liberation from the burden of everyday life, a breathing in or pure creation; it offers a view of the broad expanse of creation and its beauty; it gives us an inner peak to stand on and an intuitive sense of the Creator." Pope Benedict XVI, *Jesus of Nazareth* (New York: Doubleday, 2007), p. 309.

[11]Bruner, *Churchbook,* pp. 172-73.

[12]The "mistake" is actually the ancient heresy of the Marcionites.

[13]Notice the same pattern in Matthew 8:1. After Jesus preached his amazing message in the Sermon on the Mount, "he came down from the mountainside" and immediately encountered a leper.

[14]The word used for Jesus' transfiguration in Matthew 17:2, *metamorphoo,* is used only four times in the New Testament—two times for Matthew and Mark's story of Jesus' transfiguration, and two times for the transfiguration or transformation that every follower of Jesus will experience. Paul uses the same word in Romans 12:2, "Be transformed [or transfigured] by the renewing of your mind," and in 2 Corinthians 3:18, "And we . . . are being transformed into his likeness with ever-increasing glory." In 2 Corinthians the verb is in the present tense ("we are being changed"), suggesting the continuous process of our transformation into Christlikeness.

[15]Quoted by Gregory Wolfe, "Thirty Seconds Away," *Image Journal* (Fall 2009): 5.

[16]Dr. Seuss, *Horton Hears a Who* (New York: Random House Books for Young Readers, 1954).

[17]Paul Collier, *The Bottom Billion: Why the Poorest Countries Are Failing and What Can Be Done About It* (New York: Oxford University Press, 2008).

[18]Bruner comments, "Conversion to our child-status can be viewed as an event constantly repeated in the Christian's life. . . . The aorist imperative in this verse may mean, as is often the case with aorist imperatives, *the establishment of a rule of life.*" Bruner, *Churchbook,* p. 209. Morris adds a footnote on this verse, "It is not merely the simplicity of the child that Jesus has in view, it is even more the fact of starting life afresh, with no preconceived notions; the saying means much the same as the Johannine 'Ye must be born again.'" Leon Morris, *The Gospel According to Matthew* (Grand Rapids: Eerdmans, 1992), p. 459.

[19]Thomas Merton, *Contemplative Prayer* (New York: Image, 1971), p. 37.

[20]Bruner remarks, "From now on we should notice Jesus' repeated use of the word 'one' in the community stories. . . . It will be used repeatedly in this paragraph and the next (Mt 18:5, 6, 10, 12, 14). It is the word to watch. It stresses quality rather than quantity. It means that the special Christian contribution to community is 'passion for the individual.' . . . Jesus' expression is literally 'one of the least of these—*mikron* [in the Greek].' *Mikro*-care is Jesus' contribution to community building." Bruner, *Churchbook*, p. 213.

[21]Throughout Matthew's Gospel angels play a significant but quiet role in the story of Jesus. Depending on how you count them, there are about sixteen references to angelic activity in Matthew. Just like the true disciple, just like Joseph and Mary from chapter 1, the angels display a humble, unspectacular and almost unnoticed role in redemption. For instance, they warn and guide through dreams (Mt 1:20-24; 2:13-19), they assist Jesus after his temptation (Mt 4:11), they assist Jesus in the judgment of the earth (Mt 13:39-41, 49; 25:31, 41), and after rolling back the stone outside Jesus' tomb (Mt 28:2) they announce the resurrection (Mt 28:5).

[22]Mary Beth Sheridan, "Church-Linked Groups Challenging Abortion Laws in Western Europe," *Los Angeles Times,* June 4, 1989 <http://articles.latimes.com/1989-06-04/news-mn-2567_1_abortion-law-western-europe-roman-catholic-poland>.

[23]The Greek word for "the problem sheep" is *planomenon* (a word from which we get our English word "planet") or "wandering one." Stephen J. Nichols observes, "There are many words used to convey the notion and concept of sin in the Bible. Many of them are picturesque, perhaps none more so than the Greek word *planao,* which means 'to wander.' . . . Ancient Greek astronomers referred to these celestial bodies that they observed as wanderers about the sky. To sin is to wander, to be restless and rootless, homeless. Lost sheep." Stephen J. Nichols, *Getting the Blues* (Grand Rapids: Brazos, 2008), p. 57.

[24]Bruner states, "It is inappropriate for disciples to speculate about the place or particulars of hell. . . . [But] Jesus unmistakably teaches a future judgment, beyond the present place of mind. . . . It is not right to say that the doctrine of hell is unloving. The most loving person taught it. To warn persons of harsh consequences is an act of love. It is unloving to say it makes no ultimate difference how we live since 'God is love.' . . . Lives can be ruined, and Jesus' teaching ministry is so infused with this conviction that removing it evacuates Jesus' teaching of ultimacy. . . . Wherever the church has believed Jesus' (and the apostles') teaching on hell, her love for the world has been rekindled and Christian mission and evangelism flourished. Wherever Jesus' teaching on judgment has been for all practical purposes disbelieved, there has been a flagging of zeal to do mission or practice mercy in the world." Bruner, *Churchbook*, pp. 215, 541.

[25]As Carson remarks, "One might speculate on the pressures that prompted Matthew to include this material . . . [but] the essential factor is that Matthew insists that the demand for a disciplined church goes back to Jesus himself." D. A. Carson, *Matthew, Mark and Luke* (Grand Rapids: Zondervan, 1984), p. 31.

[26]Robert Karen, *The Forgiving Self* (New York, Doubleday, 2001), pp. 15-22.

[27]Philip Yancey, *What's So Amazing About Grace?* (Grand Rapids: Zondervan, 2002), p. 84.

[28]Karen, *Forgiving Self*, p. 21.

[29]Sandra Tsing Loh, "Let's Call the Whole Thing Off," *The Atlantic*, July/August 2009 <www.theatlantic.com/magazine/archive/2009/07/let-8217-s-call-the-whole-thing-off/7488/>.

[30]Keener, *Commentary*, p. 471. Tom Wright also notes, "The Pharisees seem to have thought that the very existence of legislation about divorce, within the law of Moses, meant that Moses was quite happy for it to take place." Tom Wright, *Matthew for Everyone, Part Two* (Louisville, Ky.: Westminster John Knox, 2004), p. 42.

[31]As a side note, Jesus' starting point and his conclusion about marriage certainly have bearing on our contemporary discussion regarding "gay marriages." The one man and one woman definition of marriage doesn't come from the lips of a repressed, hateful fundamentalist and legalist; it comes from the lips of the most loving person in history, the one who has walked with sinners and identified with the brokenhearted. The Pharisees' question provided Jesus the perfect opportunity to rebut the legalists and revise the "narrow" definition of marriage. But Jesus didn't revise it; he clarified it by advocating a very traditional understanding of marriage.

[32]Jesus provided one loophole for ending a marriage: sexual unfaithfulness (Mt 19:8). Notice he did not say that adultery *must* lead to a divorce. Jesus also believed in the power of repentance and forgiveness to heal broken hearts and broken relationships. Adultery isn't the unforgivable sin. On the other hand, repeated and unrepentant sexual unfaithfulness can destroy the Genesis one-flesh concept of marriage.

[33]In Jesus' day, his restrictive teaching on divorce and his high view of marriage served as a protection for vulnerable people—in most cases, women and children. In our culture, where most of the divorces are initiated by women, the vulnerable person could be a woman or a man; of course children rarely benefit from their parents' divorce.

[34]I thought this was an original metaphor for divorce until a friend of mine pointed out that C. S. Lewis said it long before me. In his words, "[All churches] regard divorce as something like cutting up a living body, as a kind of surgical operation. Some of them think the operation so violent that it cannot be done at all; others admit it as a desperate remedy in extreme cases. They are all agreed that it is more like having both your legs cut off than it is like dissolving a business partnership or even deserting a regiment." C. S. Lewis, *Mere Christianity* (New York: Macmillan, 1977), p. 96.

[35]Morris comments, "Matthew has completed his account of what Jesus did and taught in Galilee, and his narrative moves on to the climax in Jerusalem. . . . [Then] on his way to Jerusalem Jesus gives his disciples significant teaching [i.e., Matthew 19—25] as he prepared them for the path they would tread when his time on earth was completed." Morris, *Gospel According to Matthew*, p. 478.

[36]The Greek word in Matthew 19:6 for "joined together" (*synezeuxen*) literally meant "yoked together." It's a work image, like two oxen yoked together, moving in the same direction, plowing a field. Marriage involves much more than my happiness or even our happiness as a couple. It involves a new way to work for God, to be in mission for God by serving others.

[37]As my pastor Stewart Ruch contends, "Biblically speaking there are only two states, or two options, for followers of Jesus: you're either married or you're a celibate. But biblically there isn't a state called 'singleness.'" I agree. In our culture "singleness" means that you aren't married. It really doesn't imply anything about sexual involvement with other people. In the Bible, celibacy means that you are not married and that you are not sexually active. You are unmarried and chaste, and yet you are also called to full life of love, fruitfulness, joy and servanthood.

[38]For a discussion about divorce and remarriage (which is beyond the scope of this commentary), see Bruner, *Churchbook,* pp. 250-71.

[39]I realize that addiction specialists don't always agree on what substances or behaviors constitute a true addiction. I'm using the term in its broadest, most general sense: any habit, behavior, person or substance that controls our life, attaching our heart to something less than love for God and others, becoming unmanageable unless God intervenes with his grace and power.

[40]Whenever Jesus is addressed as "Teacher" in Matthew, it's usually a sign of insincerity or shallowness (see Mt 8:19; 12:38; 22:16; 22:24).

[41]Once again, in Matthew's Gospel the journey to and with Jesus is always attached to the journey of the Jewish people. There is one gospel/Bible story, not two stories (i.e., the harsh and irrelevant Old Testament versus the nice, hip New Testament). The God of Abraham, Isaac and Jacob is the God and Father of our Lord Jesus Christ.

[42]Although, interestingly, Jesus omits the last commandment ("You shall not covet") and instead inserts Leviticus 19:18 ("Love your neighbor as yourself"). Perhaps Jesus left coveting off the list in order to highlight it by its absence. After all, the rich young man did seem to have his ducks, or his commandments, all in a row—or so he thought. By adding Leviticus 19:18 Jesus was emphasizing this man's lack of neighbor love. Apparently the rich young ruler didn't understand his spiritual poverty (Mt 5:3). If he did, he would have been quick to mourn his sin, hunger and thirst for righteousness, and display mercy toward others.

[43]For another take on following Jesus in the midst of a celebrity culture, see Paul Metzger, *The Gospel of John: When Love Came to Town* (Downers Grove, Ill.: InterVarsity Press, 2010), pp. 47-52.

[44]See, for instance, Joseph Epstein, "The Culture of Celebrity: Let us now praise famous airheads," *The Weekly Standard,* October 17, 2005.

[45]According to Morris, this word is used thirty-one times in Matthew: "No other book has it more than Mark's 21 times. [It] means 'to hand over, deliver up' and is often employed as a technical term for handing over into custody (Acts 8:3). . . . Judas handed [Jesus] over (26:25), as did the chief priests and elders (27:2), and the people of Jerusalem (Acts 3:13). From another angle it was Pilate who delivered him up (27:26). . . . But we had our part in it too, for he was delivered up for our sins (Romans 4:25). . . . The Father did this (Romans 8:32), while in one of the most moving passages in Scripture, the Son gave himself up (Galatians 2:20)." Morris, *Gospel According to Matthew,* pp. 506-7.

[46]The Gospel of Mark, probably the original and less flattering version of the story,

doesn't mention the mother of James and John. In one way, they were probably all culpable for this brash and insensitive request.

⁴⁷Like the phrase "handed over," "the cup" was another powerful image for Jesus' passion story. In Old Testament imagery, the cup referred to judgment (Ps 75:8; Is 51:17-18; Jer 25:15-28). The shocking thing about this verse is that Jesus is about to drink the cup. The Son of God will drink the judgment of God? No wonder the disciples had a hard time grasping Jesus' meaning of his own death. See Carson, *Matthew, Mark and Luke,* p. 431.

⁴⁸Jesus' use of these terms implied a voluntary decision. It had nothing to do with a subhuman, cringing, forced and brutal system of involuntary human slavery. As a matter of fact, according to Bruner, "It is fair to say that texts like this [which emphasize voluntarily choosing the lowly path of following Jesus into a life of servanthood] gradually penetrated the idea of slavery with a new humane spirit and had the power to defeat slavery." Bruner, *Churchbook,* p. 334.

⁴⁹Benedict Carey, "Steinbrenner: The Boss Unbound," *The New York Times,* July 16, 2010 <www.nytimes.com/2010/07/18/weekinreview/18carey.html>.

⁵⁰According to Nolland, "What is true is that the donkey is no warhorse but merely a beast of burden and means of transport." John Nolland, *The Gospel of Matthew,* New International Greek Testament Commentary (Grand Rapids: Eerdmans, 2005), p. 836.

⁵¹Bertrand Russell, *Why I Am Not a Christian* (New York: Simon & Schuster, 1957), p. 19.

⁵³Neil Gaimon and Al Sarrantinio, *Stories* (New York: William Morrow, 2010), pp. 2-4.

⁵⁴As the New Testament scholar D. Marguerat observes, "Everything is excessive in this story: the incredible imprudence of the master, who, in spite of the repeated failures of his messengers, sends his only son—this is in defiance of historical realism; the homicidal act of the farmers, too, goes beyond real-life norms. But this is by design: this is the history of salvation." Quoted in Bruner, *Churchbook,* p. 379.

⁵⁴For a summary of interpretations of the wedding garment throughout church history see ibid., pp. 390-92.

⁵⁵Sam Harris, *The End of Faith: Religion, Terror, and the Future of Reason* (New York: W. W. Norton, 2005), p. 225.

⁵⁶Wright, *Matthew for Everyone, Part Two,* pp. 86-87.

⁵⁷Ibid., p. 88.

⁵⁸As Craig Blomberg says, "Two brothers make the point, seven make fun." Quoted in Bruner, *Churchbook,* p. 405.

⁵⁹By using the analogy of angels, Jesus didn't mean that we wouldn't have bodies. The entire New Testament assumes a *bodily* resurrection.

⁶⁰Bruner observes, "If David calls the Messiah 'David's Lord,' how on earth can this Messiah be merely David's son? . . . All Jesus is attempting to do is to pry open his hearers' minds to the possibility that the future Messiah will be *more* than a son of David, more than even David's glorious successor, more than we usually think possible when we think of an even eminent human father. . . . But it is enough now if readers open themselves to the Scripture's prediction of a Messiah who would be more than expected. . . . Thus if David calls the future Messiah 'Lord' it must mean that David's son is not just

David's son; in some still undefined way, David's future son, the Messiah, will be David's Lord. 'More than David is here' (McNeile, 328; cf. Mt 12:6, 41, 42). In hindsight, we now see how this can be: namely, 'David's son as man, David's Lord as God'—that is 'how.' The church's later doctrine of the two natures of Christ—Jesus both truly man and truly God—is how Jesus can be simultaneously David's son and David's Lord." Bruner, *Churchbook,* p. 425.

[61]Carson concludes, "The teacher who never attended the right schools (John 7:15-18) confounds the greatest theologians in the land." Carson, *Matthew, Mark and Luke,* p. 468. Keener also notes, "He had silenced and shamed his adversaries. Being overawed by a wise speaker's wisdom was a common motif in narratives meant to glorify their protagonist; Matthew's audience could see in Jesus their hero who could answer all the objections raised by their opponents." Keener, *Commentary,* p. 534.

[62]Notice that Jesus honors Scripture, the law, spiritual authority. He jettisons nothing except spiritual hypocrisy.

[63]Matthew 23:25 states that the inside of the cup is filled with greed and self-indulgence. Bruner notes that the Greek word for greed (*harpage*) meant "plunder." It implied "wheeling and dealing, by cheating (particularly, by dishonest methods in business)." Thus, he concludes that it matters to Jesus how we obtain our "clothes, conveniences and play things." As in Matthew 6:24-34, Jesus is an economic prophet. "It matters to Jesus how people earn their living. The Serious are living off others; what is on their plates does not justly belong to them." But, secondly, Jesus also mentions that our Pharisee-like cups contain self-indulgence (the Greek word is *akrasia*), which meant "uncontrolled sensuality, a sexual or physical sin . . . that is, by and for hedonistic pleasure." Thus, Jesus the prophet also denounced the unholy, disobedient, and person-degrading use of our sex drive. Bruner, *Churchbook,* pp. 450-51.

[64]For example, N. T. Wright concludes, "All of this related very specifically to the time between Jesus' public career and the destruction of the Temple in AD 70. . . . But the echoes of meaning rumble on in every successive generation of Christian discipleship. . . . We too may be called to live through troubled times and to last out to the end. We too may see the destruction of cherished and beautiful symbols." Wright, *Matthew for Everyone, Part Two,* p. 115. See also Craig Keener, *A Commentary on the Gospel of Matthew* (Grand Rapids: Eerdmans, 1999), pp. 563-67; Bruner, *Churchbook,* pp. 473-74; and Carson, *Matthew, Mark and Luke,* pp. 488-95.

[65]Wright observes, "The terrible times of the first century are echoed by the terrible times that the world, and the church, have had to go through many times over." Wright, *Matthew for Everyone, Part Two,* p. 119.

[66]Luke's Gospel has the most direct explanation for the much-debated phrase from Daniel about the "abomination that causes desolation." Luke simply says, "When you see Jerusalem being surrounded by armies, you will know that its desolation is near" (Lk 21:20).

[67]According the Old Testament prophets, especially Isaiah, these metaphors served as a code language for talking about huge social and political upheaval. See Wright, *Matthew for Everyone, Part Two,* p. 122.

[68]Some people interpret this to mean that the nations will mourn because they missed Jesus and now they're bound for damnation. Instead, following Zechariah 12:10 and 13:1-2, I believe that Jesus meant a mourning that leads to repentance and cleansing. This doesn't imply that everyone will repent and be cleansed; it merely holds out hope that the unconverted will finally repent and find forgiveness in Christ.

[69]See Bruner, *Churchbook,* p. 492.

[70]Keener, *Commentary,* p. 584.

[71]Here's my completely unscientific formula for the $1.8 million:

- 10,000 days divided by 250 working days per year = 40 years.
- Multiply 40 years by a very conservative annual income in the United States of $45,000 per year:
- 40 x 45,000 = 1,800,000.

[72]See Kenneth Chang, "Edward N. Lorenz, a Meteorologist and a Father of Chaos Theory, Dies at 90," *The New York Times,* April 17, 2008 <www.nytimes.com/2008/04/17/us/17lorenz.html>.

[73]Exegetes debate whom Jesus meant when he referred to the "least of these, my brothers." Did Jesus mean: (1) every suffering human being, including his followers (the universal or broad view); or did Jesus mean (2) only his followers (the specific or narrow view)? Two of my favorite Matthew scholars disagree on this issue. Keener opts for the specific-narrow view: "In the context of Jesus' teachings, especially in the context of Matthew (as opposed to Luke), this parable probably addresses not serving the poor on the whole but receiving the gospel's messengers." See Keener, *Commentary,* p. 605. Bruner holds to the universal view: "A truly spiritual Christ-centeredness—a centeredness that would surely include Christ's teaching—should lead the church to seek a truly social poor-centeredness. For Christ teaches that he is in the poor in some special—and finally decisive—way." See Bruner, *Churchbook,* p. 584. Although Jesus teaches the specific view elsewhere in this Gospel (see Mt 10:40-42), my interpretation of Matthew 25 follows Bruner rather than Keener. As Bruner summarizes, "The universal setting of the scene ('all angels,' 'all nations,' *Last* Judgment), the absence of reference to sufferings experienced '*in my name*,' the presence of the universal sufferings of humankind, the unconsciousness of the righteous that they had served *the Lord* (which they might have assumed if they had served the Lord's *messengers,* 10:41), and the ultimate judgments of eternal punishment or eternal life—all these tilt the interpretation in a universal, worldwide direction." Bruner, *Churchbook,* p. 574, italics in original.

[74]The Greek phrase *synegagete me* can be translated as "You brought me into your family circle" or "You took me into your family." See Bruner, *Churchbook,* p. 569.

[75]Compare with the secret righteousness of Matthew 6:1-18.

Chapter 5: The Death and Resurrection of Jesus

[1]"Sacrament" derives from the Latin term *sacramentum.* Some Latin editions of the New Testament use the term as a substitute for the Greek word *mysterion,* which refers to God's plan to save us in and through Jesus Christ (see, for instance, Eph. 3:2-13 where Paul mentions the word four times). The New Testament does not connect it with what we

call the sacraments (i.e., the Lord's Supper). However, we do know that early in church history theologians like Tertullian and Augustine utilized baptism and Eucharist, water and bread and wine, as sacraments that conveyed the *mysterion* of the good news of salvation. See Alister McGrath, *Christian Theology* (Malden, Mass.: Blackwell, 1997), p. 495.

[2]John Calvin, *Institutes of the Christian Religion,* ed. John T. McNeill, trans. Ford Lewis Battles (Louisville, Ky.: Westminster John Knox; 1960), p. 1403.

[3]Thomas Cahill, *How the Irish Saved Civilization* (New York: Nan A. Talese, 1995), pp. 142-44.

[4]Fleming Rutledge, *The Undoing of Death* (Grand Rapids: Eerdmans, 2005), p. 118.

[5]Matthew, Mark and Luke do not mention the disciple behind this incident; we know it's Peter only from John's account (see Jn 18:10). It's almost as if the other three writers agreed that Peter, who would fail enough by the end of this story, should at least get some slack for his ear-slicing fiasco.

[6]Notice the value they place on Jesus' life. According to the law found in Exodus 21:29, if a careless owner allowed his ox to gore a free person, both the owner and the ox were put to death. But if an ox gored and killed a slave, the slave's owner received thirty pieces of silver. In other words, when God came to the earth and walked among us we treated him like an ordinary slave. On one level, it reveals part of our sinful bent: we devalue God's glory, treating God with contempt. But this incident also quietly reveals the nature of Jesus, the glorious-humble one who stands in the place of the slaves, the oppressed and the powerless.

[7]In his delightful, compact, readable history of the world, E. H. Grombrich notes, "The history of the world is, sadly, not a pretty poem. It offers little variety, and it is nearly always the unpleasant things that are repeated over and over again." E. H. Grombrich, *A Little History of the World* (New Haven, Conn.: Yale University Press, 1985), p. 130.

[8]Dale Bruner, *Churchbook* (Grand Rapids: Eerdmans, 2004), p. 746.

[9]According to Matthew, Jesus also spoke one more time ("Jesus . . . cried out in a loud voice") right before he died (or "gave up his spirit"), but for some reason Matthew did not record the specific words (see Mt 27:51).

[10]R. T. France, *Matthew* (Grand Rapids: Eerdmans, 1985), p. 398.

[11]France remarks, "The words are, of course, a quotation of the first verse of Psalm 22, a psalm which moves from despairing appeal to triumphant faith, and the Christian reader can, with hindsight, see the appropriateness of this total message. But it is illegitimate to interpret Jesus' words as referring to the part of the psalm which he did *not* echo, as throughout the crucifixion scene, it is the suffering of the righteous man in Psalm 22, not his subsequent vindication, which is alluded to." Ibid., p. 398. At least Matthew was aware of the many elements of the Psalm that took place, not just Jesus' initial cry. And, yes, they all relate to his suffering.

[12]Other translations state that Jesus was "grieved and agitated" (NRSV) or "felt anguish and dismay" (NEB). Mark replaces Matthew's "sorrowful" with an even more intense word that could be translated as "horror . . . came over him."

[13]Matthew also wants us to know that Jesus remains the crucified one even after the res-

urrection. In the next chapter (see Mt 28:5) the angels at the empty tomb announce, "Do not be afraid, for I know you are looking for Jesus, who was crucified." The Greek verb for was crucified, a perfect participle, suggests that Jesus continually relates to us as "the crucified one."

[14]John Stott, *The Cross of Christ* (Downers Grove, Ill.: InterVarsity Press, 2006), p. 320.

[15]As Joel Green and Mark D. Baker observe in their book *Recovering the Scandal of the Cross*, the struggle with shame is often intensified in some non-Western cultures. Joel B. Green and Mark D. Baker, *Recovering the Scandal of the Cross* (Downers Grove, Ill.: InterVarsity Press, 2000), pp. 153-70.

[16]Craig Keener, *A Commentary on the Gospel of Matthew* (Grand Rapids: Eerdmans, 1999), p. 679.

[17]Richard Foster, *Celebration of Discipline* (San Francisco: HarperSanFrancisco, 1988), p. 154.

[18]Athanasius, *On the Incarnation* (Crestwood, N.Y.: St. Vladimir's Seminary, 1993), p. 55.

[19]Quoted in Bruner, *Churchbook*, p. 732.

[20]This is based on a true story found in Joe Dallas, *Lessons from San Quentin* (Wheaton, Ill.: Tyndale House, 2010).

[21]It's important to note that the Gospel stories about Jesus' resurrection weren't a case of wishful thinking, like people who claim to see ghosts or Elvis or the real Santa Claus because they desperately want and expect to see these things. The disciples didn't want or expect to see Jesus after he died. Many religious leaders emerged at the same time of Jesus, and many of these self-proclaimed "messiahs" died a violent death, but likely none of their followers ever considered the idea of a physical resurrection from the dead possible. The Greeks and Romans believed in an afterlife, but they would have considered a bodily resurrection not only impossible but repugnant. The ancient Mesopotamians were even more pessimistic about a bodily resurrection: they feared the dead coming back to life and outnumbering the living. The Egyptians were more positive but they had nothing approaching the Gospels' view of a bodily resurrection. The concept of a bodily resurrection—a real person walking around in the same body, touching and being touched, eating fish, having conversations with others—was just as difficult for people in the ancient world as it is for a twenty-first century materialist. Nevertheless, the early church made pains to say that this impossible event, this thing that no one expected or even dared to hope for, had happened and they had seen it with their own eyes. In Matthew 28:6 the angels even invite the women to "come and see the place where he lay." It's an offer to investigate the evidence. None of the early followers of Jesus believed the resurrection because it was comforting or inspiring; they believed because the evidence overwhelmed them. Thus the New Testament writers all almost dare us by saying, "You can call us liars or you can join us and enter a whole new world, but don't tell us nonsense like we had a 'spiritual experience' or we're optimistic about human progress."

[22]Carson concludes, "They still were hesitant; and their failure to understand his repeated predictions of his resurrection, compounded with their despair after his crucifixion,

worked to maintain their hesitancy for some time before they came to full faith. Jesus' resurrection did not instantly transform men of little faith and faltering understanding into spiritual giants." D. A. Carson, *Matthew, Mark and Luke* (Grand Rapids: Zondervan, 1984), p. 594.

[23]According to Carson, in its most basic sense the Greek word for nations means tribes, nations, or peoples (without distinction) or all nations (without distinction). It also certainly includes both Gentiles and Jews. Ibid., p. 596.

[24]Bruner, *Churchbook*, p. 824.

[25]Carson, *Matthew, Mark and Luke*, p. 599.

BIBLICAL. THEOLOGICAL.
CULTURAL. PERSONAL.
RESONATE.

"Reading a Resonate volume is more like a conversation than an information dump. The conversation connects my story to a much larger story . . . which is true resonance."

–MARK MILLER, author, *Experiential Storytelling*

ALSO AVAILABLE

The Gospel of John: *When Love Comes to Town,* by Paul Louis Metzger

"Paul Louis Metzger is one of the important biblical voices in our time. Here he guides us through one of the most significant biblical texts of all time. And it's really readable to boot. What's not to like?"

–ALAN HIRSCH

COMING SOON

Ecclesiastes, by Tim Keel

Lamentations, by Soong-Chan Rah

The Book of Acts, by Dan Kimball

LIKEWISE. *Go and do.*

A man comes across an ancient enemy, beaten and left for dead. He lifts the wounded man onto the back of a donkey and takes him to an inn to tend to the man's recovery. Jesus tells this story and instructs those who are listening to "go and do likewise."

Likewise books explore a compassionate, active faith lived out in real time. When we're skeptical about the status quo, Likewise books challenge us to create culture responsibly. When we're confused about who we are and what we're supposed to be doing, Likewise books help us listen for God's voice. When we're discouraged by the troubled world we've inherited, Likewise books encourage us to hold onto hope.

In this life we will face challenges that demand our response. Likewise books face those challenges with us so we can act on faith.

likewisebooks.com